D1000842

the context of contemporary theology

# the context of contemporary theology

## ESSAYS IN HONOR OF PAUL LEHMANN

*edited by Alexander J. McKelway
and E. David Willis*

JOHN KNOX PRESS
ATLANTA, GEORGIA

Scripture quotations are from the Revised Standard Version of the
Bible, copyright 1946 and 1952 by the Division of Christian Education
of the National Council of the Churches of Christ in the U.S.A.

Library of Congress Cataloging in Publication Data

BT
10
.C64

Library of Congress Cataloging in Publication Data
Main entry under title:

The Context of contemporary theology.

  CONTENTS: Allen, H. T. The life and ministry of
Paul L. Lehmann: a personal tribute.--The question of
man: McKelway, A. J. Eden revisited: hope beyond
tragedy. Willis, E. D. Rhetoric and responsibility in
Calvin's theology. Green, C. A theology of sociality:
Bonhoeffer's Sanctorum communio. [etc.]  Bibliog-
raphy:  (p.      )
  1.  Theology--20th century--Addresses, essays,
lectures. 2. Lehmann, Paul Louis, 1906-
--Addresses, essays, lectures. I. Lehmann, Paul
Louis, 1906-     II. McKelway, Alexander J., ed.
III. Willis, Edward David, ed.
BT10.C64          230          73-16916
ISBN 0-8042-0513-2

© John Knox Press 1974
Printed in the United States of America

WIDENER UNIVERSITY
WOLFGRAM
LIBRARY
CHESTER, PA

the context of contemporary theology

# Contents

# Introduction

In recent years a group of students, pastors, and teachers who had been associated with Paul Lehmann began holding regular colloquia to discuss prominent issues in contemporary theology and ethics and to examine the implications of Lehmann's thought for various theological disciplines. These meetings produced the conviction that the kinds of problems Lehmann has dealt with during his career and the perspectives he has developed merit wider communication. Hence the present volume which, fittingly enough, appears on the occasion of his retirement in 1974.

The impact of Paul Lehmann on theology in America and elsewhere during the last quarter century cannot be measured by its literary significance alone, although his bibliography contains over two hundred entries. His influence is better traced in the currency of such concepts as "contextualism," "humanization," and "the politics of God" in the theology of our time. These concepts have been used by countless others who, wittingly or not, have furthered the permeation of Lehmann's insights into intellectual life here and abroad. Unquestionably, some of Lehmann's devotees have fallen prematurely into a sort of "school" language—which is as objectionable to him as the slogans of the Barthians were to their mentor. But Lehmann has somehow managed to hold together various strands of thought and patterns of ethics and has

9

successfully avoided the reductionism which can easily beset the central figure in a group of filial critics. His place in theology is established not only by the power and imagination of his own formulations in ethics, Christology, and anthropology, but also by the seminal influence of his thought upon a whole generation of younger theologians and the effect of his style and approach upon the preaching and ministries of literally thousands of clergymen and laymen who have studied under—he prefers "with" —him.

The contributions to this volume by his students and colleagues of his own generation represent a wide spectrum of theological positions, which all focus upon issues which have been integral to Lehmann's thought. Discernible in this collection is a desire to establish new parameters and environments for theology in such diverse areas as biblical interpretation, church history, historical theology, political theology, sociology, psychology, and anthropology. While no attempt was made to solicit articles for particular themes, the contributions to this volume do seem to fall easily into four general areas which reflect major concerns of Lehmann's theology.

"Humanization" is one of those words currently in vogue which finds fundamental definition in the writings of Paul Lehmann. When he speaks of "making human life more human," he is calling not only for a new understanding of Christology, but also for a theological anthropology which can more adequately reflect that central act of humanizing grace. The first three essays take up this anthropological problem in quite different ways. In the first, the humanity of the Second Adam is discovered in the First, and a vision of man as neither fallen nor faulted emerges from a reinterpretation of Genesis 2 and 3. In the second essay, an exploration of Calvin's understanding of rhetorical responsibility and divine accommodation sheds new light on the often obscured theological humanism of that reformer's thought. In the third essay, Clifford Green discusses the social theology of Bonhoeffer's neglected *Sanctorum Communio* which offers important insight into the new humanity in Christ.

The second part of this collection focuses upon politics as a context for theological reflection. "The politics of God" is one of Paul Lehmann's best-known and most often quoted phrases. The politics of God finds expression in the politics of man when freedom, justice, and love are discovered in public life. Helmut Gollwitzer and Jürgen Moltmann present the issues of liberation and freedom as they bear upon the theological meaning of contemporary revolutionary movements. Krister Stendahl exposes the dialectical nature of divine judgment and mercy as they are experienced on either side of the revolutionary struggle. The essay on Justin Martyr by George Williams deals not only with religious and philosophical setting of Justin's thought but also with the political setting. It is placed in this section because Williams presents the Apologist's thought as an illustration of Christian protest against the dehumanization of even an enlightened totalitarianism.

Paul Lehmann has always taught that the larger context of theology, the *koinonia,* is both relative and fluid, and that theology must therefore learn to operate at the intersection of the sacred and the secular. This is particularly evident in his ethics and the indebtedness he acknowledges to the social sciences in his formulation of ethical questions. The third group of articles takes up the question of the proper relation of theology to social science. This relation may be one of "intra-mundane anonymity," in which theology engages in social-scientific description without translating issues into the language of faith (Morgan). Or theology may, while abandoning ideological absolutes, yet maintain its own distinctive witness in a dialogue with culture (Reist). Or theology may find in social science (e.g. psychology) analyses and symbols which add conceptual richness to its articulation of faith (Loder). But however different their approaches to this relationship, Morgan, Reist, and Loder share the conviction that theology cannot adequately perform its task without an appreciation and appropriation of a disciplined knowledge of human affairs.

"Probing questions, self-scrutiny, revisions of long-accepted versions, pushing into the unknown, listening to other voices— all these and more spell out the Lehmann theological method." [1] This description by H. T. Kerr says something also about the style and mood of Paul Lehmann's work, which is characterized by freshness, openness, and expectancy. Jan Lochman and Frederick Herzog both reflect this dimension of Lehmann's thought as they try to anticipate the future direction of theology. Both see Christology as the ineluctable focus of all future dogmatics. For Lochman, only a "theology of the third article," will be able to face the future challenge of political humanism. And Herzog suggests that only a new Christological anthropology will be able to respond to the revolutionary theses of "black theology."

In this way the essays in this volume offer as contexts for theological reflection the question of man, the political issue of freedom, the relation of theology to the social sciences, and the question of the future of theology. In many of the essays, the influence of Paul Lehmann is apparent. In all of them, however, questions are asked which we believe he finds important.

Quite apart from the undeniable significance of Paul Lehmann's literary contributions to theology and ethics there is "the much more subtle and personal effect of Paul Lehmann himself. [He] belongs to the rare breed of teacher who exerts charismatic and almost hypnotic influence." [2] This aspect of our subject is uniquely represented in the biographical reflections of Horace Allen, who weaves around the *curriculum vitae* of his friend and teacher something of the special aura experienced by his intimates. The volume concludes with a sermon by Eberhard Bethge. This is appropriate, not only because of the compatibility of the exegesis, but also because, for Paul Lehmann, the word of the theologian is always preparatory to the word of the preacher.

The editors wish to thank the contributors for their cooperation and patience in the long process of producing this volume and other scholars whose contributions could not be included because of limitations of space. We wish to express appreciation also to the K–V Fund, the Calvin Institute Foundation, and Davidson College for the support they gave toward the development of this volume. Finally, we wish to acknowledge the generosity of *Theology Today* in allowing the reproduction of the Lehmann bibliography prepared by Robert Mathewson, and up-dated for this collection. We are sure, however, that this list represents no final accounting, but that both the writings of Paul Lehmann, as well as scholarly commentary upon them, will increase in the years to come. Upon the occasion of his official (but certainly not actual) retirement, it is our hope and expectation that we will long enjoy the grace of his presence and the challenge of his thought.

---

1. Hugh T. Kerr, "A Paul Lehmann Festschrift," *Theology Today,* vol. XXIX, no. 1 (April 1972), p. 2.
2. *Ibid.*

# The Life and Ministry
# of Paul L. Lehmann:
# A Personal Tribute

**HORACE T. ALLEN**

In W. H. Auden's *Christmas Oratorio,* the Wisemen rather pensively admit that, "To discover how to be human now is the reason we follow this star." [1] For his pupils, friends, and fellow-travelers, this quotation may well express something of the spirit of the life and ministry of Paul Louis Lehmann. The search for humanity, which many have undertaken with his leadership, has ultimately enveloped practically every aspect of life and has not infrequently been the occasion for tears and frustration as well as rejoicing and renewal. This being the case, it will be understood that an objective account of the life, vocation, and ministry of Paul Lehmann probably cannot be written. The subjectivities of being human inevitably intrude themselves.

Paul Lehmann's early life and roots were shared by a small but stable community of German-Americans who brought to this country an experience of earnest family life, an appreciation for culture and the arts, a deep feeling for the power and formative character of faith in Jesus Christ, and loyalty to his church. His father, Timothy, was a pastor in the Evangelical Synod of North America, which later united with the German Reformed church to become the Evangelical and Reformed church. At the time of his son Paul's birth in 1906 he was located in Baltimore, Maryland. Within five years, he had moved to Columbus, Ohio, to become pastor of another bilingual congregation, St. John's Evangelical

15

his son Paul's birth in 1906 he was located in Baltimore, Maryland. Protestant Church. Such was the commitment of this family to the German language that Paul did not regularly have occasion to speak English until he entered elementary school. Even then he adopted English only at the urging of his twin brother, Timothy. A sister, Lillie, was born in 1916.

In 1928 the family moved to Elmhurst, Illinois, since the father had been elected President of Elmhurst College. Paul matriculated at Ohio State University in Columbus where he was a member of Phi Beta Kappa, and in 1927 was awarded the degrees of Bachelor of Arts, *cum laude,* and Bachelor of Science in Education. He went immediately to Union Theological Seminary in New York City from which he was graduated three years later with the degree of Bachelor of Divinity. While there he married Marion N. Lucks, also of Columbus, Ohio, whom he had known for some years and who was then teaching on Long Island. A son, Peter, was born in 1949 in Princeton, New Jersey. Paul served for two years as pastor of an Evangelical and Reformed church in Garwood, New Jersey, and then as pastor's assistant (to Dr. Paul Scherer) at Holy Trinity Lutheran Church on Central Park West in New York City.

Completion of the Bachelor of Divinity degree in 1930 led to graduate study at Union in New York where he was a Residence Fellow. Later he went abroad as Union's Traveling Fellow (1932-33), and attended the Universities of Zürich and Bonn to study with Emil Brunner and Karl Barth. It was at this time that his friendship and theological partnership with Dietrich Bonhoeffer began, first at Union in the academic year 1930-31 and then in Europe. In this same period, he began work on his doctoral dissertation which in 1936 earned him Union's Doctor of Theology degree. It was published in 1940 under the title *Forgiveness, Decisive Issue in Protestant Thought.*

In 1933 he accepted his first full-time teaching position as Assistant Professor of Religion and Philosophy at Elmhurst College. While at Elmhurst he was ordained to the ministry by the North Illinois Synod of the Evangelical and Reformed church. Also while at Elmhurst he and Reinhold Niebuhr, in cooperation with Henry Sloane Coffin, had undertaken to find a teaching post in the United States for Dietrich Bonhoeffer, only to be thwarted by Bonhoeffer himself who, after a hastily arranged rendezvous in New York, precipitiously and fatefully returned to a tormented Germany.

From Elmhurst College, Lehmann went to Eden Theological Seminary in Webster Groves, Missouri, but was there only a year when Wellesley College in Massachusetts called him to its faculty in 1941 as Associate Professor of Biblical History. There, as at Elmhurst, he exhibited an extraordinary capacity to relate to undergraduate students as a pastor. Under his influence, lives, vocations, and life-long partnerships in marriage were formed or radically changed.

In 1946, when he was forty, there occurred perhaps the sharpest shift in the direction of his life. In that year Paul Lehmann began his ministerial membership in the Presbyterian church and also a career on the faculties of Princeton Theological Seminary (1946-56), Harvard Divinity School (1956-63), Union Theological Seminary in New York (1963-74) and Union Theological Seminary in Richmond (1974- ). Having begun as Lecturer in the Social Sciences at Princeton, he ultimately became the Stephen Colwell Professor of Applied Christianity and Director of Graduate Studies. At Harvard he occupied first the Parkman Professorship and then the Florence Corliss Lamont chair. At Union in New York he began as the Auburn Professor of Systematic Theology and in 1968 was made the Charles A. Briggs Professor of Systematic Theology.

Throughout this time he was in demand for special lectureships, all of which were meticulously prepared and some of which became published works. The Thomas White Currie lectures at Austin Presbyterian Theological Seminary in 1961 became the occasion for bringing to fruition a task begun during a sabbatical year away from Princeton. It was published in 1963 as *Ethics in a Christian Context*. Later, he gave the William Belden Noble lectures at Harvard, "Jesus Christ and the Question of Revolution," which are currently being prepared for publication. His honorary degrees include the Doctor of Divinity from Lawrence College in

Appleton, Wisconsin (1949), a Master of Arts from Harvard University in 1956, a Doctor of Laws from Elmhurst College (1967), and in 1971 he was made an Honorary Doctor of Tübingen in Germany. In 1969-70 he served as President of the American Theological Society.

The first year at Princeton saw him commuting from Philadelphia as an associate editor for the Presbyterian Church's Westminster Press. John Alexander Mackay was Paul's much respected "chief" at the Seminary, and Paul proved a worthy follower of his in various revolutionary activities. It was while at Princeton and with the courageous encouragement of President Mackay that Paul Lehmann engaged in one of the most serious political battles of his life: his public opposition to the erosion of freedom in the United States, symbolized by the rise of McCarthyism. Paul Lehmann's activity as a member of the Emergency Civil Liberties Committee brought him into sharp conflict not only with the politics of the right, but also with much of the established, liberal theological community. He nevertheless stood by his own deepest sensitivities as long as the issue demanded his efforts, and the structures and strategies in which he participated were responsible to his own unique concerns and insights.

During the years at Princeton, Harvard and Union, the Presbyterian church found numerous ways to employ Professor Lehmann's talents. He attended two General Councils of the World Alliance of Reformed Churches—in São Paulo, Brazil (1959) and Frankfurt, Germany (1964)—and the All Christian Peace Assembly in Prague, Czechoslovakia.

The years which Paul's teaching career has covered have brought with them a major economic depression, two world wars, radical realignment of the world's powers, and some of the most violent upheavals in American culture and academic society that the nation has ever known. The series of theological revolutions which at the same time swept the Western church may yet amount to a new reformation and re-ordering of the church's structure and style. And throughout these years students never ceased to bring to the Lehmanns their own interior upheavals, uncertainties, disappointments and triumphs.

In the midst of all that, however, Paul Lehmann's mind and home have maintained a careful respect for the traditions of the fathers and the amenities of civilized culture. The well-chosen word, the dialectically qualified argument, the devotion to the arts, the correct dinner party, the finely-crafted prayer in morning chapel, the impeccable sense for history's value: all of these experiences and more have combined over the years to provide occasions for the experience of what it means to be human. These experiences are thoroughly congruent with Paul Lehmann's insistence upon the necessity in the church to live in intimate dialogue with society, as have been his own never-ending series of dialogues, political and personal, with the prevailing issues and crises of economics, government, art and literature. There has always been an openness not only to the issues of society but also to society's ways of verbalizing its issues: its poetry, literature and art. In convincing refutation of the theological polemic that sees its peculiar tradition as oblivious to the world and its culture, Paul Lehmann has given his students a firm grasp on poetic and political literature. Countless theological students have been introduced to *The Federalist Papers,* Karl Marx, Abner Dean, W. H. Auden, and e. e. cummings in the context of the Reformed theologizing of Paul Lehmann.

For the largest part of his life Lehmann has agonized over the meaning and exercise of human freedom in the context of political realities and institutions. He has not only agonized, he has acted. This is validated by his own suggestion, taken from both Aristotle and the Bible, that politics has something to do with keeping human life human. However thorough a scholar Paul Lehmann has been, he has never been a detached scholar. His speech abounds with both classical allusion and political metaphor. His awareness of the inner dynamics of the experience of the German nation in the thirties and forties, intensified by his theological kinship with both Barth and Bonhoeffer, provided him with a prophetic feeling for what happened to Western civilization both during and after World War II. This led inevitably to the bruising clash with the mid-century McCarthy phenomenon. It also provided a perspective from which he was able to sympathize with and support the struggle for freedom in South America. Through personal contacts, student movement activities, publications and travels, he became increasingly involved in the struggles for freedom in this country and abroad.

When the students revolted at Columbia University, Union Theological Seminary was not left untouched. Here too the students asserted a newly-defined maturity to challenge the structure of that institution. Once again Paul Lehmann found himself in the cross-fire of tradition and revolution, the individual and the community, politics and the gospel. He strove to interpret radical students to faculty colleagues, theological integrity to ideological activists, past to present, and present to past. During the upheavals of the sixties he set to work on a number of related ethical issues, such as Christian/Marxist dialogue, the matter of peace and war, and human sexuality.

Politics and music, poetry and sculpture, freedom and order are the context of the humanity envisioned in Lehmann's life and theology. Their prominence in his theological labors explains much concerning the depth of his influence upon those who have come under his tutelage.

Several other aspects of Paul Lehmann's ministry and method deserve particular attention. The affection and personal accountability felt by his students toward him over the years are rooted not only in the integrity and humility of his academic, theological and cultural involvements. There has also been the development of precisely the sort of community which is central to his theological and ethical position. Constantly he has been asked, "Where is this *koinonia?*" A partial answer may be suggested by the close association formed among Lehmann's students and colleagues. This is not to say that there were not those who were perplexed by his politics and his theology. A compelling voice always elicits strong opposition. But more importantly there was always around Paul Lehmann a nascent community of theological reflection, liturgical seriousness, and political commitment.

The theology of Paul Lehmann is difficult to categorize. He does not fit easily into any theological camp. It has been at once his genius and his burden to espouse a theological position which has invariably been at odds with its environment. Early in his career he ran headlong into the unproductive polemic of liberalism vs. fundamentalism, making enemies on both sides. He and his friend Dietrich Bonhoeffer at Union Seminary in 1930-31 found themselves virtually isolated somewhere between the biblical conservatism of the Broadway Presbyterian Church and the theological liberalism of the Riverside Church—all the while wondering at what passed for theology at Broadway and 120th Street. In a secular environment he has always seemed too "Christian" and in Christian circles too "secular." Among the Presbyterians at Princeton, for example, he was sometimes viewed as a dangerous radical. But when he went to Harvard he was incredulously received as "a Calvinist." The truth is that Paul Lehmann has always been a theological "loner."

There has also been a devotional and liturgical aspect to Lehmann's life and thought. Just as Bonhoeffer's radical social obedience was formed in the interaction of the lectionary, the liturgy and the hymns of Paul Gerhardt, so Paul Lehmann has never lost the genuine piety of his youth nor an understanding of worship as the central action of the Christian community. Though conscious of the dangers inherent in the canonization of forms of worship, he regularly has brought to his occasional liturgical duties a care and trepidation which have made his own prayers models of biblical and literary sensitivity. Even in the classroom, his opening prayers have been classics of quiet devotion.

To the surprise and delight of some of his more liturgically inclined students, his sermons have been studded with reference to the context and setting of the Sunday or the day and its appropriate ceremonies. And throughout his career he has emphasized the importance of the priestly function of the office. Thus *Ethics in a Christian Context* identifies the maturative possibilities of the Christian community with its eucharistic center. In that way he has provided for Protestants one of their most viable platforms for dialogue with a renewed Roman Catholicism. Both Lehmann and Bonhoeffer take the community at worship to be the occasion for theological reflection. In this they reflect their common theological ancestry in Karl Barth who spoke of worship as the center of the church's life, and John Calvin who described the marks of the church in liturgical terms.

For Paul Lehmann theology and worship imply a sensitivity to persons. One of the crucial components of the style of his teaching, which nicely balances his traditional reliance on the authority of lecturing, is an equally serious discipline of listening to the student. This may happen in the lecture hall or more informally elsewhere. To encourage this, seminars are always invited for tea and conversation to the Lehmann home. Students often make appointments with him for informal and personal conversation. Nothing is dismissed or ignored, and the worth of the person is always affirmed.

Politics, theology and prayer are the elements of an unusual theological career. Paul Lehmann has wedded thought to life. Thought has been lively and life thoughtful. This has proved a compelling union for eager students, who, having turned to Paul Lehmann for theological understanding, have found themselves dealing with a far greater agenda: the promise of Christ and the possibility of being human.

---

1. W. H. Auden, *The Collected Poetry of W. H. Auden* (New York: Random House, 1945), p. 431.

# the question of man

# Eden Revisited:
# Hope Beyond Tragedy

## ALEXANDER J. McKELWAY

The politics of God appears blocked by the insurrection of Adam. The new humanity is still obscured by the old, and whatever God has done or is doing to make and keep human life human seems inadequate to suppress the strange chthonian dynamism emanating from the garden. So it appears, and so much conventional wisdom, both sacred and secular, would tell us. The myth of the fall may be "broken," as Tillich said, but its power over the consciousness of Western man remains intact.

> The Lord God took the man and put him in the garden of Eden to till it and keep it. And the Lord God commanded the man, saying, "You may freely eat of every tree of the garden; but of the tree of the knowledge of good and evil you shall not eat, for in the day that you eat of it you shall die." [Gen. 2:15-17]

> Now the serpent was more subtle than any other wild creature that the Lord God had made. He said to the woman, "Did God say, 'You shall not eat of any tree of the garden'?" And the woman said to the serpent, "We may eat of the fruit of the trees of the garden; but God said, 'You shall not eat of the fruit of the tree which is in the midst of the garden, neither shall you touch it, lest you die.'" But the serpent said to the woman, "You will not die. For God knows that when you eat of it your eyes will be opened, and you will be like God, knowing good and evil." So . . . the woman . . . took of its fruit and ate; and she

also gave some to her husband, and he ate. Then the eyes of both were opened, and they knew that they were naked . . . [Gen. 3:1-7]

Little wonder that this ancient story has gripped the imagination of man as he seeks to understand himself and his world. Placed in a good and fruitful creation, we too have misused, corrupted, and polluted it—and we do not know why. Created in the image of God to live together as neighbors, friends, and lovers, we have somehow come to the place where we are more ashamed of the act of love than the act of killing. The story speaks to us because it reflects our own consciousness of personal guilt as well as our participation in a guilty world. The enigmatic figure of the snake seems to bear powerful witness to the fateful mystery of our condition. Whoever and whatever we are, we feel we are not what we should be—and the story of Adam and Eve is somehow telling us why.

So we read the story. But have we understood it correctly? Could it be that, the weight of theological opinion notwithstanding, this story is not only a story of disaster, but of promise? Is it possible that where we have seen only a portrayal of human despair, we should have seen a confirmation of man's hope?

## I. The Conception of Sin as Pride

The view of Adam as both symbol and cause of a tragic humanity was developed in Jewish Apocrypha and Pseudepigrapha[2] and finds expression in various rabbinical writings. Paul knew of the doctrine, although it is our view that he did not teach it. On Christian soil it found a severe formulation in Tertullian which was carried forward by Ambrose.[3] But it was Augustine's development of the doctrine which became normative for all subsequent interpretations. For in spite of counter tendencies in his early thought it was Augustine, in an increasingly bitter struggle with the Pelagians, who made the doctrine of original sin a dogma of Christendom. "Why were all born in sin? That we are children of Adam implies damnation by necessity."[4]

We should not be surprised, of course, to find more than a thousand years before Darwin the human predicament described as inheritance from an original pair. What was perhaps unnecessary was Augustine's location of that fault in sexuality. "We are born with desire," he wrote, "and even before we add our own guilt we are born of that damnation . . ." [5] Augustine, the monastic and reformed sensualist, was encouraged to view Adam's fault in terms of sexuality because of the references to the first couple's shame and nakedness. Yet he did not consider (nor did Tertullian) man's fleshly existence itself as the source of sin. It is not the *act* of sex itself, but what Augustine considered to be the unavoidable concomitant of that act—self-seeking and pride—which constituted the original movement of sin.

*Eritis secut deus,* "You will be like God." This promise of the serpent appeared to Augustine—and nearly every theologican after him—as the irreducible expression of blasphemous pride, the point of departure of man from God.[6]

Most theologians have accepted this definition of man's essential sin as pride. In our own day Paul Tillich has interpreted Adam's fall as a symbol of a universal (and necessary) act of pride wherein man reaches out for autonomous control of his own life. And Reinhold Niebuhr has written of the inevitable movement of man's will when he pridefully desires the higher, infinite quality of God, and thus abandons and loses his identity as his creature.

On the surface "pride" seems plausible enough as an explanation of the human predicament. Who would deny that we are corrupted and distorted and dehumanized by self-interest, self-aggrandizement, and the desire to be more than we are in the eyes of others and ourselves? And yet the idea of pride, or hubris, may be another of those Hellenistic notions which Christianity has embraced without due regard to the metaphysical baggage it brings along with it. The tragic pride of the Greek hero consists in the fact that he aspires to a state of being which, ontologically, is impossible for him. In attempting to escape the limitations of finitude he only succeeds in contradicting them, and suffers the fates and furies of a remorseless transcendence. Thus, in Greek thought, the tragic and destructive power of hubris depended upon the assumption of an absolute and eternal disjuncture and discrimination between the transcendent and the mundane, the divine and the human.

The question we must ask is whether such a dualism is characteristic of the biblical witness—especially whether it is characteristic of an understanding of Adam as the representative of man. What we must ask is whether in fact there is any valid correlation between the tragic hero doomed to a status lower than the angels and the biblical understanding of man as he finds representation in Adam. If the weight of the tradition has inclined toward an affirmative answer to this question, recent investigations of rabbinical and Pauline literature suggest the opposite.

## II. Adam: The Glorious Man

Regarding the biblical witness, Robin Scroggs, in his book *The Last Adam,* reminds us that even in the Old Testament Adam is not viewed primarily or consistently as a fallen, corrupt, or depraved representative of man.[7] The Jahwist writer of the story of the fall does not withdraw from Adam the special blessings which he had earlier been given—the "breath" of God as his special life, dominion over creation, or partnership with another. These gifts are called into question by Adam himself, but they are not withdrawn. More significant, perhaps, is the fact that the priestly author of the first chapter of Genesis feels under no compulsion to repeat the Jahwist writer's account of sin, but seems to overlook it in his portrayal of Adam as created in God's "image" and as sovereign over all other creatures. Later this same author guarantees for Adam a positive role in Israel's history as its first patriarch. (Gen. 5 and 1 Chron. 1).

This reluctance to view Adam as a man of sin separated from God is also found in Jewish apocryphal and pseudepigraphal literature. As we have already pointed out, these traditions know Adam as the author of sin. But just as significant is the fact that they know him also as the progenitor of the priestly class and a patriarch. He is seen as a representative of a glorified humanity in terms of his size, which is said to cover the whole earth, his angelic nature, and his proximity to God himself. Scroggs calls our attention to one amazing reference in I Enoch where the vision of Adam as a white bull establishes his identity with the Messiah.[8]

As W. D. Davies (*Paul and Rabbinic Judaism*) and Scroggs both show, the tendency to view Adam in a positive light is intensified in the writings of the rabbis. While the teachers of Israel certainly did speak of Adam as the man of sin, it is also true that in the Babylonian Talmud Adam is called "a great saint," and the Amora rabbi, R. Hama, can go so far as to deny any death to Adam. In another place Adam is numbered with the seven shepherds of Micah 5:5 who will arise to defend Israel. And although the rabbinical authors are usually cautious of any direct identification of Adam and the Messiah, there is the astonishing exegesis in the Midrash Rabbah in which Adam is found to have had a surplus of seventy years of life—which he wills to King David, who, according to Scroggs, stands in this context for the promised redeemer.[9]

The question we are asking is whether or not the view of Adam as primarily a fallen creature condemned for his pride is a view supported by Scripture. While the Jewish writings just mentioned are not part of the Christian canon, they do help us with an answer. These writers indicate a depth of appreciation of Adam in Israel's faith, and therefore also in Old Testament literature, which cannot be contradicted by the account of his fall. Furthermore, we cannot doubt that Jesus knew this tradition,[10] and that Paul, as a student of the Law, was trained in the very sources to which we have alluded (although, of course, not in the Talmudic form).

And yet Paul has apparently been read as if he were more of a student of Augustine than the elders of Israel! How else can we understand the astonishing consistency with which Christian theologians have misinterpreted Paul's discussion of the role and significance of Adam in the fifth chapter of Romans? Here he draws both a parallel and a distinction between Christ and Adam, which might be fairly edited in this way:

> . . . as sin came into the world through one man . . . so death spread to all men because all men sinned . . . even over those whose sins were not like the transgression of Adam, who was a

> type of the one who was to come. . . . if many died through one
> man's trespass, much more have the grace of God and . . . the
> grace of that one man Jesus Christ abounded for many. . . . If
> . . . death reigned through that one man, much more will . . .
> righteousness reign . . . through the one man Jesus Christ. . . .
> as one man's trespass led to condemnation for all men, so one
> man's act of righteousness leads to acquittal and life for all men.
> [Rom. 5:12-18]

While it is true that Paul here does hint at a sinister influence of Adam, we can only view as incomprehensible the fact that practically every commentator upon this passage has seen in it only a confirmation of Augustine's doctrine of original sin.[11]

The one exception to this tradition of interpretation is the epoch-making exegesis of this passage by Karl Barth, who, in his book *Christ and Adam,* points out that here Paul denies to Adam exactly what Augustine would grant him—the power to corrupt the nature of man. "How much more" (*pollo mallon*—he repeats the phrase twice), "how much more," Paul is saying, is the being of man secured, guaranteed, and saved by the "one man Jesus Christ." Indeed, Barth suggests that Paul is unwilling to grant to Adam even *tentative* powers of corruption, but sees him only as a *toupos tou melontos* (vs. 14), a "type of the one to come," who in his sin could only be a shadow and distorted replica of that manhood which in Christ God had determined for man from the very beginning.[12] That is to say, Adam was never simply the man he could be on his own—by virtue of his weakness. The manhood which the Gospel of John claims was "in the beginning with God" is seen here by Paul as a divine humanity which from the very beginning defines and determines not only the nature of Adam, but of his progeny. Thus, while Paul certainly differs from his rabbinical teachers concerning the basis of Adam's glory, he is no more willing than they to define him only as a lost and fallen creature in whom all men are cursed.

Still less does Paul support the notion that Adam's fault and man's sin consist in hubris, in some disastrous and inappropriate desire on the part of man to "be like God." How could this be if the only humanity granted to Adam (or the humanity he represents) is already a divine humanity, the humanity of God disclosed in his Son? The explanation of man's predicament in terms of pride—of his reaching out for a higher and more glorious being for himself—must of necessity involve the supposition that there is in his created nature indeed some lack, some inability, or unfulfillment, which forms the basis of his compulsion. Such a supposition, however, takes into account neither the tradition of a glorified Adam, expressed in both Old Testament and rabbinical literature, nor the Pauline conception of the divine humanity of Christ as the prototype of Adam's humanity.

### III. Humanistic Man: Ernst Bloch

With few exceptions theological anthropology has adopted descriptions of sin and the fall which assume a state of affairs in human being which the Christian faith itself denies. Because of this negative orthodoxy the church has found itself unable to interpret to men a more hopeful view of their own nature. If theology has been consistent in its conformity to a negative assessment of men, humanism (to risk a broad description) has been as consistent in its rejection of that view. This philosophy has said in effect: If it is really true that human being is ontologically inferior, if there really is a state of being beyond our own from which we are separated and to which we must aspire, is it not more human, more in the service of man and his progress, to encourage such aspiration than to condemn it? Should we not celebrate the Promethean element in man rather than damn it as hubris? Far from being the source of his trouble, is not pride the wellspring of his hope?

Among the many forms of contemporary humanism the one which is most interesting and challenging for theology is that of Ernst Bloch. Although he is both a Marxist and an atheist, Bloch has anticipated many of the issues of present-day theology and contributed to their development. His massive work *Das Prinzip Hoffnung* furnished much of the conceptual basis for the "theology of hope," and one of his early works, *Thomas Münzer als Theologe der Revolution,* forecast the contemporary interest in revolution.

It is, however, in Bloch's latest work, *Atheism im Chris-*

*tentum,* that the shape of his theology becomes most clear. For Bloch, the Bible is the most important document of Western civilization and the essential source of man's knowledge of himself. What is especially interesting is that he does not read the Bible as merely one example of the history of religions, but as the proclamation of man's relation to divinity. For Bloch, this relationship is seen primarily in Jesus Christ, who as the God-man represents the limitless possibilities of all men. Of course, he cannot assent to any orthodox view of Christ's "real divinity," because divinity itself for Bloch is a characteristic of man and allows for no sense of the transcendent. But it is nonetheless significant that Bloch has interpreted the whole of Scripture from a Christological perspective. For him the true and authentic message of the Bible must be traced in the leitmotiv of the new and worldly manhood of Christ. Christ is the great revolutionary who, like Moses, Amos, and other of his Old Testament prefigurations, would lead men out of the bondage of religious transcendence and into the kindgom of man. The gospel proclaims the "good news" that man can and must embrace the divine dimension of his own life and struggle to fulfill the infinite hope which is his.

It is therefore not surprising to find Bloch critical of any understanding of sin as pride or disobedience. Sin for Bloch is nothing more or less than man's lack of courage to accept himself and his world and the ultimate value of both. Operating with this hermeneutic Bloch undertakes a most daring (not to say imaginative!) exegesis of the story of the fall.[14] He interprets the snake's suggestion to Eve—*Eritis sicut deus*—as no temptation at all, but the message of the Messiah himself. "To become like God" is not the expression of destructive hubris, but the legitimate call for man to take upon himself the unlimited possibilities of his humanity. If man discovers sin in that "temptation," says Bloch, it is only because of the anti-human interpretation of the myth by the priestly editors of Genesis—who, as official custodians of transcendent religion, generally attempt to hide the real message of the Bible by the construction of the "law."

In one sense Bloch's interpretation of Genesis 3 is so fanciful as to obviate serious criticism. While the snake symbol has served for human vitality and potency in world religions, and while Jesus did liken his crucifixion to Moses' lifting up "the serpent in the wilderness," such evidence appears insufficient to support Bloch's claim for a hidden tradition of ophiolatry in the Old Testament. Nor is the claim that the priestly writers tried to counteract such a tradition by viewing the snake as evil supported by Old Testament criticism.

But in spite of exegetical problems, there is much in Bloch's interpretation that is worthy of consideration. The fact that he sees in the story of the fall a quality of life, established in creation and actualized in Christ, which makes possible and even demands the fulfillment of man's potentiality, puts Bloch clearly in the biblical tradition. And however much we may question his denial of divine transcendence, we must nevertheless admit that his refusal to view man in a hopeless and negative way, or read the Bible in that light, places him closer to a Christian understanding of man than some of his more orthodox critics.

A more serious question is whether we can discover in the confrontation of Eve with the snake the "preview of the gospel" Bloch claims. Admittedly, if Adam can be understood only in his relation to Christ, then the suggestion of the serpent is at least not *ontologically* inappropriate. The suggestion of the snake to "become like God" is hardly a Promethean impiety if man is already what he is in Christ, the God-man. But in that case the "temptation" fails as "gospel," not for what it promises, but for what, by implication, that promise denies. By accepting the snake's charge that we *become* like God, Bloch unwittingly calls into question the givenness of man's divinity.

Bloch argues for man's right to a positive and even glorious view of his own humanity. But insofar as he interprets this possibility mythologically as offered only from outside man's self-consciousness, that is, by the snake, does he not thereby imply that man does not have such a divine humanity as already established in his creation? Bloch's Adam must receive this promise from another creature; and he must fight for the divinity by revolutionary protest—he does not already have it. This means that man as such, man in the "garden," is lacking the very quality of un-limitedness Bloch would claim for him. He must turn away from what he is toward what he may be. To accept the snake's pro-posal as "good news," as Bloch suggests, is to admit a state of affairs in human being which condemns man to a new law of works in which he is burdened with the hard and even tragic labor of be-coming what he is not.

The philosophy of Ernst Bloch shares with other forms of humanism, whether economic or psychological, revolutionary or philosophical process, a necessary rejection of what man is in favor of what he will be, and the purges, terrors, and inhumani-ties which that rejection has caused are all too familiar. At this point theological and secular orthodoxies coincide. If the one re-jects human life for what it is no longer, the other rejects it for what it is not yet. In neither case is the actual life and being of man affirmed in such a way that he can accept the past and live confidently toward the future. However, such a foundation for man's understanding of himself can be discovered in the myth of the fall—if we can read that story unencumbered by either preju-dice.

### IV. The Garden of Eden: Temptation to What?

Although the first two chapters of Genesis have different authors, the editors of the book obviously intended that they be read together. We are not allowed, then, to understand what hap-pened to man in the second chapter without first seeing who he is in the first. Scroggs has reminded us that Adam in Genesis 1 is granted unlimited prerogatives over the conditions of his existence in the subjection of plants and animals to his use (1:26). These royal—even "divine"—prerogatives are confirmed in the second chapter in the privilege given to Adam to name, that is to say, "define," his world (2:19).

The point is that a sublime character is granted to man as an indelible and essential quality of his being. This is confirmed in the priestly writer's conception of "the image of God." The special quality of humanity which we associate with the *Imago Dei* is neither man's intelligence, his will, his soul, nor his moral sense, but is, as Karl Barth has shown, the fact that he exists in relation to others, and to God.[15] "So God created man in his own image, in the image of God he created him; male and female he created them." (Gen. 1:27) The unity of male and female which constitutes "man" is expressive also of the unity which binds man to God. This unity may be corrupted, but it may not be dissolved. Nor is there any suggestion in the story that this unity is dissolved. The snake is cursed, but not Adam and Eve. They must live with the results of their act, but not without the presence and grace of God—who clothes them and guarantees that the earth will still yield its fruits even if they have made it hard for themselves (3:14, 19). Some theologians, notably Paul Tillich, have argued that man before the fall was not true man, actual man, that he lived a life of "dreaming innocence" before taking the necessary, if tragic, step toward the completion of his manhood. While process and evolution are certainly not excluded, the story clearly sees creation as complete (1:31—2:2), and the man addressed by God in chapter 2 is fully human. Life with God is real life, with toil and responsibility (2:15) as well as gracious provision for needs.

What, then, could possibly have existed on the other side of obedience that man could want or need? Struggle, desire, challenge, responsibility, freedom? These he had. Goodness, dignity, a higher sense of his own being? What higher sense *could* he have desired, living as he did in an absolute and indissoluble unity with God?

"You may freely eat of every tree of the garden; but of the tree of the knowledge of good and evil you shall not eat, for in the day that you eat of it you shall die." (Gen. 2:16-17) How are we to understand this "forbidden fruit"? What is the meaning of this prohibition? Barth argues that it is not, as Augustine, Luther, and Calvin seem to suggest, an arbitrary demand for obedience by the *Deus absolutus* anxious to keep man in his place.[16] "You shall not eat, for in the day that you eat of it you shall die." It is not a desire of the father to put the child in his place that brings this stern warning, but his desire to keep him *at* his place *with* himself. It is nothing less than the gracious and loving act of a father who would keep his child back from the precipice, back from the brink of disaster.[17]

Interpretations of the "tree of the knowledge of good and evil" are many and varied. Some have seen here a prohibition against man's prideful search for the secrets of the universe—perhaps even of creation itself. But did not man already have the key to that secret? Was not the knowledge-creating function of his language already given him without impediment? Because of the sex application of the word "to know", other commentators have understood sex as the forbidden fruit. But this hardly bears consideration—especially in light of the fact that it was exactly man's sexuality which was chosen as the symbol of the image of God in him. Was the "knowledge of good and evil" then literally some kind of ethical discrimination? If we mean by such discrimination ordinary value judgments and the ordering of priorities upon which daily life depends, then we must say again that a mature man living responsibly in God's good creation already possessed that knowledge.

But if we mean by the knowledge of good and evil the will and power to impose final and absolute judgments upon the things and possibilities of that good creation, then the movement by which man attempts that may represent in the most basic way the greatest danger to his being. For what kind of knowledge is the knowledge of good and evil in a world in which all things were called by its creator "good"? In a world in which all was good and nothing denied (except a turning away from that goodness and freedom), the fruit of the tree of the knowledge of good and evil could be neither nourishing nor enlightening. It could represent only a negative possibility—a turn toward nothingness. And that is, indeed, a kind of death (3:3).[18]

That the "knowledge of good and evil" actually points to nothingness and vacuity is suggested also in the encounter of Eve and the serpent. We should note first that the identity of the snake with Satan is unknown by the Jahwist author. There is no thought here that this reptile represents a real counterforce to God, that he can offer to man a real possibility apart from

God. On the contrary, he is simply another creature of God, known for his wily and clever ways, who can dissimulate and hide the the truth. The knowledge he represents is no knowledge at all; it is only confusion and error. He is even wrong about the prohibition: "Did God say, 'You shall not eat of *any* tree of the garden'?" (3:1) Eve corrects him. They can eat of all but the one tree; but then she adds her own extravagant and erroneous judgment to God's command: "God said, '. . . neither shall you touch it, lest you die.' " (3:3) Of course, he did not say that.[19] By so expanding the prohibition Eve begins that process of self-inflicted law which she creates for herself by a lie. She moves inexorably toward the edge of reality—ever closer to the abandonment of the givenness of her being.

The snake's assurance, "You will not die" (3:4), is simply a counterpoint to the movement already begun, a movement outside the circle of being-in-God. And of course the final promise of the tempter is but a summation of the senselessness and uselessness of the whole situation. "Your eyes will be opened, and you will be like God." (3:5) *Eritis sicut deus*—evangelism? Good news? Or the worst slander upon man, the greatest hoax, quackery, a cosmic shell game, a bit of confidence-gaming whereby one is convinced that he somehow must get what he already has and is willing to pay for it! How could they desire to be "like" God when they were already made in his image? What could such an inexplicable step mean except that they had decided to turn away from who they were in their createdness, imagine they were less than who they were, and undertake an entirely fanciful assault upon a divinity already theirs.

Life after such an attempt could be nothing but what it was—shameful, hard, and deadly. "The eyes of both were opened, and they knew that they were naked." (3:7) Opened to what? Not to the beauty of their physicality, not to the goodness of their sexuality, the very image of God in them—all of that was now out of focus and distorted. Their eyes were only open in a dream; they gazed at their own illusions. They really thought that they could and must live in a world without God, that they could "hide" from him (3:8), but this too proved to be a lie. In one sense, of course, the snake was right—they did not die. But, then, they did not understand what death was because they had lost sight of life. It is not death that is hard, but living toward death, living in terms of death, living an unreal life without meaning or substance.

## V. Sin as Illusion

This is why we cannot follow Bloch in his celebration of the Promethean act of man wherein he grasps after divinity. For to do so is to celebrate an illusion. If we speak of Adam's act of sin and the sinful condition of human existence as "illusion" we must be careful to avoid the notion that this somehow dilutes the seriousness of the situation. It has been characteristic of a certain type of theology from Hegel to Teilhard de Chardin to consider the human predicament as redeemable by processes of education, maturation, or natural evolution. Sin is merely a passing state of development which must and will be superseded by clarity, truth, and virtue. Here sin is illusory in the sense that religious consciousness incorrectly assigns ultimate importance to temporary error. "Illusion" in this sense means not really there, not really important, not really indicative of something radically wrong in human existence. But the fact that man's contradiction of himself appears at every stage of history and at all levels of development, and corrupts his present and renders hopeless his future, is reason enough to object to such a trivializing of sin.

If sin and the human predicament are characterized by "illusion," this should not imply any dilution of its corruptive power in human existence. For if illusions are not real, their effects certainly are. However false and imaginary may be the misunderstanding of self which drives men to destructive and anxious self-assertion, we must nevertheless recognize such delusion as the real source of the inhumanity of man. However senseless, false, and illusory may be the inexplicable rejection of one's true and full humanity in Christ, however vain and useless our attempt to determine our own being in insufficiency and lack, the results are social- and self-destruction, which are real enough. Far from trivializing sin, a conception of its illusory nature should impress upon us the full weight of its negativity—which is that it need not have happened, that it is based upon a lie and self-deception which man has imposed upon himself. This is more than tragic.

Where sin is seen as pride, and pride is considered a rational, if impious, response to man's desire to attain a higher form of being, there is tragedy to be sure. Man is punished for his hubris and loses even the limited finitude he had. But from the perspective of the Genesis story, it is simply not possible to conceive of man as some Icarian being who must escape the prison of his finitude by a heroic, if tragic, flight of the will. Being already free for unlimited explorations of his potentialities, his flight can only be senseless and suicidal. He is absurd *because* he is fallen.

But he is more than that.

The myth of the fall is an adequate expression of both the nature and destiny of man because it represents him neither as a sinner separated from God nor as a hero reaching for transcendence, but as one who has hope beyond tragedy. To be sure, having fallen victim to his own delusions, his life may be both tragic and absurd—but it is not hopeless. Human life is not hopeless because in the final analysis it is not determined by its delusions. What man is on his own has no *fundamentum in re;* it cannot "be" over against the being of God. The judgment we bring upon ourselves is itself under judgment—and cannot stand.

> ". . . now, lest he put forth his hand and take also of the tree of life, and eat, and live for ever"—therefore the LORD God . . . drove out the man; and at the east of the garden of Eden he placed the cherubim, and a flaming sword . . . [3:22-24]

The "last word" about man belongs to God. Man may curse his life with unreality and death, but that curse itself is limited by the judgment of God. So the divine refusal to allow *that* kind of life to "live for ever" must be seen as grace and mercy rather than condemnation. At the end of our story it is God's man who sets out from innocence clothed and marked by His grace (4:15); and whatever tragedy and mortality he may encounter on his journey, the way lying east of Eden is bright with hope.

---

1. This essay was originally presented as an *Otts Lecture* at Davidson College on December 8, 1971. It was part of a symposium entitled "Three Perspectives on the Nature of Man."

2. Cf. *IV Ezra* 7:118. "O Adam, what have you done? For though it was you who sinned, the fall was not yours alone, but ours also who are your descendants."

3. Reinhold Seeberg, *Text-Book of the History of Doctrines,* Charles E. Hay trans. (Grand Rapids: Baker Book House, 1956), p. 329, footnote 2. ". . . in Adam all sinned, as it were, in the mass; for all whom he who was himself corrupted through sin begat were born under sin; from him, therefore, all are sinners, because from him we all are."

4. Quoted by Heiko A. Oberman, *Forerunners of the Reformation* (New York: Holt, Rinehart and Winston, 1966), p. 155. Cited as *In Joannis Evangelium,* Tractatus III, 12, in *Patrologia Latina,* vol. XXXV, col. 1401.

5. Eugene TeSelle, *Augustine the Theologian* (London: Burns and Oates, 1970), p. 258. Or, as he wrote to the Pelagian Julian, "Children generated from and with this evil [must be] delivered from evil . . . the guilty beget the guilty." *Against Julian,* Bk. III, Ch. 26, par. 16. See also Augustine, *Confessions,* Bk. III, Ch. 3.

6. Cf. *Confessions,* Bk. XIV, Ch. 13. The claim that Augustine's conception of sin as pride contributed to a view of human nature as ontologically "fallen" and alienated from God requires both defense and qualification. A certain line of argument in Augustine, especially present in his earlier writings, understands sin and evil as nothingness which, as such, cannot effect the status of human *being* (Cf. *Soliloquies* II/XIII/24). "If things are deprived of all good they cease to exist. So long as they are, they are good. Whatever is is good. The evil then whose source I sought is not a substance, for were it a substance it would be good" (*Confessions* VIII/12/18). On the other hand, Augustine appears to grant sin and evil standing *in re,* substantiality and actuality, when he developed his doctrine of original sin and the fleshly transmission of guilt. Thus Augustine's monism gives way to a dualism as sin comes to constitute for him a state of being over against God. (A.C. McGiffert agrees with this analysis. Cf. his *A History of Christian Thought,* Vol. II [New York: Charles Scribner's Sons, 1933], p. 91.) This line of thought was intensified in Augustine's struggles with the Pelagians, and there is no doubt that he was so

understood by Calvin and his followers as they sought patristic support for their concept of man's *status corruptionis*. Therefore, in spite of tendencies in his thought to the contrary, we are justified in interpreting Augustine's view of pride as indicative of an ontological state of privation in original humanity. (See also note 18.)

7. Robin Scroggs, *The Last Adam* (Philadelphia: Fortress Press, 1966). While Prof. Scroggs' excellent study of Pauline anthropology moves in a somewhat different direction from that taken in this essay, we are nonetheless indebted to him for extracting from the massive literature of Judaism the references mentioned below.

8. Scroggs, *op. cit.*, p. 23, I Enoch 85-90.

9. Scroggs, *op. cit.*, p. xv.

10. This is seen in the synoptic use of the phrase "Son of Man." The question as to whether or not Jesus employed this phrase (*bar nasha, ben Adam*) as a messianic title is still open. We are inclined to agree with Oscar Cullmann (*The Christology of the New Testament,* Philadelphia: The Westminster Press, 1959, p. 137 ff.) that the very ambiguity of its use in the Synoptics indicates a strong tradition which had to be honored in spite of theological confusion as to its meaning. But whether or not Jesus actually used the term, it seems reasonable to assume that its presence in first century Jewish-Christian circles indicates a willingness to translate the symbol of the representative man as a figure of hope rather than death, and further, that it was considered appropriate to ascribe such usage to Jesus.

11. Cf. John Chrysostom, Commentary on Romans 5 in *The Library of the Fathers of the Holy Catholic Church,* Vol. I (Oxford: James Park & Co.), p. 150 f.; Augustine, *Against Julian,* Bk. 6, pars. 79-80; Thomas Aquinas, *Summa Theologica,* II/I/lxxxi/I.; John Calvin, *Institutes,* Bk. II, Ch. I, Sec. 6; Martin Luther, Commentary on Romans, (WA 56, 49, 17 ff.) in *Library of Christian Classics,* Vol. XV (Philadelphia: Westminster Press), pp. 154 ff.; Friedrich Schleiermacher, *The Christian Faith* (Edinburgh: T & T Clark, 1928), pp. 166, 300, 457. (All six of Schleiermacher's references to Romans 5 interpret that chapter only as commentary on original sin.); H. Wheeler Robinson, *The Christian Doctrine of Man* (Edinburgh: T & T Clark, 1913), pp. 121, 134. Citations which show the consistency of this interpretation can also be found in R. Niebuhr, E. Brunner, Dibelius-Kümmel, D.E.H. Whiteley, and, ironically, in Johannes Monk's *Paul and the Salvation of Mankind.* But perhaps the few given here are sufficient to make the point.

12. Karl Barth, *Christ and Adam* (New York: Harper and Brothers, 1957), pp. 29 f.

13. Ernst Bloch, *Atheismus im Christentum* (Frankfurt: Suhrkamp Verlag, 1968). Cf. pp. 226 ff.

14. Ernst Bloch, *op. cit.,* pp. 231 ff.

15. Karl Barth, *Church Dogmatics* III/1 (Edinburgh: T & T Clark, 1958), pp. 195 ff.

16. *Op. cit.,* pp. 284 f.

17. *Ibid.,* pp. 258 f.

18. An interpretation of the fruit of the tree of the knowledge of good and evil as "nothing" is encouraged by Gerhard von Rad who points out that the Hebrew phase for "good and evil" was used most often as a figure of speech indicating an indeterminate "everything" which actually points to "nothing." Thus, "We cannot speak to you bad or good," means "We can say nothing to you." Similarly, "The child knew neither good nor evil," means "The child knows nothing." (*Genesis,* Philadelphia: The Westminster Press, 1961, pp. 78 ff.) Ever since Parmenides excluded non-being from rational thought talk about nothing has been a problem for theology! The "nothing-ness" so excluded he called *ouk on* (absolute nothingness), which he distinguished from *me on* (relative nothingness, which has potential being). Augustine's Neoplatonic mentor Plotinus adopted the meontic interpretation of nothingness. "Some concept of it would be reached by thinking of measurelessness as apposed to measure.... Think of the ever undefined, the never at rest, the all accepting, but never sated, utter dearth." (Plotinus, *The Enneads,* trans. Stephen MacKenna, London: Faber and Faber, Ltd., 1962, i.8.3.) John Hick speaks of this as a "positive and active interpretation arising from the felt experi-ence of evil." (John Hick, *Evil and the God of Love,* London: Mac-millan, 1966, pp. 48, 49.) And while Augustine objected to this view, his later substantive definition of sin as inherited fault appears re-lated to it. (See note 6.) But if our interpretation of Genesis 1-3 is correct, theology must understand sin and evil as absolute vacuity. It may well be, as Karl Barth seems to suggest (CD III/1), that the nothingness to which we refer is peculiarly a theological concept. Because it represents a break in the created order, sin and nothingness can have no place in any philosophical system or principle of thought. In this Parmenides was right. But faith knows this nothingness as that which God overcomes in his creation and continues to defeat by the determination of his grace.

19. Von Rad, *op. cit.,* p. 85.

# Rhetoric and Responsibility in Calvin's Theology [1]

**E. DAVID WILLIS**

E. DAVID WILLIS

While it has become almost commonplace to say that Calvin's thought is dialectical, what is meant by that term differs widely with interpreters. It can mean that Calvin is best seen as a precursor and nourisher of the dialectical, or neo-orthodox, theologians of this century like Barth.[2] This line of interpretation has helped by breaking an earlier pattern of presenting Calvin as a prototype of Protestant scholasticism, or even of presenting him as a syllogistically fixated logician who, in the quiet frigidity of his heart and study, was concerned above all about constructing the first Protestant system of doctrine. I do not want to minimize the contributions made in Calvin research by this particular line of dialectical interpretation.

There is another sense of dialectic, however, which I do wish to oppose as misleading.[3] It is that Calvin's thought is dialectical in that he is primarily to be understood as a product of late medieval logic, especially in the form of diastatic nominalism, which—according to this interpretive strain—accounts for what are to be taken to be the unresolved conflicts, the complex of opposites, the sharply disjunctive qualities, in his thought. Surely there is also some grain of truth even in this perspective. But it does not do sufficient justice either to the wide diversity to be found in late medieval nominalists or—and this is the particular interest in this article—to the rhetorical tradition of

Christian humanism not only in Calvin's *style* but in the *content* of his theology and anthropology.[4] Calvin's thought is not primarily characterized by dialectical diastasis but by rhetorical correlation.

Calvin obviously was influenced by late medieval intellectual (and social, economic, and political) currents. The question is which of those currents influenced him most, judging from the references he makes to other texts, thoughts, and authors. There has been a tendency, born of the one-sided historiography which treats the last medieval period as a decline from the "high" Middle Ages, to see the Reformers *primarily* as products of what is variously, and often loosely, referred to as nominalism, Scotism, the Occamist tendencies, etc. According to this scheme, Luther is not really to be blamed, therefore, if he reacted so fiercely to Roman Catholic theology because, poor fellow, the only theology he knew well was the nominalist sidetrack, not the real Catholic thing! This kind of perspective is applied also to Calvin in spite of the fact that we have far less direct evidence in Calvin's own citations that he thoroughly studied the late medieval theologians than we do with Luther. Yet Calvin continues to be identified with nominalism (a) because his emphasis on the divine will seems to be so similar to Scotus, and (b) because anyone who continued to follow the Augustinian monk Luther as closely as Calvin did on grace and justification must have been led there at least indirectly also by nominalism.

I am going to leave aside the entire question, being pursued especially by Heiko Oberman, of the extent to which there was far greater vitality and variety among the nominalists than would warrant treating their period mainly as a decline from "high" scholasticism.[5] I will call attention to the facts that (a) the Renaissance humanism which appeared also in the late medieval period constituted at least as much of an influence in the circles in which Calvin moved as did the school theology of the diastatic nominalists, and (b) if we are to judge from Calvin's own citations and references this Renaissance humanism was far more influential on him than was nominalism. This does not mean that the humanist's influence was less theological than the nominalist's. To accept such a distinction would be to admit a judgment which the Christian humanists above all did not want to allow, namely that Christian theology was to be considered as best represented by the theologians of the Sorbonne and their favorite authors. The Christian humanists considered that their movement *ad fontes* was a form of a theology which was more, not less, Catholic than the endless squabbles of those whom they called the "theologasters," "sorbonists," and "sophists." [6] And in this they were largely correct. Their cry was not just *ad fontes* but *Christium praedicare ex fontibus*. They recovered many of the ecumenical perspectives of the patristic period which had been abandoned by Latin and European theology, as it accommodated itself to the feudal setting of activity. Calvin's grounding in Christian humanism, and in the rhetorical tradition which was part of it, constitutes therefore an element of the catholicity of his thought and theology.

## Two Rhetorical Traditions

Rhetoric, like dialectic, has several meanings. There are at least two main rhetorical traditions. Before we identify certain rhetorical characteristics in Calvin's thought, we must first specify what rhetorical tradition we are speaking about and, second, say something about the legal and patristic studies through which Calvin was brought into that tradition.

There is a positive and a negative sense of rhetoric, senses which are with us today and which go back to the debate in classical times over the function of argumentation and persuasion in public life. The question was this: when the public, whether as jury or political assembly, is brought into the process of determining justice and executing wise statecraft, with what attitudes and techniques does the person skilled in verbal communication hinder or facilitate that process?

Almost from its emergence in the sophists as a discipline, there have been two competing conceptions of the purpose of rhetoric. As C. S. Baldwin puts it,[7] the one concentrates on rendering the speaker effective in winning a case or persuading his audience, quite apart from a prior consideration about the truth or falsity of the case. The art of persuasion in this light is preeminently a matter of putting one's argument, whether it be true or false, in *the best possible form* to make it acceptable to one's hearers. Form of presentation and stylistic considerations become the preoccupation of the rhetorician so conceived. It is this view of rhetoric which has given it its commonplace negative connotation and which bears the brunt of Socrates' criticism in the *Gorgias*.

The other conception of rhetoric concentrates not on rendering the speaker effective but the *truth* effective. It approaches the discipline as a positive explication of how the truth becomes powerful in human affairs. This theory of "rhetoric as the energizing of knowledge, the bringing of truth to bear upon men" [8] is expressed by Aristotle, who understands the discipline to be larger than that of its sophistic representatives against which Plato reacts.

Cicero goes beyond both Socrates' and Aristotle's treatment of rhetoric. He teaches that rhetoric trains men for sharing in the right governance of the state and that the training of the orator includes his moral formation. Cicero agrees with Aristotle's more positive evaluation of the discipline, but he criticizes Aristotle for separating too sharply the task of rhetoric from that of philosophy. In each case, Cicero attempts to hold the ideal of joining rhetoric and philosophy. He therefore praises those practicing lawyers who, before Socrates, claimed the title of philosopher. ". . . The followers of Socrates cut the connection with the practicing lawyers and detached these from the common title of philosophy, although the old masters had intended there to be a marvellously close alliance between oratory (*dicendi*) and philosophy (*intellegendi*)." [9] It was their competence for practical philosophy (the study of life and ethics which refused to let philosophy be taken over by those who were learned but who deliberately shrank from political affairs and chose not to communicate effectively in terms which were persuasive to the common man) that validated the orators' claim to the title of philosopher.

> . . . To us belong—assuming that we are really orators, that is persons competent to be retained as leaders and principals in civil

actions and criminal trials and public debates—to us, I say, belong the broad estates of wisdom and of learning, which having been allowed to lapse and become derelict during our absorption in affairs, have been invaded by persons too generously supplied with leisure, persons who actually banter and ridicule the orator after the manner of Socrates in Plato's *Gorgias,* or else write a few little manuals of instruction in the art of oratory and label them with the title of Rhetoric—just as if the province of the rhetoricians did not include their pronouncements on the subjects of justice and duty and the constitution and government of states, in short the entire field of practical philosophy.[10]

This positive, Ciceronian, rhetorical tradition did not die out with the close of the ancient world but was one of the main elements included in the transformation of classical into medieval culture. The outlines of the history of rhetoric in the Middle Ages have been provided by several scholars. McKeon, for example, traces reduction of rhetoric to medieval preaching and diplomatic and court correspondence (the *ars dictamini* and *ars gravimini*) and the reassertion of rhetoric as a broader discipline with the Renaissance movement to classical sources. In Harbison's words, the activity of the Christian scholar in the age of the Renaissance and Reformation constituted a reassertion of rhetoric and grammar over dialectic and speculative philosophy.[11] The Renaissance meant in part a recovery of the fuller Ciceronian ideal of rhetoric. It involved both a re-reading of the so-called pagan treatises on rhetoric and a rediscovery of the use to which the early Christian theologians put the rhetorical tradition in formulating the gospel for the Graeco-Roman world.

### How Calvin Was Related to This Tradition

Whether Calvin was influenced more by his study of the classical rhetoricians themselves or by his study of the early Christianized rhetorical tradition is a matter of debate. It is really a question of which side of French Christian humanism is emphasized, i.e., the editing and study of the classical so-called pagan sources or the editing and study of patristics—a dichotomy which we must take care not to draw more sharply than did the Renaissance figures themselves.

Before turning to the patristic influences, I want to acknowledge parenthetically that rather than making him "legalist," as so often is supposed, Calvin's legal training was one of the most important sources of the rhetorical humanism which helped shape the content of his theology. The legal training he had was that of the innovative Renaissance law professors (for example, d'Etoille and Alciati) who were creating such a stir in France, and this involved a recovery of classical models which challenged the prevailing medieval models. It was a legal training [12] which included a reassertion of the role classically given to the lawyer's training as rhetor who exercised the art of persuasion as the best means of discerning and applying justice in individual cases. Rather than strengthening the idea of a God who rules by demanding "legalistic" obedience to his arbitrary and imperial-like decrees (the role Calvin's legal training is often asserted to have played in his theology), Calvin's humanistic legal training strengthened the view that God is one who accommodates himself to human weakness to restore men to their lost freedom, to persuade them of their vindication in Christ, and to inform, delight, and move them to live out their adoption as free sons. One can point, obviously, to a certain tendency in Calvin strictly to enforce the civil laws for which Geneva was particularly noted, either to its praise or blame. Cities like Geneva saw, at the end of the fifteenth and throughout the sixteenth centuries, the influx of peasants into cities as a part of the rise of the bourgeoisie. The civil magistrates (like those in Geneva even before Farel and Calvin came there) sought, with what seem to us to be minute codes, to regulate life in these crowded cities. Calvin was an uncompromising supporter of these laws, especially since: (a) he had to keep Geneva diplomatically secure as a refugee city; (b) he had to make Geneva an instrument of the ecclesiastical discipline necessary to the success of the Reformed movements in countries (especially France) where they were being persecuted; and (c) he had to make it clear that contrary to what Protestantism's opponents were only willing to judge from the specter of Muenster and from Luther's implication in the bigamy case of Philip of Hesse, the

Protestant doctrine of Christian liberty was not a rationalization to justify antinomianism. Surely Calvin's legal training imbued him with a concern for the right ordering of society and for making the transition from individual justification to societal sanctification. The content and extent of his Geneva rectitude one may well object to; but his claim that the gospel has something to say about the whole of human life, including its political, economic, and social dimensions, is as correct now as it was then.

Calvin frequently cites directly certain patristic sources. In doing so he acts as a representative of those French Renaissance scholars who turned their attention to the early Church fathers as much as to the pagan sources. There is considerable difference among the Christian humanists about how Christian philosophy comes about, and there is considerable latitude in the way they related intellect and will. They are joined, however, in the conviction that self-knowledge and human happiness are not to be divorced from the knowledge of God, and that this knowledge involves a conversion of the will by divine instruction and persuasion. In this conviction they are heirs not simply of classical pagan learning but of that portion of the medieval tradition which kept alive the patristic effort to integrate classical learning and Christian doctrine transforming the one by the other.

Augustine is the father to whom Calvin has special recourse,[13] and it is in Calvin's reading of him that we find the primary source of his rhetorical theology. In Augustine, Calvin found the ancient rhetorical tradition turned to the true philosophy of Christ. One of Augustine's chief contributions is that he extended and altered the Ciceronian tendency in the rhetorical tradition and used this latter to shape a distinctively Christian eloquence.[14] While Baldwin perhaps overstates Augustine's innovation by underestimating the way the Cappadocian Fathers used the rhetorical tradition, he does not go far enough in seeing the theological significance of Augustine's use of rhetoric. Augustine carries on the enterprise of developing a Christian paideutic tradition, as Werner Jaeger has pointed out. This Christian *paideia* is similar to Greek *paideia* in that it concentrates on reinterpreting the cumulative written wisdom of a people. But the literature whose interpretation is crucial for the Church is that of the writings of the Old and New Testaments rather than Homer.[15] Perhaps of equal importance is Augustine's theological conviction, which permits and validates this enterprise, that God through Christ is the initiator of an educational process which brings man to wholeness. Christ uses the Christian *paideia* to instruct, persuade, and move his people from pride to humility, from love of self to love of God. Christ is the truth which rhetoric makes powerfully effective among men. Put this way, Augustine's renewal of the rhetorical tradition is no less than a way of describing, responding to, and transmitting revelation. In his use of rhetoric to expand the tradition of a Christian *paideia,* Augustine offers a model for subsequent Christian humanists, including Calvin, in their effort to turn classical learning to the service of Christian theology. He shows how Christian theology can use classical wisdom to enrich the Church's appreciation of its own literature.

## Instances of Calvin's Rhetorical Theology

So far I have indicated something about the positive rhetorical tradition and Calvin's probable connection with it. Now we turn to examine its function in Calvin's theology. We are here not so much interested in the form of his argument or literary style as we are in the influence of the rhetorical tradition upon three major areas of his thought. These areas go to the very heart of his theology: his views of faith as persuasion, of knowledge as efficacious truth, and of revelation as God's persuasive accommodation.

*The Believer's Persuasion* ". . . he alone," says Calvin, "is truly a believer who, convinced by a firm conviction that God is a kindly and well-disposed Father toward him, [really, "persuaded by a solid persuasion" etc.: *qui solida persuasione . . . esse persuasus*] promises himself all things on the basis of his generosity; who, relying upon the promises of divine benevolence toward him, lays hold on an undoubted expectation of salvation." [16] Calvin defines faith as "a firm and certain knowledge of God's benevolence toward us, founded upon the truth of the freely given promise in Christ, both revealed to our minds and sealed upon our hearts through the Holy Spirit." [17]

In these definitions, Calvin distinguishes true faith from the doctrine of implicit faith which he feels is "ignorance tempered with humility." [18] "Faith rests not on ignorance, but on knowledge. And this is, indeed, knowledge not only of God but of the divine will. We do not obtain salvation either because we are prepared to embrace as true whatever the Church has prescribed, or because we turn over to it the task of inquiring and knowing. But we do so when we know that God is our merciful Father, because of reconciliation effected through Christ [2 Cor. 5:18-19], and that Christ has been given to us as righteousness, sanctification and life." [19]

Calvin also distinguishes true faith from the doctrine of unformed faith or assent to all the necessary articles of faith. It will not do just to know that the gospel stories are true. Some people are moved by some taste of the Word and become convinced themselves that they truly believe. But this sort is not true faith, for those who have it ". . . persuade themselves that the reverence that they show to the Word of God is very piety itself, because they count it no impiety unless there is open and admitted reproach or contempt of his Word. Whatever sort of assent that is, it does not at all penetrate to the heart itself there to remain fixed." [20] Over against these alternatives, therefore, Calvin argues that faith is such a knowledge of God's will and benefits that it becomes the personal application of them to one's own condition. Being sealed on the heart, becoming a matter of firm conviction—these are other ways of saying that the gospel becomes a matter of inward and effective persuasion. He says, "We add the words 'sure and firm' in order to express a more solid constancy of persuasion. For, as faith is not content with a doubtful and changeable opinion, so is it not content with an obscure and confused conception; but requires full and fixed certainty, such as men are wont to have from things experienced and proved. For unbelief is so deeply rooted in our hearts, and we are so inclined to it, that not without hard struggle is each one able to persuade himself of what all confess with the mouth: namely, that God is faithful." [21]

*Knowledge as Truth Becomes Efficacious* Truth is measured in the rhetorical tradition not primarily by logical coherence or propositional clarity but by its power to change those whom it grasps. This rhetorical tradition regarding truth's fruitfulness, and not just impatience over scholastic disputation, is an important basis for Calvin's rejection of speculative theology and philosophy. True knowledge is experiential and ethically active. Today we might say, if we felt compelled to use contemporary terms, it is existentially real and compels us to a new life–style. Calvin says that those who are unchanged have only a pretended knowledge of Christ, no matter how learned and fluent their talk about the gospel.

> For it is a doctrine not of the tongue but of life. It is not appre-hended by the understanding and memory alone, as other dis-ciplines are, but it is received only when it possesses the whole soul, and finds a seat and a resting place in the inmost affection of the heart. . . . it must enter into our heart and pass into our daily living, and so transform us into itself that it may not be unfruitful for us. The philosophers rightly burn with anger against, and reproachfully drive from their flock, those who when they profess an art that ought to be the mistress of life, turn it into sophistical chatter. With how much better reason, then, shall we detest these trifling Sophists who are content to roll the gospel on the tips of their tongues when its efficacy ought to penetrate the inmost affections of the heart, take its seat in the soul, and effect the whole man a hundred times more deeply than the cold exhortations of the philosophers. [22]

This experiential character of true knowledge is echoed throughout Calvin's work as he consistently contrasts speculative sophistry with the kind of knowing engendered by the twofold instrument of God's teaching, Word and Spirit. The knowledge of God to which we are called is "not that knowledge which, content with empty speculation, merely flits in the brain, but that which will be sound and fruitful if we duly perceive it, and if it takes root in the heart. For the Lord manifests himself by his powers, the force of which we feel within ourselves and the benefits of which we enjoy." [23]

*Revelation as God's Persuasive Accommodation* God's purpose through his dealing with men is to bring them to the maturity he wills for them, and he educates and persuades them to that end.[24] Far from maintaining a view of a lofty God who is untouched by human weakness and changeableness, Calvin presents a view of God who as a loving Father strategically adjusts his dealings with his people in order to inform, delight, and move them (cf. the three classical aims of rhetoric) to doing his will, which represents both his glory and their highest good. A favorite term used for this revelatory activity is "accommodation." [25] God accommodates himself to our lowly condition, and the story of this accommodation is the history of the economy of his covenantal purpose. He keeps hope alive in his people by freshly adapting the promises of his covenant to different epochs and conditions of his people.[26]

> . . . God ought not to be considered changeable merely because he accommodates [*accommodaverit*] diverse forms to different ages, as he knew would be expedient for each. . . . if a householder instructs, rules, and guides his children one way in infancy, another way in youth, and still another in young manhood, we shall not on this account call him fickle and say that he abandons his purpose. Why, then, do we brand God with the mark of inconstancy because he has with apt and fitting marks distinguished a diversity of times? The latter comparison ought to satisfy us fully. Paul likens the Jews to children, Christians to young men (Gal. 4:1 ff.). What was irregular about the fact that God confined them to rudimentary teaching commensurate with their age, but has trained us through a firmer and, so to speak, more manly discipline? Thus God's constancy shines forth in the fact that he taught the same doctrine to all ages, and has continued to require the same worship of his name that he has enjoined from the beginning. In the fact that he has changed the outward form and manner, he does not show himself subject to change. Rather, he has accommodated [*se attemperavit;* Fr. 1545, *accomodé*] himself to men's capacity, which is varied and changeable." [27]

We might think that Calvin would, as he moved chronologically away from the early period usually most associated with his classical humanism, stress this category of persuasion less and less. But in replying to questions put to him by Laelius Socinus [28] ("How is it that the true believer often doubts and that the unbeliever often shows signs of faith?"), Calvin relies more heavily than ever on the terms of persuasion to explain what he means by faith. There Calvin's argument (which itself may have been less than persuasive to Socinus!) is, in effect, that the difference between true and false faith is a matter of the degree of depth and constancy with which one experiences the assurance of his being adopted by a merciful God. The elect are more deeply and lastingly imbued with assurance of their being adopted by a merciful God, whereas the reprobate may taste some assurance, but only fleetingly and superficially. "Although faith is a knowledge of the divine benevolence toward us and a sure persuasion of its truth, there is no wonder that the awareness of divine love vanishes in temporary things [or "in the temporary ones": *in temporariis*]. Even if it is close to faith, it differs much from it. The will of God is unchangeable, I admit, and his truth ever remains in agreement with itself. Yet I deny that the reprobate proceed so far as to penetrate into that secret revelation which Scripture vouchsafes only to the elect." [29] The following lines indicate that by this secret revelation Calvin means the Spirit of adoption, i.e., the Spirit assuring men that they are adopted: ". . . however deficient or weak faith may be in the elect, still, because the Spirit of God is for them the sure guarantee and seal of their adoption [Eph. 1:14; cf. 2 Cor. 1:22], the mark he has engraved can never be erased from their hearts. . . ." [30]

But how does a person know if he has the Spirit of adoption as opposed to a spirit of self-deception? Calvin's explanation of the difference between true and false faith seems, at this point, to have reference to a fairly arbitrary and inscrutable will of God. Calvin's insistence on the immutability of the divine will is mitigated, though not enough, by his rhetorical humanism. There is in Calvin's thought (and in Augustine's) a juxtaposition of two insights about God's dealings with men. One insight focuses on God's adaptive and accommodative strategy to persuade into mature freedom; the other focuses on the fact that this adaptive strategy is effectively applicable only to those whom God has chosen from the beginning so to deal with, a number fixed by the immutable will of the immutable God.

This latter conception, that it belongs to the very essence of God to be unchangeable, is of course not limited to Calvin and was—and many persons would still say is—an indispensable affirmation of Christian orthodoxy. Calvin never really questioned this basic assumption of God's immutability. Indeed, he has to defend his teaching against those who charged that with his emphasis on the divine accommodation Calvin introduced the idea that God is affected by emotion or his purposes are changeable by man's actions. My point is that the equation between the divine and the immutable which Calvin inherited was mitigated by this other insight—that God persuasively accommodates his purpose to man's persuadability. Calvin was not able to expand this insight, as I think we must today, to argue from the variety of God's dealing with men that God himself changes in some sense in his relation to his changing creation. As it is, Calvin sometimes uses the very argument about God's accommodation in order to guard against the thought that God himself changes. That is, it is only our weakness which necessitates the biblical anthropomorphisms which attribute human emotions to God.[31] This is a point at which Calvin has a very contextual view of the Scriptures. God's work does not speak uniformly to all situations but addresses itself to varying situations and accommodates itself to varying capacities of apprehension.

Calvin wants—as a good follower of Augustine—to insist upon the principle of God's undeserved favor. But that the identification of the experience of grace should be as arbitrary as Calvin suggests here was a bad detour for Christian doctrine. Surely the debate is misplaced if he makes this arbitrary will dominant merely to spell out the difference between the true and the false feeling of being adopted and forgiven. In Calvin's reply to Socinus and, earlier, Bolsec, he tries to make a more ambitious point about election than he attempted earlier. Earlier his doctrine of predestination served a subordinate role to account for the observation that some men hearing the gospel respond to it and are changed by it, while others, also hearing, do not respond and remain unchanged. But in this reply he accepts a different ground of debate and attempts now to answer the question as to how one can tell the difference between those who really think they experience the Spirit of adoption, but actually do not, and those who really think they experience the Spirit of adoption, and actually do. In attempting this answer, Calvin almost claims that the difference is known from the constancy and intensity of this feeling, a teaching which in the seventeenth and eighteenth centuries could serve to reinforce the introspection which emerged in pietism from other quarters.

Even so, Calvin's answer is not an absolute one, since he does base his argument on an examination of the phenomenon of faith as experienced, as that experience is constantly being corrected from a reinterpretation of Scriptures.[32] More important, however, is that fact that his argument does not rest on introspection. He points out that to have the seal of the Spirit of adoption means to live as an adopted son. The internal experience and the outward ethical response are indissolubly linked. Living as an adopted son means above all serving one's fellows out of the spirit of love and in Christian freedom, rather than out of a sense of compulsion and with a bad conscience. ". . . as a persuasion of God's fatherly love is not deeply rooted in the reprobate, so do they not perfectly [solide] reciprocate his love as sons, but behave like hirelings." [33] The love of God which is shed abroad in our hearts through the Holy Spirit (Rom. 5:5, cf. vulgate) is ". . . the love that generates the above-mentioned confidence that we can call upon him [Cf. Gal. 4:6]." [34] In other words, the assurance of faith (which is equivalent to the persuasion by God's Word and Spirit) is the firm conviction of one's adoption by a loving Father (or, to use Tillich's paraphrase, the acceptance of one's acceptance). The life of free and delighted obedience to God and service of men which flows from this new sense of one's worth before God (or new self-image, we might say today) is a confirmation of our inward experience of adoption.[35]

This persuasion which is faith is the same thing as being moved from trying to serve God out of a sense of compulsion (being bound by a bad conscience) and serving him in the Spirit of freedom as a son (having the testimony of a good conscience).[36] The persuasion, then, of God is to dissuade men from acting out of fear and with bad consciences and to move them to delight to obey him freely with good consciences. This use of conscience as the forum for judging one's relation to God (as judged and forgiven and set free) is another example of the function of the rhetorical tradition in Calvin's thought. That is, for Calvin, man is above all created for free obedience to God, and as such is always persuadable. God leaves to men—even in their rebellion—a conscience which bears witness to their incompleteness apart from him and to their experience of being reconciled to him. Conscience is the instrument of man's self-knowledge, whereby he perceives himself either destructively as one condemned by an angry judge (and thus lives and worships idolatrously) or constructively as one assured of his acceptance by a loving Father. Self-knowledge, then, stands in correlation to the knowledge of God, the two knowledges together constituting practically the whole of knowledge, as Calvin remarks at the beginning of the *Institutes*.

## Conclusion

If one reads Calvin looking for signs of the diastatic nominalism he is sure dominates his thought, he will emphasize the sharp distinction Calvin sometimes draws between the human and the divine, reason and revelation, grace and nature, and justification and sanctification. On the other hand, if we are alerted to Calvin's location in the rhetorical tradition, we can see how many of the polar elements of his thought are correlatively joined. God and man are not primarily seen by him as statically irreconcilable entities or as unrelatable types of being. Rather, God and man are seen together in a continual story of the one's effort persuasively to relate himself to the other and of the other's growing self-knowledge and maturity as the subject of his persuasive history. God remains God; and man's being really human depends on God's remaining God in relation to him. But God is God *for* man by his self-accommodation to human capacity. Calvin's thought is not determined by the philosophical principle, as often alleged, of *finitum non capax infiniti*. Calvin's thought is centrally that God does indeed accommodate himself to our capacity. *Humanitas capax divinitatis per accommodationem.* That is, God begins with our incapacity, makes himself small to adjust to it, and by his gracious action of strategic self-limitation, transforms us so that we are increasingly united to God himself in Christ.

---

1. This article is from a paper originally presented under the title "Dialectic and Rhetoric in Calvin's Theology" at the American Academy of Religion, meeting in New York, October 1970.

2. Here see especially W. Neisel, *The Theology of Calvin,* tr. H. Knight (Philadelphia: The Westminster Press, 1956), but also Thomas Torrance, *Calvin's Doctrine of Man* (London: Lutterworth Press, 1952), and Thomas Henry Louis Parker, *Calvin's Doctrine of the Knowledge of God* (2nd ed.; Grand Rapids, Mich.: W. B. Eerdmans, 1959).

3. Cf. Alexandre Ganoczy, *Calvin: Théologien de l'Eglise et du Ministère* (Paris: du Cerf, 1964), and D. Willis, "Notes" on the latter in *Bibliothèque d'Humanisme et Renaissance,* 30, 1968, pp. 186-198. Cf. also Ganoczy's *Le Jeune Calvin: Genèse et Evolution de sa Vocatrice* (Wiesbaden: Steiner, 1966). Ganoczy's studies on Calvin's view of conciliar authority are especially useful.

4. It is Francois Wendel's emphasis on the Development of Calvin's thought which makes his *Calvin: Sources et evolution de sa Pensée Religieuse* (Paris: Presses Universitaires de France, 1950) so useful, though one should not overlook the earlier works of Emile Doumergue (*Jean Calvin* [7 vols.; Lausanne: G. Bridel and Co., 1899]). Josef Bohatec in *Bude und Calvin* (Graz: Böhlaus, 1950) has been most helpful in setting Calvin in the context of the wide and diverse circle of humanism: but cf. also especially E. H. Harbison's treatment of Calvin in *The Christian Scholar in the Age of the Reformation* (New York: Charles Scribner's Sons, 1956, and André Biéler's in *La Pensée Economique et Sociale de Calvin* (Geneva: Libr. Univ., 1959). On Calvin's humanist setting, cf. also C. Trinkhaus, "Renaissance Problems in Calvin's Theology," *Studies in Renaissance,* I (Austin: University of Texas Press, 1954); Egil Grislis' paper on "The Humanism of John Calvin" read at the Spring Conference of the American

Society of Church History, Louisville, Ky., April 19, 1969; and Ekkehard Mühlenberg, "The Ciceronian Tradition and the Implementation of Civil Virtue by Zwingli, Calvin and Melancthon," paper read at the American Society of Church History, meeting in San Francisco, December, 1973. Also V. L. Nuovo, "Calvin's Theology: A Study of its Sources in Classical Antiquity," Thesis, Columbia Univ., N.Y., 1964. More than anyone else so far, Quirinus Breen has dealt with Calvin's humanism in his relation especially to his Seneca Commentary (*John Calvin: A Study in French Humanism* [Grand Rapids: Wm. B. Eerdmans, 1931]) and with the way the rhetorical tradition influenced Calvin's *style* of argument in the *Institutes* ("John Calvin and the Rhetorical Tradition," *Church History*, 26, 1957, pp. 3-21). For his treatment of rhetoric in Melanchthon, see Breen's "The Subordination of Philosophy to Rhetoric in Melanchthon," *Archiv für Reformationsgeschichte*, 43, 1952, pp. 13–28). Cf. also other essays in Breen's *Christianity and Humanism* (Grand Rapids: William B. Eerdmans, 1968). Of the many works on the history of rhetoric, those which have been especially useful for this paper are R. McKeon, "Rhetoric in the Middle Ages," *Speculum*, 17, 1942, pp. 1-32; C. S. Baldwin, *Medieval Rhetoric and Poetic* (New York: Macmillan, 1928); J. E. Siegel, *Rhetoric and Philosophy in Renaissance Humanism* (Princeton: Princeton Univ. Press, 1968). Cf. also H. Gray, *History and Rhetoric in Quatrocentro Humanism*, Ph.D. Diss., Radcliffe College, 1956, and Beryl Smalley, *English Friars and Antiquity in the Early Fourteenth Century* (Oxford: Blackwell, 1960). Also W. S. Howell, *Logic and Rhetoric in England, 1500-1700* (New York: Russell & Russell, 1961). Though not specifically on rhetoric, Paul Kristeller's work (e.g., in his *Eight Philosophers of the Italian Renaissance* [Stanford: Stanford Univ. Press, 1964]) has been helpful in redefining Renaissance humanism and in locating the role which Christian piety played in that humanism. Cf. also Lewis W. Spitz' judgement that "... the Florentine Platonism which Mutian learned to know represented an effort at a constructive theology in the service of Christian piety and in opposition to Averroism, lifeless scholasticism, and the half-stoic eudemonistic religiosity or irreligiosity characteristic of a small segment of Italian humanism." (*The Religious Renaissance of the German Humanists*, Cambridge, Mass.: Harvard University Press, 1963, p. 136).

5. Cf. especially Heiko A. Oberman, *The Harvest of Medieval Theology: Gabriel Biel and Late Medieval Nominalism* (Cambridge: Harvard University Press, 1963).

6. For a classic example of this, see Erasmus' "Reply to Martin Dorp," May, 1515. In Erasmus' theological lineage in the ancient Christian humanism, see P. G. Bietenholz, *History and Biography in the Work*

*of Erasmus of Rotterdam,* Travaux d'Humanisme et Renaissance, (Geneva: Droz, 1966), Vol. 87, pp. 35 ff.; and Ernst K. Kohls, *Die Theologie des Erasmus,* 2 Vols. (Basel: F. Reinhardt, 1966), Vol. 1, pp. 176 ff.

7. C. S. Baldwin, *op. cit.,* pp. 2 ff.

8. *Ibid.,* p. 3.

9. *De Oratore,* 3, 19, 73; trans. H. Rackham, Loeb Classical Library (Cambridge, Mass.: Harvard Univ. Press), II, pp. 58-59.

10. *De Oratore,* 3, 31, 122 *ibid.* pp. 414-17. For a discussion of the Ciceronian model of relating rhetoric and philosophy, see Siegel, *op. cit.,* ch. 1, and Albert Michel, *Rhétorique et Philosophie chez Ciceron* (Paris: Presses Universitaires de France, 1960).

11. Cf. Harbison, *op. cit.,* p. 43. According to Harbison, Valla exemplified this "triumph of grammar and rhetoric over dialectic, of the historical over the philosophical attitude" better than anyone else of his generation.

12. Cf. Breen, *op. cit.,* pp. 183-199, esp. pp. 193 ff.

13. The best study of the relation of Calvin to Augustine remains L. Smits. See above all, L. Smits, *Augustin dans l'oeuvre de Jean Calvin,* 2 vols. (Assen: Van Gorcum, 1957-8).

14. Cf. McKeon, *op. cit.,* and especially the section on Augustine, pp. 5 ff. Augustine's assimilation and reapplication of Cicero constituted one line of intellectual development in the Middle Ages concerning rhetoric. This Augustinian rhetorical current McKeon describes as the tradition of philosophers and theologians who found in Augustine a Platonism reconstructed from the Academic and Neoplatonic philosophies (conscientiously reversing the process by which they were derived from Plato's doctrine) and formulated in terms refurbished and simplified from Cicero's rhetorical distinctions" (*ibid.,* p. 4). "The influence of rhetoric on Augustine was by reaction and assimilation; he differentiated two eloquences and two arts, much as Plato has proved rhetoric to be a psuedo art in the *Gorgias* and yet had illustrated to be the method the true rhetoric based on dialectic in the *Phaedrus*" (*ibid.,* p. 5). At the beginning of his *De Inventione,* Cicero describes the way wisdom and eloquence are to be held together for the good of the state. By doubling these terms, Augustine was able to argue, as McKeon puts it, that "The wisdom and eloquence of the world are to be contrasted to eternal wisdom and eloquence, for not only are there two kinds of things, temporal and divine, but two kinds of words, the external words instituted and used by men, which have no correspondence to things except by designations and no controllable influence on our thought except by the context of other words, and the internal words by which a master teaching within us teaches the truth. Whether things be treated as signs or signs as things, only the

eternal meanings and realities are important; knowledge of temporal things and of the arts is chiefly useful for the interpretation of the language and symbolism of Scripture, and the sacraments are signs adapted to the mutability of human sensibilities but are immutable in their significance of the changeless things of God" (*ibid.*, pp. 6-7). Cf. Henri I. Marrou, *Saint Augustin et la Fin de la Culture Antique* (Paris: E. de Boccard, 1938), esp. chapters 3, on rhetoric, and 6, on Christian eloquence; Marie Comeau, *La Rhétorique de Saint Augustin d'après le Tractatus in Iohannem* (Paris: Boivin, 1930); H. R. Niebuhr's treatment of Augustine under the type which sees Christ as the transformer of culture, *Christ and Culture* (New York: Harper, 1951), ch. 6, esp. pp. 206 ff.; H. Hagehdahl, *Augustine and the Latin Classics*, 2 vols. (Göteborg: Univ. of Göteborg Press, 1967), Vol. 2, pp. 553-558; M. Iestard, *Ciceron dans la Formation et dans l'Oeuvre de Saint Augustin* (Vol. 1 of *Saint Augustin et Ciceron*) (Paris: Etudes Augustiniennes, 1958); A. Cutler, "Augustine and the Transvaluation of the Classical Tradition," *The Classical Journal,* 54, 1958, pp. 213-220.

15. Werner Jaeger, *Early Christianity and Greek Paideia* (Cambridge, Mass.: Harvard University Press, 1961). Cf. also Henri I. Marrou, *Histoire de l'Education dans l'Antiquité,* 2nd ed. (Paris: Editions de Seuil, 1950), pp. 139 ff. On the civilization of paideia.

16. *Institutes,* 3, 2, 16; John Calvin: *Institutes of the Christian Religion,* ed. John T. McNeill, trans. Ford Lewis Battles, (Philadelphia: Westminster Press, 1960), 2 vols. (henceforth McNeill), p. 562; *Opera Selecta Calvini,* ed. Peter Barth and W. Neisel (Munich: Kaiser Verlag), 5 vols., 1936 ff. (henceforth *OS*), 4:26-27.

17. *Inst.* 3, 2, 7-1539; McNeill, p. 551; *OS* 4:16.

18. *Inst.* 3, 2, 2-1539; McNeill, p. 545; *OS* 4:11.

19. *Inst.* 3, 2, 2-1539; McNeill, p. 545; *OS* 4:10.

20. *Inst.* 3, 2, 10; McNeill, p. 554; *OS* 4:20.

21. *Inst.* 3, 2, 15; McNeill, p. 560; *OS* 4:25. Cf. also in the same section, "Here indeed is the chief hinge on which faith turns: that we do not regard the promises of the mercy that God offers as true only outside ourselves, [extra nos tantum veras esse arbitremur] but not at all in us; rather that we make them ours by inwardly embracing them."

22. *Inst.* 3, 6, 4-1539; McNeill, p. 688, *OS* 4:149-50. Sophists here is equivalent to the dialecticians of the schools, the "scholastici" or "sorbonists." Cf. also the same usage in *Inst.* 2, 3, 10 and *Inst.* 1, 17, 2 (and note 7, McNeill, p. 214).

23. *Inst.* 1, 5, 9-1539; McNeill, pp. 61-62; *OS* 3:53.

24. Calvin speaks of all the signs God used in Israel's tutelage, "*apte quadrabant and rationem docendi*" (*Inst.,* 1, 11, 3; *OS* 3, 90-91). Cf. also *Inst.* 2, 11, 5 and 4, 1, 24.

25. Cf. R. Hofmann, "Accommodation," "*Realencyklopädie der Protes-*

*tantische Theologie und Kirche,* I (Leipzig: Hinrichs 1896), pp. 127-130. J. Reumann concentrates on the background to the shady sense of accommodation or "expedient policy in business, rhetoric and morals" in his *"Oikonomias* as 'Ethical Accommodation' in the Fathers, and Its Pagan Backgrounds," *Texte und Untersuchungen,* 78 *(Studia Patristica,* 3), (Berlin: Akademie Verlag, 1961), pp. 370-379. Cf. also on accommodation in Calvin, E. A. Dowey, *The Knowledge of God in Calvin's Theology* (New York: Columbia Univ. Press, 1952), pp. 3-17.

26. Cf. the similar teaching in Irenaeus, that God's economy is the continuity of history. "It is one and the same *oikonomos* who rules the whole household, giving to the slaves and the underdeveloped a suitable law, but to free men and to those who through faith are justified, imparting corresponding rules and opening up to the children the riches of their inheritance . . . namely, the Word of God, our Lord Jesus Christ" *(Adv. Haer.* 4, 14, 2). Calvin says even that "The same Church existed among them [the Jews], but as yet in its childhood." *(Inst.* 2, 11, 21.) This is a better way of putting the relation between Israel and Church, and anticipates Barth's view that the one community of God exists in two forms, Israel and the Church.

27. *Inst.* 2, 11, 13–1543; McNeill, pp. 462-63; *OS* 3:435-6.

28. Cf. D. Willis, "The Pressure of Laelius Socinus on Calvin's Doctrine of the Merits of Christ and the Assurance of Faith," *Italian Reformation Studies in Honor of Laelius Socinus,* ed. J. A. Tedeschi (Florence: Le Monier, 1965), pp. 231-241.

29. *Inst.* 3, 2, 12-1559; McNeill, p. 556; *OS* 4:21-22.

30. *Inst.* 3, 2, 12; McNeill, p. 556; *OS* 4:22.

31. "Shut up as we are in the prison house of our flesh, we have not yet attained angelic rank. God, therefore, in his wonderful providence accommodating himself to our capacity, has prescribed a way for us, though still far off, to draw near to him" *(Inst.* 4, 1, 1, McNeill, p. 1012; cf. *Inst.* 4, 1, 8). Also, ". . . the mode of accommodation is for him to represent himself to us not as he is in himself, but as he seems to us." *("Haec est porro submittendi ratio, ut se talem nobis figuret, non qualis in se est, sed qualis a nobis sentitur.") (Inst.* 1, 17, 3-1539; McNeill, p. 227; *OS* 3. 217-218)

32. Cf. a treatment of experience in Calvin's theology in Charles Brooks Partee *The Providence of God and the Wisdom of Man,* Th.D. Diss., Princeton, Princeton Theological Seminary, n.d., pp. 25 ff.

33. *Inst.* 3, 2, 12-1559; McNeill, p. 557; *OS* 4:22.

34. *Inst.* 3, 2, 15-1559; McNeill, p. 557; *OS* 4:22.

35. "The object [goal: *scopus*] of regeneration, as we have said, is to manifest in the life of believers a harmony and agreement [*symmetria et consensus*] between God's righteousness and their obedience, and

thus to confirm the adoption that they have received as sons. [Gal. 4:5; cf. II Peter 1:10] (*Inst.* 3, 6, 1, McNeill, p. 684; *OS* 4:146)

36. Cf. *Inst.* 3, 19, 5 where Calvin, in describing the second part of Christian freedom, contrasts the free obedience of a son, assured of the Father's approval even of his incomplete work, and the fearful obedience of a slave.

# A Theology of Sociality:
## Bonhoeffer's *Sanctorum Communio*

**CLIFFORD GREEN**

That *Sanctorum Communio* [1] is a work in ecclesiology is an orthodoxy of Bonhoeffer studies. This orthodoxy embraces a wide range of interpreters, and is the more striking because the interpreters agree in this matter despite their disagreement on many other major issues. Thus the orthodoxy encompasses, on the one hand, those like Hanfried Müller and John Phillips who regard Bonhoeffer's first book as a preliminary, or even an obstacle, to the theological development which led to the so-called "secular theology" of the *Letters*.[2] On the other hand, it includes those who, like John Godsey and Eberhard Bethge, argue for a much more integral relation between the thought of the "early" and the "later" Bonhoeffer.[3]

It would be foolish to deny that *Sanctorum Communio* is indeed an ecclesiological work. To dispute this would be to fly in the face of its very title, and to ignore the conspicuous size and detail of its culminating fifth chapter on the church. The orthodoxy must be corrected, however, not for what it asserts but for what it ignores or minimizes: the comprehensive and ambitious theology of sociality found in this book. Bonhoeffer himself specifically drew attention to the comprehensive import of sociality for his theology when he wrote in the preface:

The more theologians have considered the significance of the

> sociological category for theology, the more clearly the *social intention of all the basic Christian concepts has emerged.* Ideas such as "person," "primal state," "sin" and "revelation" are fully understandable only in relation to *sociality.*[4]

This is a programmatic statement for *Sanctorum Communio,* as I shall argue here. It is also programmatic for his other early writings, as one can initially see from the way "the sociological category" and "sociality" function in them both explicitly and implicitly.[5]

Bonhoeffer's assertion about "the social intention of all the basic Christian concepts" provides the theme for the present interpretation. But we immediately confront the fact that *Sanctorum Communio* is Bonhoeffer's most complex, demanding, and probably most neglected book. Even his doctoral adviser, Reinhold Seeberg, is said to have had difficulty with its sophisticated conceptuality and intricate argument.[6] This has become more esoteric with the passage of forty years, and more elusive through the editing and translating process.* Our theme, therefore, will be developed as follows. Section I argues that a "theology of sociality" is the comprehensive context for ecclesiology. Sections II and III present the major components in the complex category "sociality" by focusing on the Christian concept of *person* in its individual and corporate meanings. Section IV shows how Bonhoeffer's under-

---

*The first edition (Berlin: Trowitzsch und Sohn, 1930) cut the original manuscript about 20 to 25 percent. About half of this material was printed as an appendix in the third German edition (Munich: Chr. Kaiser, 1960). On this the English translation was based (London: Collins, 1963, as *Sanctorum Communio;* New York: Harper & Row, as *The Communion of Saints*). It incorporates in the text the material from the German appendix and thus corresponds more closely than other versions to Bonhoeffer's original, as Ronald Gregor Smith claims in the translation note. But it is a distinct redaction and incomplete—not "the work . . . in its original unabbreviated form," as the dust jacket proclaims. It combines revisions and transitions with the original material these were designed to replace. Some footnotes similarly overlap, and English footnotes frequently do not give all the details in the notes of even the third German edition. A critical edition and a revised translation are sorely needed. Fortunately, the original manuscript is extant and will soon be available on microfilm from the Board of Microtext of the American Theological Library Association.

standing of creation, sin, revelation, and church is developed in terms of sociality. Section V concludes with some brief observations about the significance of this theology of sociality for Bonhoeffer's later life and thought, and for our contemporary situation.

## I

Several clear indications show that his theology of sociality is Bonhoeffer's comprehensive concern. First, the statement in the preface that "person, primal state, sin and revelation" are fully understood only in terms of sociality is programmatic because it precisely points to the very structure of Bonhoeffer's whole argument. The Christian concept of the person is the subject of chapter 2, and primal state (i.e., creation), sin, and revelation are treated in chapters 3 through 5 respectively. In each case, these major Christian doctrines are expounded in terms of sociality. Creation is discussed in terms of the primal community, sin in terms of the broken community, and revelation is treated as the restoration of human sociality in the new humanity of Christ who is present in the Christian community. The whole range of theological subjects is involved, and ecclesiology is set within this comprehensive framework. It is not an overstatement to describe the work as an introduction to a Christian theology of sociality.

Second, the Foreword to the original manuscript supports this reading. After stating that his method is interdisciplinary and seeks to make insights of social philosophy and sociology fruitful for the theological consideration of the church, Bonhoeffer states: "the problem of *a specifically Christian social philosophy and sociology,* therefore, can also be designated as the fundamental problem" of the work.[7] Obviously, a Christian social philosophy built upon basic theological concepts and setting forth their "social intention" must give an important place to the Christian community, the church. But this does not mean that its exclusive concern is ecclesiology. Bonhoeffer's wider purpose leads him to treat a broad range of theological subjects: doctrines of God, creation, sin, Christ, revelation, and Spirit. It involves him with many anthropological subjects, such as the Christian understanding of person, community, society, history, and ethics. His argument is not restricted to traditional questions in ecclesiology, such as worship, preaching, sacraments, ministry, church authority, pastoral care, and so on. If ecclesiology is taken to be the exclusive concern of *Sanctorum Communio,* one cannot explain the detailed discussion of so many subjects which fall outside the doctrine of the church. But when sociality is seen to be the basic category for the whole argument, then it is apparent why these subjects are discussed and why the Christian community necessarily has a central place.

Third, early in the text Bonhoeffer states that he intends to present "a Christian philosophy of *Geist*" which will give direction to a "Christian social philosophy" and hereby "overcome and supersede idealism's philosophy of immanent *Geist*." [8] Idealism in its various forms, he argues, is a philosophy of "immanent *Geist*"; it understands man as an instance of universal reason, and its epistemological preoccupation with the subject-object relation informs its whole anthropology. But the epistemological subject-object relation is not a sociological category, and therefore idealism can neither give essential value to the individual nor adequately understand human community. A different "social basic relation" must be posited as the foundation for a Christian social philosophy which seeks to overcome idealism. [9]

But even the critique of idealism is another indication of Bonhoeffer's relation to a philosophical tradition much concerned with human social experience. His very use of the term *Geist* and his critique of idealism point to Reinhold Seeberg and Hegel in the near and distant background of the argument. "Sociality" was an explicit and significant category in Seeberg's theology. [10] Hegel, who had influenced Seeberg, is well known for what John Hermann Randall has called his "fundamental socializing of all the concepts for dealing with human experience," thus overthrowing the individualism and social atomism of the Enlightenment. [11] Bonhoeffer critically appropriates from both Seeberg and Hegel in arguing his own position.

Finally, it is sociality which distinguishes Bonhoeffer's approach to the issues of modern theology. Aware of the theological problems deriving from the impact of Kant and post-Kantian epistemology, he did not seek a breakthrough via an alliance with neo-Kantianism or existentialism, as his older contemporaries in the dialetical theology of the 1920's were doing.[12] Rather he sought with *sociological* categories to develop a new conceptuality for dealing with theological subjects such as transcendence, Christology, creation, sin, revelation, and faith. Not the epistemological context but human sociality holds most theological promise.

The content of Bonhoeffer's argument, which follows, substantiates these indications that sociality is his comprehensive concern. In moving to discuss the central idea of the book, the Christian concept of *person,* we first consider person from the perspective of relations between individuals in social life; then we examine how Bonhoeffer uses the concept of person to interpret the corporate, or collective, dimension of social life. Various components in the complex category of sociality will thus be identified. Further, the discussion of both individual and corporate dimensions of social life shows how Bonhoeffer uses his concept of person to interpret *Geist,* thus pursuing his aim of developing a Christian social philosophy in place of the idealist philosophy of immanent *Geist.*

## II

Bonhoeffer develops the concept of person as the key to interpret *Geist* both individually and corporately.[13] Person, used both individually and collectively, means for him the socio-ethical, historical person. The definition strongly emphasizes ethical will in its anthropological and theological presuppositions.[14] Bonhoeffer insists equally on the irreducible, independent integrity of the individual person, and on the fact that this person exists essentially in relation to others. His paradigm is not *cogito ergo sum,* but "I relate ethically to others, *ergo sum.*"

The human person always exists in relation to an "other." Human being is therefore essentially relational and social; man is person as related to others in human communities. Granted that the person is an individual, that he has abilities of his own such as willing, reasoning, and knowing, man nevertheless only realizes his full humanity as a person essentially related to others in human communities.

Within this framework of ethical voluntarism, Bonhoeffer accepts what he describes as a general, metaphysical concept of *Geist,* which understands man as self-conscious and spontaneously acting. *Geist* is therefore interpreted by his theological concept of the person in the historical decisions of social-ethical relationships. In social life persons encounter one another with ethical claims which must be answered by responsible decisions.

More particularly, as independent and individual willing beings, men constitute limits, boundaries, or "barriers" (*Schranke, Grenze*) for each other.[15] Negatively, this means that their egotism and dominating pretensions are checked and halted as they run up against the countering wills of others; this cannot happen in the function of *Geist* as reason (since reason in principle is limitless and unbounded), but it does happen in the confrontation of ethical wills. Positively, encounter with the "other" as "thou" constitutes man as a distinct, ethical self. In contemporary parlance, the encounter contributes to the formation of one's ethical identity. The "other," furthermore, who wills and affirms the self in love, is a creative source of life for the self. Here the other person as thou "limits" the I in the positive sense of contributing human resources to the self from "outside." Given this concept of the person whose individual being essentially arises in historical, ethical encounters with others, Bonhoeffer concludes that this relation of I and thou is the social basic-relation (*soziale Grundbeziehung, Grundverhältnis*).

The theological basis for this relational anthropology of self and other is given, Bonhoeffer argues, in the Christian view that man is always man before God as the divine "Other." As created, as sinner, and as redeemed, man is always human in relation to God, encountered by God in his Word. Precisely as an individual person, man is never alone, isolated, or self-sufficient. The theological basis of the anthropology is apparent in the following important passage.

> It is a Christian perception that in the moment of being moved, of standing in responsibility, of passionate ethical engagement, . . . man is created as a conscious person. The concrete person grows out of the concrete situation. Here too the encounter occurs completely in *Geist*, as in idealism. But here *Geist* means something other than in idealism. For Christian philosophy the human person originates only in relation to the divine which transcends him, contradicting him and overcoming him. A self-sufficiency [*Fürsichsein*] of *Geist* in the sense of idealistic individualism is unchristian. . . . The Christian person arises only from the absolute duality of God and man; only in the experience of the barrier does the self-knowledge of the ethical person originate.[16]

While man's being in relation to God establishes that human existence is always relational, Bonhoeffer also means that the socio-ethical relation to the human "other" is precisely the form in which men encounter the divine "Other." Transcendence is interpreted in terms of sociality. "The concepts of person, community and God have an essential and indissoluble relation to one another." [17] Within this theological view of man in his social relationships, God is both the one who establishes the other as thou, and the divine Thou who encounters the self in the ethical limit and claim of the human "other." "God is a Thou for us, that is, active will standing over against us." [18] But since transcendence is to be understood in terms of sociality, Bonhoeffer boldly states: "the thou of the other man is the divine Thou." [19]

### III

Bonhoeffer uses his concept of person to interpret the corporate, or collective, dimension of social life. The philosophical tradition, particularly in Hegel, had applied the concept of *Geist* to corporate life as well as to individual existence. Bonhoeffer, similarly, does not use person as a category limited only to individuals. It is, rather, a model which, while first expounded in terms of individual persons in I-thou relations, is fundamental to his interpretation of corporate life. A social community—family, church, people, nation—and its "objective *Geist*," therefore, is considered as a "collective person." In its most universal use the category of person is even applied to humanity as a whole in the concept of the *Menschheitsperson*. Indeed, this application is crucial to the whole discussion of creation, sin, Christ, and the church; both Adam, as created and fallen, and Christ are representatives (*Stellvertreter*) or prototypes for the modes of being of humanity as a whole.

Here Bonhoeffer's "personalism" must be distinguished from the use of the I-thou relation found in Martin Buber, Eberhard Grisebach, Friedrich Gogarten, and Emil Brunner. In their inter-subjective personalism the I-thou relationship prevails between individual persons. Bonhoeffer, however, uses person as both a corporate and an individual concept. The I-thou relation is fundamental not only to relations between individual persons, but also to relations between individuals and social groups, between one social group and another, and ultimately to the relation between God and humanity as a whole; he builds up his argument to the position where humanity as a whole is seen as the "I," personified by Adam and Christ, standing before God as "Thou."

Like individual persons, human communities [20] are constituted, Bonhoeffer holds, by willing. When men will in the same direction, willing has a mutual or reciprocal character; each must will and intend the person of the other and be himself willed and intended by the other. From this co-willing, human social forms arise. Bonhoeffer develops a typology of social forms by appropriating and modifying the well-known categories of Ferdinard Tönnies, "community " (*Gemeinschaft*) and "association" (*Gesellschaft*).[21]

Typologically considered, in *Gemeinschaft* people will one another and their common life as ends in themselves, giving rise to a "structure of meaning." Examples of such communities are families, friendships, peoples and nations, even mankind as a whole, and—in a special sense—the church. In *Gesellschaft* people will one another and their common life as a means to a rational end, as in business corporations, universities, political organizations; such willing constitutes the association as a "structure of purpose."

When people will together in communities and associations there arises the phenomenon of "objective *Geist*," objective or social spirit. What is "objective *Geist*"? When we describe the "spirit" of a social group by speaking of its "mentality," "mood," "ethos," or "culture," as in phrases such as "the suburban mentality" or "youth culture," we are referring untechnically to the social phenomenon expressed by the concept "objective *Geist*." Discussing Hegel's view of this concept, a noted historian of philosophy writes:

> . . . It is "objective spirit" that displays both Hegel's grasp of fact and his originality of insight at their highest. Objective spirit is the direct ancestor of the "cultural heritage" and "social process" of our own social sciences . . . It is Hegel's most suggestive and fertile idea, his major philosophical discovery. It signalized the definite overthrow of eighteenth-century individualism, and made it impossible for nineteenth-century social science to take seriously the atomism of the Enlightenment.[22]

Bonhoeffer would agree with this evaluation. While attacking Hegel's subordination of the individual person to the social process, he appreciated Hegel's perception that human life is inescapably corporate.

> The tragedy of the whole idealistic philosophy was that it did not ultimately break through to personal *Geist*. But it was its tremendous perception (especially in Hegel) that the principle of *Geist* was something objective beyond everything individual, that there was an objective *Geist*, as the *Geist* of sociality, which was something in itself as the counterpart to all individual *Geist*. Our task is to affirm this without denying the other, to retain the perception without joining the error.[23]

Bonhoeffer insists that the "spirit" of a social structure—family, university, corporation, nation—is a reality *sui generis*. While it arises from the interaction of the individual wills of the members of a corporate group, and is real and operative only in those individual persons, it nevertheless has a distinctive character and identity which is not identical with any given individual. It is trans-individual, a reality *sui generis*, and not simply reducible to the aggregate of the individual wills from which it arises. The willing of every individual contributes to the character of the objective *Geist*; reciprocally, individual willing is itself affected by the objective *Geist* of the particular social structure. Illustrations of the point can easily be found in considering the life of a family, a college, or a congregation.

Having appropriated the Hegelian concept of objective *Geist,* Bonhoeffer now makes a crucial transformation of it. He asks, By what conceptual model should we interpret the social spirit of communities? [24] Shall we regard social life fundamentally in terms of the dynamics of consciousness whereby mind comes to self-realization? Bonhoeffer rejects this Hegelian option, for which the subject-object schema would constitute the social basic-relation. Or does the Marxist concept of class provide the key? Do family, race, and nation give suitable models for understanding communities? Bonhoeffer answers by taking his idea of person, in the social basic-relation of I and thou, as the conceptual model most appropriate for a theological interpretation of the life of communities. The objective *Geist* of communities—family, people, nation, mankind, church—is to be interpreted as a "collective person."

To speak of a community's spirit as *Kollektivperson* is not here a piece of social magic, hypostasizing the social spirit into a super-person and thus elevating it into a superior status and authority quite autonomous from individual wills and divorced from the concrete responsibilities of particular persons. On the contrary, the reason for applying the model of the person to communities is to guarantee that they are ascribed the same ethical-historical character as the individual person. Similarly, it emphasizes that persons are not private individuals but that they have responsibility for the socio-ethical life of their communities.[25] Indeed, it is precisely in individual persons that the call to corporate ethical responsibility is heard; in responding to it these persons act on behalf of the whole community. Bonhoeffer gives as an illustration the prophets of Israel who both speak the word of Yahweh's justice and judgment to the people as a whole and in themselves repent in behalf of the whole community. Another illustration is provided by Bonhoeffer's own life; his personal response to the national crisis in Germany under Hitler is a perfect example of acting upon this aspect of his own theology of sociality.

It is not only individuals, then, but communities as such in their corporate activities which must hear the word of God in their own historical situations. The community as such is an "I" addressed by the divine "Thou." [26] Through persons who act in the name of and for the sake of the corporate body, the community must respond in ethical responsibility. "God does not want a history of individual men, but a history of the *community* of men; but nor does God want a community which absorbs the individual into itself, but a community of *men*." [27]

To complete the theological argument, Bonhoeffer universalizes his concepts of community and person. Every community, understood as a *Kollektivperson,* is embraced in a more comprehensive one. Hence "humanity is the universal community [*Gesamtgemeinschaft*] embracing all communities." [28] Humanity—mankind as a whole—is the *Menschheitsperson,* the "humanity-person." Here the argument reminds us of Paul and Irenaeus: Adam and Christ are seen as prototypes; they are "representatives" or "personifications" of two fundamental styles of human being. Around these two representatives Bonhoeffer develops the whole Christian drama of creation, fall, and redemption.

How are these all-embracing concepts—universal community, *Menschheitsperson,* Adam, Christ—related to the personal life and social communities in which people live their concrete history? We live in our specific communities each having its own distinctive ethos. These communities range all the way from the most direct and intimate communities, such as families and friendships, through wider communities, such as people and nation, to the most universal community of mankind—humanity as a whole. Bonhoeffer acknowledges the great variety of character and culture which distinguishes these communities, which vary from place to place, nation to nation, culture to culture, and endure through successive historical periods. Yet in this rich and changing diversity of human spirit, common dynamics are evident. Theologically understood, these dynamics are "mutations" of the social basic-relation of I and thou as seen in creation and the "primal community," in sin and the "broken community," and in redemption and the community of the new humanity. Adam "personifies," as

prototype and representative, both the created person and community, and the isolated person and fragmented solidarity of
humanity in sin. Christ "personifies" the new person in the new
humanity. In other words, Adam, created and fallen, represents a
fundamental and universal mode of human being which is operative in all the individual and corporate life of humanity. Christ,
likewise, is a mode of personal and corporate being in which all
people may be restored to their authentic humanity. The diversities
of human experience exhibit the universal dilemma and promise of
our common humanity in these two primal names.

## IV

Having constructed this conceptuality of sociality, theologically appropriating and modifying ideas from various social philosophers and sociologists, Bonhoeffer uses it to present the
Christian drama. We now see how primal state, sin, and revelation
are presented in this theology of sociality.

The primal community (an ontological construct, not a
chronological designation) is man as created in community with
God and with others. Understood from the revelation in Christ,
the primal community is a community of mutual love. As the
divine love rules by its serving, so man serves by his loving.[29]
The will of God and man relates to others by loving. There is an
identity of direction and purpose in divine and human willing.
Man's community with God is actual and real in the community
of men with one another. The creature loves and serves the
Creator by the common service of mutual love in the human
community.[30] Love and service of God in community with God is
not an individualistic possibility. The divine community takes form
in human sociality, in the human community where men not only
relate to other individual persons but also to the community as a
whole. In all aspects of his life, not only in his ethical will, "man
as *Geist* is necessarily created in a community." [31] Adam is the
symbol and representative of created man. He is the prototype
of the individual person and is the "collective person" of the
primal community. He "stands for" the person and community
whose spirit is one of service to God by mutual love to men. He

personifies the group culture (objective *Geist*) of the primal community as a community of love.

With sin the broken community appears. Sin does not cancel the sociality of man, but makes it self-contradictory. When the primal community is broken, self-seeking replaces love, demanding replaces giving, and the self uses the other instead of loving him. Mutual love is perverted into an isolated self-love.[32] "Sin is . . . the will which principally affirms only itself as a value and not the other, and which acknowledges the other only in this perspective." [33] The will of the other is dominated by the will of the self.[34] Thus the primal community is brought into profound inner self-contradiction. Sociality is now a solidarity of egocentric individualism.

Bonhoeffer wisely rejects the view that a *Gesellschaft* is merely a sinning *Gemeinschaft*. Having given both social types an essential place and function in creation, he now defends *Gesellschaft* against this reactionary accusation. What he does argue is that sin perverts the purposive character of instrumental associations, so that through the evil will operating in them they become "institutions of systematic exploitation of one man by another." [35]

Sin, finally, has a universal, corporate character which is as inescapable as individual responsibility.[36] Adam, and every man, is at once individual and corporate humanity. Fallen Adam represents and personifies individual and corporate sin in a humanity which now wars against itself and whose humaneness is disintegrated.

Now, as in Irenaeus' doctrine of recapitulation, Bonhoeffer presents the revelation of Christ as the "collective person" who embodies and inaugurates the new humanity. This new humanity is no mere potentiality, but a *reality* in the person of Christ, and this reality is actualized historically and socially by the Holy Spirit.[37] As Bonhoeffer thus comes to discuss the church, it is imperative to see that his well-known formula, "Christ existing as the congregation," is a commentary upon his view of Christ as the *Kollektivperson* of the new humanity.[38] The new humanity of Christ, socially concrete in the Christian church, is presented in the third act of the drama of all mankind from creation, through fall, to reconciliation. This ecclesiology is concerned with the rehabilitation and renovation of genuine humanity for all mankind. The word of Christ is not only a word to the church, but his presence in the church creates a new social reality of mankind that is a paradigm, a promise, and a challenge which encounters mankind in all its life. Bonhoeffer's view of Christ as the new Adam is a deliberate way of relating Christ and the church to humanity as a whole. It is not a way of confining Christ to the church, or of encouraging any complacent, ecclesiastical self-preoccupation and self-righteousness. He states, accordingly, as he does again in the 1933 Christology lectures, that the history of the church is the hidden center of world history.[39]

Like all human social structures, the church has its distinctive social or "objective *Geist,*" and is to be understood as an ethical "collective person." How are these, as human phenomena, related to the Holy Spirit and Christ as the *Kollektivperson* of the new humanity? The objective *Geist* of the church as a *Kollektivperson* is *not* identical with the Holy Spirit. It is the "bearer" of the Spirit of Christ,[40] the latter creating and making effective its own forms—word and sacrament—in the social life and spirit of the empirical, human community of the church. Again, as an ethical collective-person, the church is not equivalent to Christ himself. Christ is contemporaneously present in the congregation in word and sacrament, but freely and creatively present. The gospel of the cross and resurrection encounters the church, breaking it up and building it up. The presence of Christ is not the essence of the church as an assured and possessed attribute or a static being. Understood on the model of the ethical person in social relations, the life and spirit of the church is continually in historical encounter with the person of Christ.[41] The *sanctorum communio,* continually created by the present reality of Christ and his Spirit, is the *peccatorum communio* engaged in the dynamics of human renovation by the new humanity of Christ.

This encounter and these dynamics create, Bonhoeffer contends, a distinctive sociological form. The church is a Spirit-community as a community of love.[42] This is not the simple and unambiguous love of the primal community, nor is it the perfected love of the eschatological Kingdom. Yet, created by the serving of the divine love, the Christian community is a genuine actualization of the divine love which transforms the egocentricity and power-seeking of the old humanity. As such it is a real anticipation and instrument of the eschatological Kingdom. In ever and again encountering the present Christ, the church is a laboratory of the new humanity. Its group dynamics, so to speak, are those of justification and sanctification. It is not engaged in a struggle against the world.[43] Rather, the Christian community as the new-humanity-of-Christ-being-actualized is engaged, to use Paul Lehmann's terminology, in the humanization of man—man whose humanity is at war with itself in the ambitions and strife of power and dominance. The signs of Christ's presence are the transformation of the posture of sin into the co-humanity of love which actively wills, affirms, serves, and bears the other, and in "active being-for-one-another" [44] where love voluntarily and vicariously identifies with and suffers for others, intercedes for others, and forgives others.[45]

These observations leave much to be said about the ecclesiology of *Sanctorum Communio,* yet they are enough to demonstrate that it is only intelligible in the more comprehensive context of the theology of sociality to which Bonhoeffer draws his reader's attention in the Preface.

## V

An understanding of Bonhoeffer's theology of sociality both illumines the work itself and shows it to be formative for his later thought and life in many ways. It establishes that a strong ethical concern was at the heart of his theology from the beginning. It highlights a strangely neglected aspect of his whole theology, namely, his theological anthropology and soteriology. It shows how a profound appreciation for the historical character of human experience was as central in his earliest theology as in his later life and writings. It discloses the roots of much in his final writings, such as the concepts of "deputyship" and "mandates" in his *Ethics,* and the socio-ethical interpretation of transcendence in the Christology of the *Letters.* Biographically it shows the theological rationale for Bonhoeffer's participation in the ecumenical movement. This participation was distinguished by an insistence that the movement should first clarify its theology of the church and then, as the church, act ethically for the sake of humanity—especially in the cause of peace. It also reveals much of the theological impetus in his willingness to take personal responsibility for the corporate life of his church and nation, first as a leader in the Confessing Church and then as a member of the resistance movement.

There are, to be sure, theological and methodological problems in this first book. The interaction of theology, social philosophy, and sociology would certainly have profited by a much more serious use of empirical, historical, and theoretical insights coming from sources such as Weber, Troeltsch, and Marx. Related to this is the problem of theoretical, abstract theology. Much as Bonhoeffer insisted that the *sanctorum communio* is not to be sought apart from the visible, empirical church, it is difficult to believe that his own church in Germany corresponded to the ecclesiology in his theology. Indeed, history soon proved how little this was the case, and Bonhoeffer's implementation of his ecclesiology in the Confessing Church and at Finkenwalde led him further and further away from the official church. Again, his emphasis on man as essentially ethical, salutary as it is, left his doctrine of creation and his anthropology underdeveloped in the dimension of creation as nature, and of man as body with an instinctual and emotional life.

Such problems do not obscure the fact that, despite its formidable terminology, *Sanctorum Communio* still encounters the contemporary American church with radical questions. No one can read Bonhoeffer's ecclesiology as an apology for the bourgeois institutional church of his time or our own. From this theological base Bonhoeffer predictably found himself in a minority opposition to an ecclesiastical institution which found the *Zeitgeist* more attractive than the Spirit of Christ. In our own time the churches might learn some simple lessons from this erudite and academic treatise: that they must abandon once and for all their socially-conforming individualism and their paralyzing ethical and political neutrality; that the Word of Christ which creates the new humanity will not be heard in a spiritualistic, religious ghetto but only in active engagement in the decisive, historical conflicts of our common social life; that self-preservation as a primary goal is a denial of the serving love of Christ, a delaying tactic foreboding death; that the new humanity of Christ is one throughout the world, overcoming the primitive and destructive loyalties of nation, class, and race. If such sharp words would be heard and acted upon, the churches could find themselves transformed and enlivened by the strange, new spirit of the *sanctorum communio*.

---

1. For details of texts and published editions, see the excursus with text. Abbreviations used: SC—German edition, 1969; SCe—English translation, 1963; SCms—original German manuscript, 1927. In a number of quotations I have used by own translations rather than the published version. Since this essay was first written, several Bonhoeffer studies have appeared: Ernst Feil, *Die Theologie Dietrich Bonhoeffers* (Munich: Chr. Kaiser; Mainz: Grünewald, 1971); Heinrich Ott, *Reality and Faith: The Theological Legacy of Dietrich Bonhoeffer* (Philadelphia: Fortress Press, 1972); André Dumas, *Dietrich Bonhoeffer: Theologian of Reality* (New York: Macmillan Co., 1971).

2. Hanfried Müller, *Von der Kirche sur Welt* (2nd ed.; Hamburg: Herbert Reich, 1966), and "Concerning the Reception and Interpretation of Dietrich Bonhoeffer," in *World Come of Age,* ed. Ronald Gregor Smith (Philadelphia: Fortress Press, 1967), esp. p. 184, though cf. p. 207, n. 6; John A. Phillips, *Christ for Us in the Theology of Dietrich Bonhoeffer* (New York: Harper & Row, 1967).

3. Cf. John D. Godsey, *The Theology of Dietrich Bonhoeffer* (Philadelphia: Westminster Press, 1960); Eberhard Bethge, *Dietrich Bonhoeffer* (New York: Harper & Row, 1970), esp. pp. 58 ff., pp. 38 ff., through cf., for example, p. 59, where Bethge notes the importance of sociality for Bonhoeffer's thought.

4. SCe p. 13, italics mine.

5. Cf. *Act and Being* (New York: Harper & Row, 1961), with its references to the "sociological category" on page 16 and *passim; Creation and Fall* (New York: Macmillan Co., 1967), particularly the interpretation of the *imago Dei* as an *analogia relationis; Christ*

*the Center* (New York: Harper & Row, 1966), and the discussion of this in my article "Sociality and Church in Bonhoeffer's 1933 Christology," *Scottish Journal of Theology*, Vol. 21, No. 4 (December 1968), esp. pp. 419-431. A thorough discussion is found in my dissertation, *"The Sociality of Christ and Humanity: Dietrich Bonhoeffer's Early Theology,"* 1927-1933, available on microfilm from University Microfilms, Ann Arbor, Michigan.

6. Cf. Fritz Figur, *I Knew Dietrich Bonhoeffer*, ed. Wolf-Dieter Zimmermann and Ronald Gregor Smith (New York: Harper & Row, 1969), p. 55.

7. SCms, italics mine; the next paragraph continues with the statement quoted about the social intention of theological concepts.

8. SC 230, SCe 27–28; cf. SC 20.

9. SC 20-22, 230; SCe 26-28.

10. Cf. his *Christliche Dogmatik* (Leipzig, 1924-25), I, 505-506, 507 ff.; II, 327-328, 350. The origins of Bonhoeffer's interest in sociality are complex. The set of categories he uses to explicate sociality was not simply taken over from Seeberg, but hammered out in debate with others; not least among these was Max Scheler, from whom the idea of *Gesamtperson* was appropriated and modified—cf. *Act and Being*, 121, n. 1.

11. John Herman Randall, *The Career of Philosophy*, Vol. II (New York: Columbia University Press, 1965), p. 315.

12. Cf. his criticisms in *Act and Being* of efforts along these lines by Barth, Bultmann, and Gogarten.

13. "Person" remains a pivotal concept in following works. In *Act and Being, Dasein,* replaces *Geist* as the main anthropological category; *Dasein,* nevertheless, is interpreted as "person." In the 1933 *Christologie* the main anthropological category is *Existenz,* again understood as "person."

14. The voluntarism of Seeberg, and of others such as Dilthey (cf. *Act and Being*, pp. 140, 143, n. 1), is clearly influential here.

15. SCe 31 ff.

16. Cf. SC 27-28, SCe 31; cf. SC 26-27, SCe 30, where Bonhoeffer's ethical-social concept of *time* elaborates on the historical nature of the human person.

17. SCe 22.

18. The printed texts, which omit the *Du* are corrupt at this point; cf. SC 231, SCe 34.

19. SCe 37.

20. Here, as often in Bonhoeffer's text, "community" is a general term referring generically to human corporate life and social structures; the more specific, technical use is discussed later.

21. SCe 56 ff.

22. Randall, *op. cit.*, 314-315.
23. SC 47, SCe 49.
24. *Gemeinschaft*, in the specific sense discussed.
25. Since Bonhoeffer regards an institution or association *(Gesellschaft)* as a means to an end, it follows—since persons can never be regarded as merely instrumental—that his theory cannot treat associations as "ethical collective persons." This raises the serious problem that precisely the most powerful social institutions—of business, government, communications, education, labor—are not constituted as ethically responsible in their very essence. Here I can only indicate the problem, and not discuss how Bonhoeffer would reply to this criticism.
26. SCe 82 ff.
27. SCe 52.
28. SC 79, SCe 84.
29. SC 37.
30. SC 233-234.
31. SC 39; cf. the discussion of language, will, and emotion as evidence of the essential sociality of human spirit, 43 ff.
32. SCe 71, 81.
33. SC 254-255, SCe 82.
34. SC 56, SCe 55; cf. SC 24, SCe 28, where the critique of "dominance" is applied to the idealist concept of *Geist* as mind. The centrality of power and dominance in this description of sin, incidentally, explains why the concept of "barrier" is so important in Bonhoeffer's account of the ethical person in the I-thou relation.
35. SC 254-255, SCe 82.
36. SCe 72-85.
37. Note Christ as "person" and the Holy Spirit as *Geist. Sanctorum Communio* is Bonhoeffer's most trinitarian book, though characteristically the trinitarianism functions anthropologically; it is not developed in terms of the classical trinitarian doctrines, as in Barth, though these are presupposed.
38. SC 80, SCe 84-85.
39. SCe 146.
40. SCe 148.
41. SCe 147.
42. SCe 118 ff., 125 ff., 134, 178-185. Note that Bonhoeffer does not understand the church as an example of the ideal type *Gemeinschaft* as previously defined. In his technical terms it combines and surmounts the types *Gemeinschaft, Gesellschaft,* and *Herrschaftsverband;* cf. Promotions Thesis 7, *Gesammelte Schriften* (Munich: Chr. Kaiser, 1966), III, 47.
43. SCe 199.
44. SC 131. This formulation of "active being-for-one-another" *(tätig*

*Füreinander)* unmistakably anticipates the celebrated phase in the *Letters,* "being-for-others."

45. SC 127 ff., 131 ff.; SCe 126 ff., 129 ff.; on spirit-community *(Geistgemeinshaft)* as community of love *(Liebesgemeinschaft),* see especially SC 118-136.

politics

# The Gospel and the Struggle for Freedom[1*]

**HELMUT GOLLWITZER**

In the history of the church to the present the heralding of "inner freedom" has been a substantial part of the gospel and a central motif of the Christian proclamation. But this message has been discredited by the fact that it was and is used in the interest of the privileged to make "external freedom" a matter of indifference for the underprivileged, to quell the desire for it, and to cripple and defame the struggle for it. Thus the proclamation of "inner freedom" has been an ideological means of maintaining the status quo—in the same way that sermons against violence have been addressed to the suppressed (but not the supressors) in order to wrench their weapons from their hands. Only the privileged man who fights to see that all disadvantages are done away with, and who is willing to lose his privileges in this struggle, can speak unideologically of the victory of "inner freedom" over "external freedom."

The proclamation of inner freedom can be misleading, as seen, for instance, in Helmut Thielicke's thesis that a change in structures must be preceded by a change in individuals. Thielicke holds that the change in the individual is the "explosive, which finally must force change in the structures." "The changed heart is the bud of world change." [2] Apart from the fact that here a monolineal

---

* Translated by Julius S. Winkler, Davidson College.

causality has replaced the dialectical relation between individual and corporate structures, which is possible only by a massive disregard of Marxism, it is astonishing that Thielicke is not afraid of being refuted by history precisely on his own example of slavery. The institution of slavery remained in "Christian" countries until the middle of the nineteenth century. However indispensable may have been the moral preparation of Christian involvement (John Wesley, Wilberforce, and even Harriet Beecher Stowe), this did not suffice for the peaceful dissolution of slavery. A bloody civil war was necessary in the United States in order to extirpate merely its legal form while its content—suppression, exploitation, and inequality—continued. In this case, inner freedom did *not* lead to the actualization of external freedom.

And the same was true in the early church. Why did the spread of Christianity, accompanied by spiritual strength even to martyrdom, *not* so undermine the institution of slavery that it finally would have collapsed? Especially must this be asked of a church which had rid itself of the hindrances of eschatological imminentism and political irrelevance. That this was a fateful failure of Christianity from Constantine on cannot be denied. The continuing assertion of Thielicke and many others that a revolution of hearts creates a revolution of structures (and the latter only in a peaceful way) is not universally applicable, and appears, at least in many cases, to have been refuted by history. For this reason, this assertion can only appear as bourgeois illusion and as counter-revolutionary appeasement of the suppressed.

The struggle between inner and outer freedom in the early church was reflected in the contrast between the new world of God, called "the kingdom of God," and the old world, or the contrast between the social life of the Christian community and that of the surrounding culture. Conversion to the Christian faith implied belonging to a community with a common, new way of life. Faith in Jesus was a confession of one whose appearance had begun a new movement of God to *all* people to save them from old corrupting life-styles and structures. Thus, the early Christian community declared its "Lord" the one who determined and made possible a common life here and now—under the conditions of the old aeon, within the context of the relationships prevailing in the old world.

It was inevitable, then, that the institutions of that old world be called into question by the evangelically based humanism of the Christian community. That community believed itself to be a community of brotherhood. It believed that no human being was excluded from brotherhood, but rather destined for it, for each one is loved by God in Christ and destined for living together in the kingdom of God. Concerning the institutions of the old world, it followed that one could either no longer participate in them, as, for example, the excluded professions (military, prostitution, the theater), or there had to be a different kind of living together within their framework, according to the criteria of brotherliness. Thus, in comparison to other sectarian communities of the day, the Christian community demanded a more radical change on the personal level (the commandment to love, freedom of the individual, eschewing of violence), but a less radical change on the corporate level where public law and social structures were concerned. They were neither communistic nor abolitionist by ecclesiastical *or* civil law.

And yet, the brotherhood of the Christian congregation stood in contrast to the competition and class warfare of the older, deficient society. It challenged the inevitability of the structures and institutions of the old society—the "truth" of that society. For its part, the older society disputed the viability of the new. It asked: Is anticipation of the new possible, given the stipulations of the old? And if a new way of living together within the old institutions is possible, to what extent is it possible, and in what way?

The Christian community answered that the manifestation of the new *within* the old must be possible, if what the gospel claims is true, namely, that the proclamation of the kingdom of God not only gives hope for future joy, but is also supposed to effect present change (metanoia)—because the death and resurrection of Jesus have already made present the kingdom of God and his Spirit. We are thus no longer obligated to live as flesh after flesh, but rather, can, through the Spirit, kill the "deeds" of the flesh

(Rom. 8:13) and can place our members, which have up to now been at the disposal of impurity and lawlessness, at the disposal of "righteousness for sanctification." (Rom. 6:19) Thus the possibility of the Christian life was immediately a questioning of the Christian belief itself. That question could only be answered by an act of faith—and faith means: seize and live the promised possibility of that new life.

In faith the Christian community undertook the adventurous effort to anticipate the new life by brotherly life in the *familia Christi,* by anti-authoritarianism which rejected rulers and hierarchies, and by placing social and other privileges for the use of all, especially for the underprivileged.

The new community did not represent the perfect life, because it existed in an unchanged world. The church still is subject to the conditions of the old aeon in which it is rooted. It still is subject to the stipulations of a deficient society and an unregenerate humanity. The consequence of this situation is that both the new community and its members also participate in self-preservation through the battle for existence and competition and mutual repression. They too become objectively guilty in their involvement in the lives of others. For that reason the Christian community must affirm the regulations of a deficient society and must express itself in a readiness to get its hands dirty too, for its life is woven into the political and social battle and its contradictions.

Why, then, the failure of the early church to achieve external freedom? It is necessary to remember that a historical-materialistic analysis prohibits a moralistic verdict on earlier generations. Not everything is possible at all times. The productive situation corresponds to the available productive forces and can be overcome only in accordance with further development of those forces. Antique society was based on slavery; its abolishment lay on neither the economic nor the moral horizon. For just that reason the plan for a brotherly community of all people leaped far beyond this horizon—and was at the same time, in that the members remained masters and slaves, affected in its realization by that horizon. And yet, universal abolition of slavery should have become a process with moral pressure emanating from the expanding Christian community. The same applies to later epochs. But there was no strong ecclesiastical counterweight to the extensive spread of socage over free peasants, to the introduction of slavery in the new colonies, or to the slave trade in the new world. On the contrary, the church furnished theological justification for these things.

It has been accepted for centuries that the church responded in this way because, after Constantine, its leadership had been taken over by the upper levels of society. Under this influence, the redirection of life demanded by the gospel became limited to particular points of political morality, to resistance against the development of a tribute system, and to official (ecclesiastical) marriage ethics. Under this leadership the spiritualization and individualization of the Christian message and ethic were promoted. Similarly, they promoted the dogmatization of Christianity (that is, the understanding of faith as the acceptance of doctrine) and concealed the social implications of the gospel, which had been clearly seen by the early church. "When Christianity was not doctrine, but only a few scanty sentences—which, however, were expressed in life—then God was closer to reality than when Christianity became doctrine. Every increase and embellishment of doctrine removes God further." [3] The church had lost a total view of the commandments of Jesus. "Of the commandments of Jesus, the only one actually impressed on the consciences of millions of Christians is the one concerning neighborly love, in the sense of helping a stranger in need. In general, the man who confesses Christianity passes over, completely unperturbed, the many other demands of Jesus, such as the renouncement of riches, power, honor, etc., although these demands represent the precise intention of Jesus and are in his view fulfillable." [4] The improprieties resulting from the church's functioning as an agency of the upper classes were partly removed by the Reformation. Yet despite this, the church, even under Luther, was not able to break with individualization and dogmatization which, especially in Calvinist regions, maintained the identity between the church and the bourgeoisie. Since the middle of the nineteenth century, socialism has asked the church the question as to whether it can free itself from a Babylonian captivity to the upper classes and take the part of the lower classes. For only through the promotion of those interests can society be truly directed toward brotherhood.

Given the framework determined by the continuance of slavery and economic disparity, the early Christians *could have* formed esoteric communities in which such differences were abolished—although such communities, like the Essenes, would only have been ineffective curiosities. The early Christians did not, however, because they understood themselves to be called not only out of the world, but also into it; they did not think in terms of a salvation egoism, and kept open the possibility of possessing slaves. This meant, in the first place, that the Christians did not conceive of their new life as depending upon formal, and thus externally fulfillable, law. Rather, being already a community of freedom, they trusted the effect of the liberating spirit of Jesus to break the inner bond of social privilege by speaking through the gospel and by creating unity within this new way of living together.

In the second place, the church's attitude toward structures of injustice meant that they had taken the privileged into their common life, in which all were responsible for all. This inclusion influenced the individual class consciences of congregational members. This was an event of unprecedented humanization of class relationships exactly at a time when such relations were inhumane and legalistic. Downtrodden slaves were recognized as humans with equal rights and were instilled with a new consciousness of self, and slave owners had to learn to use their privileges as occasions for service to the underprivileged. Both were furnished inner liberation from the external class situation by means of the proclamation of the gospel and community living. The privileged had to learn to use their privileges as if they did not possess them (1 Cor. 7:29-31), and the underprivileged were supposed to recognize themselves as liberated beings desipte poverty and dependence. Formerly responsible only to others, they were now responsible to themselves, and even as slaves under strange powers (1 Peter 2:18) or in the mines or galleys, had to prove themselves men who serve others in the context of the development of their own humanity. For this community the path led from inner freedom to free self-expression and was independent of the exterior framework of social and legal freedom. The gospel as an affirmation of such inner liberation is of greatest significance precisely in situations where there is an external lack of freedom which cannot be overcome (prison, concentration camp, sickness, slavery). It is important to note that the early church's maintenance of the distinction and independence of inner freedom from external freedom did not imply a disinterest in external freedom or a willingness to accept its absence. Rather, it had as a consequence the wish for external freedom and was the presupposition for the struggle for it.

This can be supported on several grounds. The assertion that the external circumstances of bondage necessarily make people slaves or that the absence of liberties has as a consequence the impossibility of *freedom,* and that therefore talk of inner freedom is an ideological appeasement in the struggle for external freedom, can be proven invalid. While external bondage does indeed produce massive inner bondage, it does not do this as a matter of course. Martyrs and confessors of every sort in chains and faced with death, and the joyful letters of Paul and many others are glowing proof to the contrary. Rather, in these examples we see an absolute conquest of the consequences of the lack of freedom, namely, fear, cowardice, despair, and servility. In their stead came ascendancy over the situation, joyfulness, frankness, tenacity, responsibility, courage, hope, humanity. Where those in servitude rise up to do battle for their liberation, they must first have arrived at such inner liberation. Therefore, the assertion that inner freedom is either impossible or insignificant under the conditions of non-freedom strikes at the roots of the socialist struggle. That struggle goes on because people in chains become inwardly free and thus begin to fight.

On the other hand, external freedom does not guarantee inner freedom. Of course, free circumstances favor a free disposition, as unfree circumstances favor a servile disposition. We are constantly under the influence of external circumstances (which Thielicke ignores, as if it were unimportant), their mitigations as well as their temptations, their help as well as their hindrance. Aeschylus said, "Half of man's virtue is lost in servitude," to which we answer, "Yes, but not automatically; it is lost only if he has nothing else which protects and helps him." Conversely, free circumstances do not automatically produce free people. There are endless possibilities for being an enslaved human being inwardly, and thus showing oneself a slave, even under free circumstances. Man can lose half his virtue and more, even in freedom.

This relation between inner and outer freedom does not necessarily produce indifference toward external freedom, either one's own or other people's. Slavery often carries with it the temptation to give up even one's inner freedom and hinders as well any manifestation of that freedom in service to others (which is the desire of the truly free man, the man freed also from himself). He who is inwardly free can bear external non-freedom, can resist its temptations, and even as a slave express his freedom in love. But he cannot for that reason wish the slavery; he will also desire external freedom. Likewise he desires external freedom for others, for he sees how external enslavement on a large scale makes people captive inwardly. It cripples them in character, takes away the richness of life and the possibility of doing good for each other, and throws them back on their own egoism. He will thus fight to make freedom and liberty coincide, and he will do this through his own inner freedom.

The early Christian community could hold both freedoms together in the same way that Paul promised the freedom of the bound one to the slaves (1 Cor. 7:22). A proof of the reality of the brotherhood of that early congregation is that Paul, the privileged one, the free *civis Romanus,* could say this to slaves, apparently without fear that they would sullenly reject it ("It's easy for you to say that") or suspect it as an effort to dull their sense of self-interest before the interests of the ruling classes. And here we encounter the one stipulation under which an externally free man may, in the presence of the externally bound man, believably point to "being free in Christ." That promise is believable only if the brotherhood between the two is intact and if the solidarity between the privileged and the unprivileged is manifested in the former, freely subjecting his privilege to the latter.

We can understand the early Christians' attitude toward the structures of injustice in the world only if we remember that although they lived as collectives different from the surrounding world, they were not sequestered sects. An important feature of that early community was self-consciousness about being isolated from and yet open to the outside world. Brotherly behavior was not limited to the internal life of the congregation, to the brothers in faith. The congregations were supposed to "do good toward all men" outwardly as well as inwardly (Gal. 6:10). Indeed, Paul did add: "but mostly toward one's fellows in faith." But he certainly does not mean that Christians should do good only to their fellows in faith—and do good to others only as a kind of gratuity, if they have time for it. No, he simply means that the benevolence of Christians will most likely begin in their own ranks, and spread from there outward. If real brotherliness is not practiced in the community, then, accordingly, it will not be offered to those "outside."

Church history has verified that beginning with the Constantinian era, the congregations living as collectives of genuine brotherly life disappeared in the mass of a Christianized population. The church then became an institution of the ruling society, and the effect of brotherly life on society also disappeared. When that happened, the ones "outside"—the Jews and the heathen—did not feel the brotherliness of the Christians, but rather the murderous arrogance of the salvation-possessor toward the supposed unholy ones.

The struggle for social change and human freedom in the early church must finally be seen in the context of the New Testament's parabolic reference to the function of light and salt

(Matt. 5:13-14). The image of light describes a working out of self, a radiation beyond one's own life and realm. The image of salt describes a wasting of self in the surrounding world, without regard for self-maintenance, as if the community were an end in itself. The new communal life-style, through which the members derived help for their own lives, was not supposed to make them into a new privileged class, but rather was for the benefit of "everyman." Where brotherly congregations live genuinely, they awaken (far beyond their immediate area and thus also among non-believers) a taste for brotherhood, freedom, tolerance. They open up the imagination for new possibilities of social life, for anti-authoritarian solidarity, and spoil the taste for traditional ruling and exploiting structures. The early Christian community understood itself, according to the New Testament witness, as detached *from* the old surrounding world by means of a new life-style, and as open in a missionary way *to* the world. As permeating salt and radiating light, and as a critical counterimage to the old structures, they could not leave the old world the way it was.

Today, socialism is raising the question of how we are to approach the realization of a free, brotherly, masterless, and unified society. We are asked how we are to overcome a privileged society which is the result of the old order of deficiency. The model of the early Christian community may suggest at least the outline of an answer. The gospel implies, according to the early church's concept of brotherliness, a tendency toward socialism, that is, a break with class structures, be they feudal or bourgeois-capitalistic. And this means for the group gathered together by the gospel, for each congregation and each individual, a struggle to relate the dynamics of inner and outer freedom as it impinges upon the new order and the old. Thus the Christian community must discover where and to what extent the overthrowing of a class society is possible and needful today, and what can and must be done to that end. And because the Christian community, now as in the early years of its growth, is both separated from and part of the world in which it lives, it must also discover with which social and political groups, regardless of their origin or motives, it must necessarily cooperate to achieve this goal.

1. This essay is from the lecture "Die gesellschaftlichen Implicationen des Evangeliums: Blick auf das Urchristentum," given at the Free University of Berlin, May 25, 1970.
2. Helmut Thielicke, "Können sich Structuren bekehren?" *Zeitschrift für Theologie und Kirche* 66 (1969) pp. 113 f.
3. Søren Kierkegaard, *Tagebücher,* 1854.
4. Konrad Farner, *Theologie des Kommunismus* (Frankfurt: Stimme Verlag, 1959), p. 22.

# Justin Glimpsed as Martyr
# Among His Roman Contemporaries

GEORGE H. WILLIAMS

Justin the Martyr is the oldest Apologist whose works survive *in extenso*. He emerges therefrom a quite distinct personality. Indeed, he is the most ancient Christian outside the New Testament that we can readily visualize. Through his extant writings and the acts of his martyrdom, his countenance peers at us from the bottom, as it were, of church history with the extraordinary directness of a black and gold-leaf miniature at the base of some broken funereal flask from a Christian catacomb in Rome.[1]

Justin was not a lone intellectual among the early converts who happened to have survived the upheavals and wreckage of history. In his own day, he was esteemed by fellow Christians widely. In Gaul Irenaeus used his writings.[2] Tatian, his convert and pupil in Rome, ending his own career as an Encratite, in Syria recalls the animosity of a Cynic philosopher who may have informed on Justin.[3] In North Africa, Tertullian first refers to him as (the) martyr,[4] by which Christian honorific he has entered the calendar of the saints—in the East, where he was born for June 1, and in the Roman Church, of which he was a member when he was martyred, for April 14.

As we gaze back at that quaint miniature, the earnest black and gold countenance of our most venerable *doctor ecclesiae,* an apologist and a martyr, Justin comes into focus as rigoristic, opinionated, and of only median intellectual force. He is not the kind of ancient Christian with whom most of us today would feel at ease theologically or temperamentally. We must make an effort to rejoin his company. Justin's six pupil companions at his trial in 165/166 and martyrdom were Chariton, "a Christian by the ordination of God"; Euelpistos from Cappadocia, a slave in the palace or public works of Marcus Aurelius, who had learned to be a Christian from his parents and afterward "used to listen with joy to the words" of his philosophical teacher; Hierax, a slave dragged from his parents in Phrygia; Paiōn, who had first learned his noble confession from his parents; and Liberianus, presumably the only native Italian, who denied that he had no sense of religion, as the prefect inferred, but felt bound to worship "the only true God." [5] Hierax, possibly reflecting the teaching of his master, when questioned by the prefect as to his birth and parentage, replied that his earthly parents were dead in far-off Iconium but that the "true father" of all believers in any case was Christ and that their common mother was faith. In that international community of faith and rebirth in Christ which was the church, earthly nativity and parentage was of but minor significance, for many had let kith and kindred go to become the offspring of Christ.

But Justin does, in fact, preserve for us the name of his own father, Priscus, and his grandfather, Bacheios (*I. Apol.* 1). The Greek-speaking family of Justin went back to the Roman colonization of the Samaritan capital, resettled by Vespasian's legionaries and renamed Flavia Neapolis (modern Nablus), with a temple built by Hadrian. Though born of Gentile stock, Justin, perhaps even before he came to know what had once been preached in the environs of Nazareth, was already familiar with the fact that the indigenous Samaritans as well as the Jews (whose sacred city was put to flames for the second time when he was about thirty-five) were worshipers of the same God and held the Pentateuch in common. But Jews, under Barkochba, who led the revolt against Roman imperial authority and whom Justin mentions (*I Apol.* 31), and the Samaritans (*I Apol.* 53), did not present to him in his youth the kind of religion and ethical discipline that at the time could appeal to his philosophically inclined temperament. Justin (c. 100–c. 165), the third-generation scion of martial colonists of Flavia Neapolis, had presumably the accumulated family means and the intellectual motivation to engage in higher studies in quest of philosophy. However stylized his retrospective account (*Dial.* 2) may be,[6] the recorded sequence of his philosophical peregrination is plausible: Stoicism, Aristotelianism, Pythagoreanism, and Middle Platonism.

Justin's final conversion to scriptural philosophy took place apparently in Ephesus. It is not entirely clear whether Justin's last teacher of philosophy, the sagacious Platonist, had "lately settled" as a teacher in Samaria or in Ephesus. But it was almost certainly in Ephesus that the definitive philosophy, "philology," the love of the Logos made flesh, became his. Justin recalls the conversion in two different contexts. In conflating these two recollections we have the fullest description of his conversion to Christian philosophy.

In *II Apology* Justin stresses as foremost the influence on him of the exemplary behavior of Christians, some of whom he must have seen put to death in a public square or arena in Neapolis or, more likely, Ephesus. He writes:

> I myself used to rejoice in the teachings of Plato and to hear evil spoken of Christians. But, as I saw that they showed no fear in face of death and of all other things which inspire terror, I reflected that they could not be vicious and pleasure-loving [12].

The other recollection of his conversion is the climax of the aforementioned rehearsal of his philosophical peregrination (*Dial.* 2-7). After leaving the haunts of the Platonist, Justin was wont to fill himself with quietness, shunning the path of men, strolling in a certain field overlooking the sea, presumably in the environs of Ephesus. It was on one such stroll that an old man followed him, described by Justin as of "meek and venerable manners." The old man explained his presence to Justin in perhaps intentionally vague and symbolic language as one looking for members of his household about whom he had become concerned. From the ensuing dialogue, which began in the language of Pythagoreanism and Platonism, moving toward more explicit references to the Holy Spirit, to the Divine Word, to the prophets, and to Christ as the incarnate God who might be beheld and heard (as the God of Plato could never be), it is clear that the questing old man was himself a philosophically schooled Christian or the symbol of such a quest. Surely he was not an elder or teacher of the church of Ephesus. Justin never refers to him again. Justin reports that a flame was kindled in his soul, a love of the prophets and the "friends of Christ" took possession of him, and he, "after being initiated" (*Dial.* 8) through baptism, set about to "live a happy life" as a true "philosopher."

Retaining the frayed oblong woolen outer garment (*tribon pallium*) of the philosopher (*Dial.* 1.2) in his new office as teacher in the School of Christ, Justin went twice to Rome, the second time establishing his school in his rooms upstairs in the house of one Martin, near the Timothian bathhouse (*Acta*). It was while in Rome during either the first or the final sojourn—which, all told, he considered quite a while ("all this time")—that Justin composed *I Apology, II Apology,* and his literary recollection of what purports to have been a dialogue once engaged in with a Hellenistic Jew and his companions back in Ephesus. The *Dialogue* (25.5) refers to *I Apology.* The dates and circumstances of all three writings are under ever-renewed scholarly scrutiny.[7]

*I Apology* (c. 151-155) is addressed to the "Emperor Titus Aelius Adrianus *Antoninus Pius* [137-161] Augustus, Caesar; and to his [adopted] son Verissimus the philosopher [Marcus Aurelius, 161-180], and to Lucius [Verus] the philosopher, the natural son of Pius . . ." In *I Apology* Justin refers to Marcion, to Felix, governor of Alexandria (150-154), and to his writing "150 years after Christ's birth" (*I Apol.* 46). *II Apology* 3 refers to Prefect Lollius Urbicus, who had sentenced Ptolemy, a teacher, and two others to death. Ptolemy was the teacher of the Christian wife of a dissolute and angry pagan.

A plausible theory,[8] explaining the fragmentary "chapters" at the end of each Apology as the outer address on the envelopes of formally submitted protestations, suggests that *I Apology* was in fact an *epistula* in the technical sense, sent in 150 to the imperial chancery *ab epistulis,* and that *II Apology* was technically a *libellus* (cf. *biblidion, II Apol.* 14.1) sent in 156 to the subdivision of the chancery *ab libellis* in connection with the denunciation of Justin's group by a Cynic teacher (of whom more presently). In any case, the two Apologies and the *Dialogue* along with the authentic *Acts* of martyrdom and a few fragments are all that survive of the rather considerable literary corpus of the winsome teacher and apologist.

From these documents and related material we know not only considerable detail about Justin himself but also about his death. The life and thought of Justin are brought into extraordinary relief, given his antiquity, by our knowledge of seven or eight personalities around him.

In seeing Justin among his contemporaries—his companions, adversaries, and neutral observers—we will have primarily a frame, made up of pieces from the life and thought around him, that can help toward a definition of the central figure,[9] in whom we contemplate indeed the mystery of a Christian in the moment of decision in face of the sovereignty and claims upon him of the society about him.

1. *"Trypho," the Gospel-Reading Jew.* The Trypho of the *Dialogue* was presumably a Hellenized Jew with whom Justin had once carried on an extended scriptural debate in Ephesus, but was also a representative figure of the kind Justin encountered in Rome on the margins of the Christian community.[10] Since Trypho is in part at least also a literary creation, known to us in any case wholly through Justin, what he represents in Justin's theological milieu in Rome is more important than the personal biography of the Jew of Ephesus; but we at least should have certain incidental details before us first.

Trypho had fled the war in Palestine (*Dial.* 1.3; 16.2) and had spent much time in Greece, notably Corinth (*Dial.* 1.3), where he had been taught "in the school of Socrates" by one Korinthas before coming to Ephesus. Clearly the second destruction of Jerusalem in 135 (*Dial.* 108.3) had undermined some of Typho's confidence in the faith of his fathers and he was open to what Justin was saying, if the present text is in any way a literary reconstruction of authentic reminiscences. Trypho, like Justin,

used only the Septuagint. Trypho had not felt himself bound by
the rabbinical warning to refrain from discussion with Christians
(*Dial.* 38.1; 19.4), had come to know "the commandments
given . . . in what is called the Gospel," finding them both "admirable" and almost too difficult to keep (*Dial.* 10.2); and he
did not for a moment have to be persuaded that the common
charges of immorality against Christians were but popular tales
unworthy of credence (*Dial.* 10.2). Although Trypho occasionally
accused Justin of tendentious misquotation, artifice, and even blas-
phemy, he was for the most part genial. He summed up his positive
reactions and those of his companions to the interfaith dialogue
in the gymnastic portico of Ephesus in c. 135 thus:

> I confess that I have been particularly pleased with the confer-
> ence; and I think that these [associates in debate] are of quite
> the same opinion as myself. For we have found more than we
> expected, and more than it was possible to have expected. And
> if we could do this more frequently, we should be much helped
> in the searching of the Scriptures themselves. [*Dial.* 142.1]

Justin left Ephesus right after the dialogue, perhaps already determined to establish his own school of Christian philosophy in Rome.

In Rome Justin was faced as a teacher by challenges to his
theology not only from philosophical pagans but also from various kinds of Christian teachers whom he regarded as heretical or
even worse (2 below) and from various kinds of Jews, with
several circles of whom he felt closer than he did with aberrant
Christians. Justin, plausibly on the basis of recollections, in due
course produced our present comprehensive apology for *scriptural*
Christianity to win over prospective Jewish and Judaizing seekers
of the truth in his Roman milieu and perhaps to oppose the Gnostic
Christians who disparaged the Old Testament and its prophecies.
He was even prepared to call Trypho and his companion friends,
in contrast to Gnostic and other aberrant Christians in the same
city, with whom he disdained to have any contact (*Dial.* 35.5;
cf. 80; 82.3; 3). Justin in some ways felt closer to some Jews
like Trypho than to even "many Christians of pure and godly
mind" (*Dial.* 80.2), because like the Jews, he along with Christians
"right-thinking in all things" held that with the resurrection of

the flesh and reanimation there would be a millennial rule of Christ in a rebuilt Jerusalem (*Dial.* 80.5).

Trypho and his colorless, unindividualized companions, who enter, leave, laugh, and occasionally scoff (*Dial.* 8.3; 9.2; 57.4; 58.2; 82.1; 118.5; 122.4; 123.7; 142.1; 3), must represent a type of Jew within range of intellectual contact, even teaching and apologetic, whom Justin hoped to convert before the imminent advent of Jesus a second time in judgment (*Dial.* 28.2), along with pious pagans. Although Justin drew up his own list of some seven heretical sects of Jewry, including Sadducees and Pharisees (*Dial.* 80.4), most of these are much less in his mind than the following seven circles of importance to him in the interfaith dialogue in Rome.

It will be helpful to visualize the sectors of Jewry of which Justin was aware: (1) Hellenistic Jews who in their synagogues anathematized Christians (*Dial.* 16.4) and enjoined their brethren to have no contact with them (*Dial.* 38.1); (2) Jews who, having once accepted Jesus as the Christ, relapsed to Moses but who might still have been saved by repentance, in contrast to apostate Gentile Christians (*Dial.* 46.4); (3) Christian Jews (by birth) who accepted Jesus as the Christ but who compelled Gentile converts to live in accordance with the law or refused to have communion with then (*Dial.* 47.1; 2; 3); (4) Jews who accepted Jesus as the Christ, maintained the ceremonial laws of Moses as well as "those ordinances in the Old Testament of the practices of righteousness and of piety which are everlasting and in accordance with nature" (and therefore to be observed also by Gentile Christians), but who did not impose the ceremonial law on fellow Christians of Gentile origin and willingly joined them in conversation and at meals (*Dial.* 47.1; 2); (5) Christian Gentiles who complied with the Jewish legalistic demands of group three (*Dial.* 47.1); (6) Christians of Jewish antecedents who refused to follow anything but the moral law of the Old Testament and did not perpetuate the rite of circumcision for their Christian progeny (*Dial.* 23.3); and (7) Jewish proselytes of pagan background and *phoboumenoi ton theon* who were initially attracted to, and versed in, the moral law of the Old Testament and practiced at least some of the ethical code of Hellenistic Jewry. However, they hovered between a definitive submission to Judaism through the painful rite of circumcumcision and a no less decisive incorporation into that plenary and painless Christian "Judaism" through baptismal "circumcision" in Jesus as the Messiah and Lord of the Law (*Dial.* 10.4; 25.3; 70.1; 106.1; 122.2).[11]

Given the sustained concern of Justin in his *Dialogue* with the applicability of the Law, the fulfillment of the promises of the prophets, and his recurrent discussion of God-fearers, proselytes, circumcision, and baptism, it is plausible to see in Trypho and his companions figures not too far from number 2 above, for Trypho was in any case familiar with gospel and Christian usage. More important, in arguing with Trypho he was no doubt primarily concerned to argue against Christian Jews in number 3 above and especially to make converts from among number 7 above, while interdicting their conversion to any aberrant form of Christianity (Gnosticism) which seemed to belittle the Law or to spiritualize the promises of the prophets and thus to disparage the resurrection of the flesh and the millennial kingdom centered in Jerusalem rebuilt and enlarged.

2. *Valentinus.* Of the several schools of aberrant Christians mentioned by Justin (*Dial.* 35; 80; 82), the group of which he must have been most aware was the large body of followers of Valentinus.[12] Born in Egypt and educated in Alexandria, Valentinus under Bishop Hyginus opened a school in Rome which flourished from c. 136 to c. 165. Like Marcion, who was concerned with the creation of an expurgated Lucan-Pauline canon and who was excommunicated from the Roman Church in 144, Valentinus, "an able man both in genius and in eloquence," the presumed compiler of the recently discovered *Gospel of Truth,* c. 140, also broke away from the main church in Rome. He was "indignant" that another had obtained the episcopal dignity by virtue of his being a confessor.[13] Valentinus employed the background of a platonic pleromal and phenomenal world as well as an elaborate cosmogony of thirty paired Aeons.[14] Against this background he distinguished the unredeemable hylics in the world from church members—the psychics who were the merely

baptized and the pneumatics who were fully redeemed by the laying on of hands in the Spirit (*apolytrōsis*). Large though his following was in Rome, Valentinus left for Cyprus.[15]

Justin, who mentions other Gnostics besides Valentinus and who wrote a lost *Adversus Marcionem,* was primarily alarmed at the Gnostic repudiation of the Old Testament God of creation and prophecy (*Dial.* 35.5; 80.4) and at the Gnostic denial of the eschatological resurrection in the false assumption that souls ascend to heaven at the very moment of death (*Dial.* 80.4).[16] Justin's lost *Syntagma,* widely thought to have been used by Irenaeus and Hippolytus in their refutation of heresies, may have been composed entirely against Valentinus and Basilides.

3. *The Encratite Tatian Among the Pupils of Justin.* In our imagination we can enter the academic chambers of Justin. Under direct questioning from the prefect as to where the seven Christians before him met for study and worship, Justin was evasive in order to protect the larger company of fellow Christians. He resorted to a theological generalization about the God of the Christians as uncircumscribed, filling unseen the heaven and the earth and "therefore to be worshiped by the faithful everywhere." Under further questioning he was willing to tell at least where he and his apprehended students were wont to meet, namely, in his own apartment. When anyone wished to come to him, he said, he imparted to that one the doctrine of truth. He averred that he knew of no other meeting place than that in all Rome. Though his own dwelling served daily as a school and on the Lord's Day possibly for the meeting of a house church, surely he must have known of other places of Christian assembly in the city.

Justin's description in *I Apology* of a weekly and a paschal eucharist suggests familiarity with the main body of worshiping Christians in Rome. Yet clearly his instruction was of a private sort without official approbation or oversight of the bishop in Rome. The bishop at the time of Justin's martyrdom, himself to die a martyr, was Anicetus (c. 155–c. 166), like Tatian, a Syrian. Born in Emesa, Anicetus as pontiff received the Jewish-Christian historian Hegesippus,[17] and also Bishop Polycarp of Smyrna, the latter in Rome to discuss the Quartodeciman (Judaizing) dating of Easter as presumably observed in Rome by the Eastern Christian colony there, for whom Polycarp was the selected irenic spokesman.[18] Justin, leading presumably the life of an ascetic celibate, quartered in what was at once his home and his school, belonged to the choir (*chōros*) of charismatic teachers whose functions were still largely independent of the bishop, constituting at the time a free-lance order in the larger Christian community in Rome. One gains the impression from Justin and his companions in martyrdom and from other indications that his school was something between an advanced catechetical center and a one-man philosophical hall. His pupils indicate that they came to him for advanced instruction only after they had learned Christianity from their parents or otherwise.

That Justin had able students is evidenced by Tatian, born c. 120 in Syria, who wrote his *Discourse to the Greeks* in defense of the barbarian Christians soon after his conversion.[19] Tatian's programmatic Encratism carried further the strong moralism of Justin himself, who based his Christian code on the Sermon on the Mount, which he quoted extensively. After breaking with the church in Rome (c. 172),[20] he left for Syria and completely repudiated all Greek philosophy; in his rigorism he came to regard marriage as adultery, while in the eucharist he substituted water for wine. Hence his followers were called both "Abstinents" and "Watermen." In Syria he prepared his harmony of the four Gospels, the *Diatessaron,* long to be used in the liturgy of the Syrian Church to which he returned.

4. *The Cynic Crescens.* Both Tatian and Justin himself (*II Apol.* 3) indicate that the teacher-apologist and his school incurred the enmity of a certain otherwise undocumented Cynic philosopher, Crescens.[21] This Cynic teacher, with a Latin name, came from Megalopolis in Arcadia, where long before in the third century B.C. another Cynic (Kerdias) had boldly proposed to distribute the wealth of the powerful among the virtuous poor.[22] Although there were indeed still atheists among the Cynics in the days of Marcus Aurelius and Justin, some of their number were professed Christians. This philosophical sect was sometimes recom-

mended to contemporary Christians because of their discipline or neglect of the body and earthly possessions, their disdain for civil authority, and their dedication to the reform of mankind through the espousal of universal brotherhood. Epictetus in his *Discourses,* discussing the calling of the ideal Cynic, spoke of him as "devoted to the service of God," ready to suffer patiently the discipline of Zeus, "messenger and scout and herald of the gods." [23]

From Justin and Tatian we get, to be sure, an entirely different picture of their Cynic competitor Crescens, whose blackness in their characterizations, however, derives from enmity which may have followed upon an earlier phase of more amicable interchange with him. Crescens is described as "unphilosophical and vainglorious," a would-be teacher who had come to make "his nest in the great city," and as one who, though he may have read some Christian writings, did not understand them, even acted so as not to be taken for a Christian, and cravenly sought to capture the applause of the masses by calling Christians "atheistic and impious." The breach widened between the rival teachers on the question of how to overcome the fear of death, and the public disputations between them were increasingly so noised about that Justin could even imagine that they might already have come to the notice of he emperor. Justin openly avowed that he expected any time to be denounced by Crescens to the public authorities and to be put into the stocks. His pupil Tatian expressly declared that Crescens endeavored "to inflict death" *inconsistently* [24]—as though it were an evil which he otherwise professed to hold in contempt— upon both the teacher and the most illustrious pupil in the school near the Timothian bathhouse. Referring to these two passages in Justin and Tatian, Eusebius of Caesarea would later allow surmises to coagulate as fact and would state that it was precisely Crescens the Cynic who informed on Justin and brought him before the prefect of the city,[25] although the *Acts* themselves are silent as to the source of the indictment.

5. *The Prefect Q. Junius Rusticus and His Rhetorical Rival, the Jurist Marcus Cornelius Fronto.* About the Roman magistrate before whom Justin was thus arraigned we have details that make the encounter especially poignant. The *praefectus urbi* in this

period was a major functionary, representing the might of the emperor within the jurisdiction of the imperial capital, with soldiers under his command. In Roman antiquity, the prefect of the city had administered Rome in the absence of the king. Under the early Republic the prefect had been the representative of the consulate, the supreme magistracy of Rome, whenever both consuls were absent from the city; but with the rise of the praetorship, the office of prefect was gradually eclipsed and survived in fact only as an honorific of ornamental value on the occasion of a major Roman holiday when the regular magistrates would be out of town. Then, beginning with Augustus, the prefect of the city became increasingly the personal representative of the *princeps,* and by the time of Justin's hearing he was again, as once in the period of the kings, the chief metropolitan magistrate under the sovereign, now eclipsing both the consul and the praetor. The *praefectus urbi* from 163 to his death in 167/8 [26] was Q. Junius Rusticus, who had been serving as an honorific consul since his appointment by the Emperor Antoninus Pius in 161 and his reappointment by Marcus Aurelius in 162.[27] Rusticus was so devoted to his emperor that he was said, by the jurist M. Cornelius Fronto, mentor and correspondent of Marcus Aurelius, to be willing "to lay down his life" even for "the Emperor's little finger nail." [28]

It is just possible that it was against attacks of this Fronto of Cirta in Numidia in his lost *Adversus christianos* that Justin composed his *II Apology.*[29] Fronto's speech in a judicial suit is presumably the earliest attack on Christianity of which we have record:

> On a fixed day they assemble together, children, sisters, mothers, people of both sexes and of all ages. After much feasting, a dog, fastened to the lamp, is encouraged by some pieces of meat thrown to it to spring violently beyond the length of its chain. The lamp, which would have been an inconvenient witness, is overturned and extinguished; after this riot and indecency reign supreme.[30]

Fronto and Rusticus were both teachers and then mentors

of their philosophically-minded imperial tutee. Fronto's excessive caricature of Rusticus' sedulous loyalty to the Emperor may have come partly out of his realization that Marcus Aurelius had, in fact, changed in about his twenty-fifth year from Fronto's tutelage in the new rhetoric to that of Rusticus, who stressed instead Stoic sobriety and restraint in both speech and conduct.

Marcus Aurelius, when he came later to compose his *Meditations* in his camp at night during the Marcommanic War, would devote the seventh paragraph of his first book to looking back summarily on what he owed to his Stoic tutor Rusticus, Justin's judge, in the inculcation of the virtues of forthrightness in speech and fairness in judgment of all kinds:

> From Rusticus [I learned] to get an impression of need for reform and treatment of character; not to run off into zeal for rhetoric, writing on speculative themes, discoursing on edifying texts, exhibiting in fanciful colours the ascetic or the philanthropist. To avoid oratory, poetry, and preciosity,[31] not to parade at home in ceremonial costume or to do things of that kind; to write letters in the simple style, like his own from Sinuessa [in Campania], to my mother.[32] To be easily recalled to myself and easily *reconciled with those who provoke and offend, as soon as they are willing to meet me.* To read books accurately and not be satisfied with superficial thinking about things or agree hurriedly with those who talk round a subject. To have made the acquaintance of the *Discourses* of Epictetus, of which he allowed me to share a copy of his own.[33]

It is apposite to have this full description of Junius Rusticus, who brought about Justin's martyrdom, because theologically, ethically, legally, and psychologically it is important to participate in the religio-political complexity of the encounter between the Christian apologist and the good and even devout pagan magistrate who condemned him by the authority of a likewise good and devout pagan sovereign. Marcus Aurelius characterized Rusticus' influence on his life as that of a Stoic magistrate who was ever ready to be reconciled with offenders, and who was diligent to determine facts, being distrustful of superficial thinking and hurried inferences. Something of this sobriety and forthrightness is, indeed, reflected in the laconic questioning of Prefect Rusticus in the surviving *Acts*.

Seated in judgment, Rusticus opened the hearing with a programmatic sentence: "Your first duty is to believe in the gods and to obey your Emperor." After ascertaining that Justin and each of his six companions were in fact self-confessing Christians all, and after showing perfunctory interest in where they were accustomed to assemble and their extraordinary confidence in the afterlife (eventual resurrection and reanimation) displayed by their spokesman, Rusticus duly warned them of the penalty for their obduracy and proceeded with the by-now long-since routinized test of civic loyalty: "Well, let us get on to the immediate business that lies before us. Come here all together, and with one accord sacrifice to the gods!" Justin recoiled at the very thought of falling "from piety into impiety," alluding to "the more terrible judgment seat of their ultimate *Kyrios* and Master"—an asseveration in which each of the other six concurred. Thereupon Rusticus pronounced sentence: "Let those who have refused to sacrifice to the gods and to yield to the command of the Emperor, be scourged and led away to suffer the punishment of decapitation according to the laws." [34]

The provisions of the law were apparently the same as under Trajan when he, just about fifty years earlier, instructed Pliny the Younger as provincial governor how he should deal with the same "pertinacity and inflexible obstinacy" of Christians in Bithynia.[35]

6. *The Stoic Emperor Marcus Aurelius.* What we know about the attitude toward Christians on the part of Marcus Aurelius Antoninus (161-180), by whose authority Rusticus condemned Justin and his six companions to be flogged and executed, centers in their inexplicable obstinacy, which vexed him.

The unusual violence and large number of martyrdoms reported by Eusebius for the period 161-168 may be connected with an imperial edict of about 167 ordering sacrifices to the gods for the whole of the Empire to win their help in the tragic situation caused by the devastating plague in Rome in 165 and possibly by the threat of the German war. This general edict in line with Roman tradition was not an expressly anti-Christian measure, but it produced action by mobs, informers, and possibly by some officials.[36]

In his *Meditations* and elsewhere Marcus Aurelius referred to Christians perhaps as many as five times.[37] He may well have been thinking of Christians, for example, when, arguing that the use of the mind is no necessary mark of a good man, he observed: "To have the mind [*nous*] as guide to what appear to be duties belongs also to men who do not believe in gods, who betray their own country, who do anything and everything once they have locked their doors." [38] More specifically, Marcus Aurelius referred to Christians when he reflected on the admirable readiness of the purified soul of a noble pagan to be released from the body— whether for extinction, diffusion, or personal immortality—in contrast to the ignoble readiness of the martyr-minded Christian to die, irrationally overconfident of a life hereafter:

> This resolve [the Emperor writes of noble pagans] . . . must arise from a specific decision, not out of sheer opposition (*psilen parataxin*) like the Christians, but after reflection and with dignity, and so as to convince others, without histrionic display.[39]

The reference to "histrionic display" is of interest. The Emperor, defending the outer reaches of Roman civilization in his headquarters at Caruntum (near modern Hainburg), may well have here alluded to the heavily attended and widely publicized apotheosis by self-immolation on the part of Peregrinus Proteus during the Olympian games in 165,[40] the conventional date, by chance, for martyrdom of Justin. Marcus Aurelius could readily have confused this fiery self-sacrifice with Christian martyrdom because Lucian, who circulated a satirical account of this alleged imposter, recounted how Peregrinus had first become a Christian before reconversion to Cynicism. And we have already noted in connection with the Cynic Crescens, who frequented Justin's public discussion groups, that in ascetic life, Cynicism and Christianity had indeed something in common which even their respective proponents, not alone their enemies, recognized.

Even though the somewhat ungrammatical phrasing in the foregoing passage from the Emperor's meditations that contains the word "Christians" may be an interpolation,[41] there can be no doubt about the persons whom the mediating Emperor mainly had in mind. And what he distrusted in Christians was what he considered their *unreasoned* resistance, for the whole point of his meditation was to admire precisely those nobler, reflective souls who are ever ready to depart the body without any assurance as to what might be the eschatological outcome. It would appear that what the Stoic Emperor found insupportable in Christians—not primarily because he was charged as emperor with the maintenance of civil order, but because he was a philosopher—was the indisputable and seemingly irrational confidence of these ancient witnesses of Christ about exactly what would happen to the good and to the wicked after death.

If the prefect of the city had chanced to report to Marcus Aurelius verbatim the words of Hierax, companion of Justin, "Our true father is Christ, and our mother is faith in Him," the imperial philosopher, himself an adoptive son of Emperor Antoninus Pius, might, by a stretch of religious imagination, have been able vaguely to understand how Christians thought of themselves as sons of God through Christ or even sons of Christ, as Hierax had put it. But the Stoic Emperor never could have understood the Christian faith of these witnesses, so potent in transmuting their eschatological hope both into the substance of communal charity and into the rigidity of their quiet courage and forthrightness in the face of death. Although he might have understood elitist Valentinus' belief in the direct immortality of the *souls* of pneumatic Christians, he would have been baffled at Justin's belief in an imminent resurrection of the flesh and reanimation of such humble saints as Justin's companions to co-rule with Jesus Christ from Jerusalem as the capital of a millennial realm destined to supersede Rome.

The rationality, the freedom, and the austerity of both Marcus Aurelius and Justin were thus of a different order, however closely in certain other respects they approximated one another.

7. *Galen, Philosopher-Physician.* During the sojourn in Rome of the Christian teacher of philology, Justin from Neapolis, there lived in the same city the pagan physician and philosopher, Galen from Pergamum, who was charged with the health of the son of Marcus Aurelius (Commodus) and who lived in Rome from 162 to 166, i.e., in the time of Justin's execution. (He returned to the capital in 169, dying there in 199.) From Galen's pen we have a number of fragmentary references to the Jewish and Christian communities in Rome and elsewhere.[42] He knew of their schools, to which he referred disparagingly: "If I had in mind people who taught their pupils in the same way as the followers of Moses and Christ teach theirs—for they order them to accept everything in faith, I should not have given you a definition." [43] But if Galen was critical of Christian pedagogy, he was highly appreciative of Christian morality:

> . . . we see the people called Christians drawing their faith from parables [and miracles], and yet sometimes acting in the same way [as those who philosophize]. For their contempt of death [and its sequel] is patent to us every day, and likewise their restraint in cohabitation . . . They also number individuals who, in self-discipline and self-control in matters of food and drink, and in their keen pursuit of justice, have attained a pitch not inferior to that of genuine philosophers.[44]

Although Galen does not in the surviving fragments of reference to Christians mention Justin in the same city with him, he may well have heard of the execution of the teacher of Christ or of teachers and pupils like him and his companions. Thus a faint echo of the proceedings under Marcus Aurelius comes down to us from an unexpected medical source transmitted in Muslim translation.

\*     \*     \*     \*     \*     \*

The references of contemporaries in Rome—Galen, Marcus Aurelius, Rusticus, Crescens, Tatian, Valentinus, and "Trypho"—to Justin directly or to the select community of which he was a part, sharpen our focus on the mystery of what it was to be a Christian in the world but not entirely of it in the capital of the

Empire in the year 165. For the most part our frame around the image of Justin Martyr has been composed of good men in their day—physician, magistrates, religious philosophers—some of them much closer to us in temperament or vocation than Justin the Martyr.

Especially is the mystery and the tragedy of this approximation palpable as we contemplate the emperor-philosopher, meditating on the Logos of world order, and the teacher-philosopher, dying in fealty to that same Logos believed to have become flesh as the sacramental high priest of the eucharistic fellowship in the new covenant, and eschatologically king with an invisible sovereignty above that of all rulers of the world. The tragic mystery is all the more poignant, too, when we turn from what Justin said on trial before a Roman magistrate about Jesus to what he said to the philosophical emperor himself long before the trial—about the Romans and their empire and also about the Greeks and their wisdom, when he was soberly directing apologies to emperor and imperial associates.[45]

Almost as if Justin knew what vexed Marcus Aurelius most about Christians, who took reason for a guide only to be irrationally resistant to traditional authority in civil and religious matters, he opened his *I Apology* to the Emperor Antoninus Pius and his two adoptive sons, one of them being Marcus Aurelius, with an appeal to reason:

> Reason [*nous*] directs those who are truly pious and philosophical [he said] to honour and love only what is true, declining to follow traditional opinions, if these be worthless. For not only does sound reason direct us to refuse the guidance of those who did or taught anything wrong, but it is incumbent on the lover of truth, by all means, and if death be threatened, even before his own life, to choose to do and say what is right. [*I Apol.* 2]

Justin's faith in what was dogmatically and morally right, which was the hard core of the vexing obduracy of all Christians in the eyes of Marcus Aurelius, was based on what Jesus judged by Pilate, in the tradition of John the Evangelist (19:11; cf. *I Apol.* 36.5), had said about himself (as the Son) in relation to the creator and king of the universe by whose power Pilate governed. Before becoming a Christian, Justin had long been seeking a word from this God whom he already knew or at least intuited. He was already a convert to monotheism, a devotee of the Creator God, as it were, philosophically inferred and abstracted, before he came to know his personal envoy or servant, Jesus Christ. It is even possible that Justin was helped toward monotheism not only by his study of philosophy but also by his Samaritan environment, for he claimed the Samaritans as his "own people" (*Dial.* 120.6),[46] although he on principle opposed circumcision. What made Justin a devotee of Jesus Christ was that the prophets were the fulfilled heralds of Jesus; that Jesus himself had put forth in his lifetime on earth his authenticated credentials as the definitive Word of the one true God made flesh; and that the apostles in their turn were his authoritative emissaries, foretelling his second advent in judgment. In a surviving fragment of his lost *Contra Marcionem,* Justin declared with startling specificity: "I should not have believed the Lord Himself [Jesus Christ], had he proclaimed another God than the Creator." [47] It is clear from everything that Justin said that he believed in free will and hence in moral accountability, that he used his rational powers to the limits of his capacity, and that at the same time he was unswervingly certain about the divine credentials of Jesus Christ and of both his prophetic anticipators and his apostolic proclaimers. He was certain of this for the reason that these very prophets of the old covenant and apostles of the new, and above all Jesus himself, referred creation, salvation, and all providential sustenance to that one and only God.

It is extraordinary that just as the emperor and the prefect had a strong sense of moral accountability, so Justin had a very strong sense of the place of the Roman Empire in God's providence. In his universal providence God, according to Justin, had not only prepared old Israel for the first advent of the pre-existent Christ, long foretold by the prophets inspired by "the Spirit of prophecy," but through the power of the Roman Empire he also prepared the entire civilized world and all nations for the emissaries of Christ, who were enjoined to enroll converts to the gospel, subjects of the kingdom to be established with power at the imminent second advent.

Justin was prepared to see even in the military standards of the Roman imperial army a providential anticipation of the symbolic shape of the cross and therein an emblematic consecration of Rome's universal sway. After seeing in the sail, the plow, and even the erect posture of man, the foreshadowing of the triumphant cross, he writes more specifically of the Roman Empire:

> And the power of this form is shown by your own symbols [he said to the emperors] on what are called *vexilla* and trophies, with which all your state possessions are made, using these as the insignia of your power and government, even though you do so *unwittingly.* [*I Apol.* 55.6]

Justin minimized the role of Pontius Pilate and hence the Roman government in the events leading up to the crucifixion (cf. *Dial.* 17, 32, 93, 102-103), even when he cites the *Acts of Pontius Pilate* (*I Apol.* 35.9).[48] Justin is alone among the Apologists to have used "tree" for "cross." The typological value of "tree" made it preferable. Justin thus combined in a theologically pregnant term the cruel cross and the fruitful tree of Paradise, the tree of life.[49]

Justin understood the persecution of Christians as instigated by still unsubdued demonic forces of the fallen angels, using magistrates, philosophers, Jews, heretical Christians, and even relations and friends (*Dial.* 35; *I Apol.* 56-57), despite Christ's victory over demons (*Dial.* 30, 49, 111, 121, etc.). Justin was convinced that the diminutive community of faith of which he was an initiated member was in league with a cosmic Power and Person that could even bring the persecuting empire into providential service for the salvation of all mankind.

Justin had thus an extraordinary respect for Roman authority and enjoined obedience and loyalty to Caesar in the terms of Matthew 22:20-21 (*I Apol.* 17). He recoiled at the thought that so august an administration, which his own Christ had said should be obeyed in all things properly of concern to Caesar, should be tainted, however so little, by a tax on prostitution (*I Apol.* 47). Throughout the Apologies Justin addressed the emperors as a collective personage, the deed of any one being construed as the work of all. Thus, addressing the emperors of his own day, Justin could say that when Jesus appeared *"you* began to rule the Jews" and that after the crucifixion Judea "was straight-away surrendered to *you* as spoil of war" (*I Apol.* 32). It was part of God's plan, Justin believed, that Christ should make his first advent as a subject of the Roman Empire (*I Apol.* 32.3-4; 63.16), and it was right that the Temple with its superseded sacrifice had been destroyed by Roman legions (*Dial.* 45.1; 42.2; 110.16). And far from holding that the emperor had no competence in the realm of religion, Justin even demanded that he punish heretical Christians "who are not living pursuant to these [Christ's] teachings, and are Christians only in name [heretics]" (*I Apol.* 16.4; cf. *Dial.* 35.5).

Justin could not know that his own theology would one day be looked back upon as archaic, inchoate, if not heretical. Justin from a later perspective was certainly a rigorist and his catholicity was only embryonic.

God was to him God the Father and Creator, the only Unorig-inate or Unbegotten Being; but though Justin distinguished between the internal and external Logos of God the Father and sometimes called the Logos the preexistent Christ,[50] he could not think of the Logos as without beginning, and he often confused or identi-fied the Logos and the Holy Spirit (*I Apol.* 33). Moreover, Justin could not conceive of God the Father and Creator as creating from nothing (*I Apol.* 10). Christ was for Justin the Word made flesh, born of the Virgin, with blood not of human seed but "of divine power" (*I Apol.* 32). Justin was also a millennialist, as-sured that there would be a resurrection of the dead and the rule of Christ from Jerusalem, which would be appropriately rebuilt, "adorned, and enlarged" (*Dial.* 80).

But whatever a later Christianity would think of Justin as a theologian, the authentic and abiding core of Justin's Christianity was surely his conviction in moral freedom and accountability and the divine authority of the moral code committed to his people of the New Covenant by Christ, the Lord of redeemed humanity, the *only* begotten Son and Ambassador (*Apostolos*) of God the Father and Creator, who, working through the Word present everywhere before and since the advent of the Son, prepares men in all cultures (*I Apol.* 5; 46) through the gift of *love* and *faith* to witness to his sovereignty in their lives. For this transcendent person Justin lived and was prepared to die. He was a martyr to Christ, a new kind of power and person in the brooding evolution of humanity. Justin thought of God's preparation of mankind for the reception of his redeeming Word as embracing all. Mankind he divided into pagans on the first level, then Jews, and finally Christians, who restored the original loving, monotheistic faith of primordial man (*Dial.* 108-110).

In *I Apology* Justin said to the Emperor:

> . . . though death is decreed against those who teach or at all confess the name of Christ, we everywhere both embrace and teach it. . . . Ye can do no more than kill us: which indeed does no harm to us, but to you . . . [*I Apol.* 45]

In his trial Justin said, to the same effect, to the Emperor's prefect: "No right-thinking person falls away from piety to impiety."

By *eusebeia* Justin meant piety toward the Word, the pre-existent Christ, and the Christ indwelling every witness to him, every martyr. In *II Apology* he had written:

> And those of the Stoic school—since so far as their moral teaching went, they were also the poets in some particulars, on account of the seed of the word implanted in every race of men—were, we know, hated and put to death. . . . For . . . the devils have always effected that all those who anyhow live a reasonable and earnest life, and shun vice, be hated. And it is not at all remarkable if the devils are proved to cause those to be much more hated who live not according to part only of the Word diffused [among men], but by the knowledge and contemplation of the *whole* Word, which is Christ. . . .
> He was and is the Word who is in every man. . . . Not only

philosophers and scholars believed, but also artisans and people entirely uneducated, despising both glory, and fear, and death. [*II Apol.* 8; 10]

What was in essence the difference between the piety of Justin and what we, if not Justin, in fairness would be willing to call also the piety of the Stoic chief magistrates of Rome?

With respect to the afterlife, some of today's theologians have programmatically repudiated immortality, while many others are probably at best more like Marcus Aurelius, entertaining the same three eschatological possibilities mentioned by him in his *Meditatations* and finding Justin's fourth and distinctive view of resurrection and reanimation for millennial rule particularly difficult. With respect to *pietas,* Justin had once for all sworn fealty in a solemn baptismal covenant to a person, to Jesus Christ foreseen by the prophets and vouched for by the apostles and experienced morally and sacramentally in the communion of faith. The Stoic magistrates were self-disciplined students of an august and universal power and were obliged by Roman law and cumulative Roman custom to make certain religious claims about the emperor's person and his impersonation of the power of Rome. Yet, no more than Justin had Marcus or Rusticus any real faith in the ahistorical divinities of the pantheon or in the divine epiphanies of pious legend, except as these gods and their cultus, local or empire-wide, provided sanctions for the ecumenical commonwealth. And Justin, for his part, was scarcely less concerned than they with order and moral probity.[51] But the sovereignty in the name of which Justin felt free to criticize that state was the sovereignty of One who had created the cosmic order, had established the Roman Empire itself, and had sent his Son as plenipotentiary to redeem all mankind with a new law and accordingly a new and inward covenant.

Justin was therefore unreservedly loyal to a unique person who had entered history, bearing the credentials of messianic expectation and preparation among an elect people. Christ was no ephemeral epiphany of divinity but a person, transforming lives like his own, a person to whom the Magi came in the mystery of the manger, who grew in wisdom and stature, laid down a new law upon the mount, and ruled from the tree, which was the cross,[52] subversively fulfilling the legitimate claims and expectations of every elect race, ruling class, and imperial commonwealth and thus transcending them and freeing all men with him.

---

1. The flask bottom is a distinctive type of Roman funereal portraiture. A gold-leaf portrait of a person or a couple was commonly presented to him or them on some notable occasion, as a birthday or wedding. It formed the base of an ornamental flask or bowl. At the death of the owner it was broken as part of the funeral ceremony and the medallion-like miniature was imbedded in the fresh mortar of the grave of the deceased as a means of identification.

   The following biographical miniature brings no new data, but by placing the martyred theologian among his contemporaries in Rome, it may bring closer the reality of that conviction which sustains martyrdom. The portrait first sketched in a commemorative service in Andover Chapel at Harvard Divinity School, where Paul Lehmann once served, is now dedicated to him in recognition of his creative association with a modern theologian, teacher, and martyr, and with the publication of the definitive life of that martyr against the demonically omnipotent state of our age.

2. In *Adversus haereses,* iv. 6.2, Irenaeus quotes Justin's lost *Adversus Marcionem.*

3. *Oratio ad Graecos,* 18 f.

4. Tertullian, *Adversus Valentinianos,* 5, where he says that he drew upon "Justin, philosopher and martyr."

5. The *Acta* are to be found in Otto (below, fn. 6). (For the place of Justin's martyrdom in the larger setting, see W. H. C. Frend, *Martyrdom and Persecution in the Early Church* (Oxford: Blackwell, 1964), esp. pp. 249-251.)

6. Niels Hyldahl holds that Justin's conversion autobiography is literary convention and that Trypho is a wholly fictitious character, *Philosophie und Christentum* (Copenhagen: Munksgaard, 1966). Cf., however, Merrill Young, "The Argument and Meaning of Justin Martyr's Conversion Story," Harvard Th.D. Thesis, Cambridge, 1972, and less directly concerned with the personality of Trypho, regarded nevertheless as more than a literary fiction, see Theodore Stylianopoulis, "Justin Martyr and the Mosiac Law," Harvard Th.D. Thesis, Cambridge, June, 1974.

7. The critical texts used for the *Dialogue* and the *Apologies* are Johannes C. T. Otto, ed., *Iustini philosophi et martyris Opera quae feruntur omnia,* 2 vols. (3rd ed.; Jena: H. Dufft 1877), the first volume in two

parts with extensive notes, and the *Acta,* constituting volumes in the *Corpus Apologetarum Christianorum saeculi secundi;* and Edgar Goodspeed, ed., *Die ältesten Apologeten: Texte mit kruzen Einleitungen* (Göttingen: Vandenhoeck and Ruprecht 1914), to be supplemented by his *Index Apologeticus sive clavis Iustini Martyris operum aliorumque Apologetarum pristinorum* (Leipzig: J. C. Hinrichs 1912). For the translations of the *Apologie* and the *Acta* into English, the standard version in the American edition of *The Ante-Nicene Fathers,* I (Buffalo: The Christian Literature Publishing Co., 1885), has been adduced (into which the chapter subdivisions of Goodspeed and occasional modifications of the translation have been introduced without notice), and for the translations of the *Dialogue,* that of A. Lukyn Williams has been adduced, *Justin Martyr: The Dialogue with Trypho: Translation, Introduction, and Notes* (London: Madras, 1930).

8. Arnold Ehrhardt, "Justin Martyr's Two Apologies," *Journal of Ecclesiastical History,* III (1953), pp. 1-2. Gustave Bardy considers *II Apology* as composed in 161, "Saint Justin et la philosophie stoicisme," *Recherches de Science Religieuse,* XIII (1923), pp. 491-510; XIV (1924), pp. 33-45. See also Bardy's magisterial article Dictionnaire de Theologie Catholique, VIII:2 (1925), coll. 2228-2277. Paul Keresztes strengthens Ehrhardt's theory of two distinct Apologies by his close analysis of the literary structure of each, "The Literary Genre of Justin's First Apology," *Vigiliae Christianae,* XIX (1965), pp. 99-110, and "The 'So-Called' Second Apology of Justin," *Latomus,* XXIV (1965), pp. 858-869.

9. An attractive portrait of Justin within the frame is that of Henry Chadwick, "Justin Martyr's Defense of Christianity," *John Rylands Library Bulletin,* XLVII (1964/5), pp. 275-297.

10. See my related study, "The Baptismal Theology and Practice in Rome Reflected in Justin Martyr," *The Ecumenical World of Orthodox Civilization: Russia and Orthodoxy, Essays in Honor of Georges Florovsky,* 3 vols., ed. Thomas Bird and Andrew Blane (The Hague: Mouton Press, 1974), III, pp. 9-34.

11. Dieter Georgi for another center (Corinth) and for a century earlier has extensively analyzed the forms of the Jewish mission and of the Christianization of this mission in *Die Gegner des Paulus im 2. Korintherbrief; Studien zur religiösen Propaganda in der Spätantike* (Neukirchen-Vluyn: Neukirchener Verlag, 1964), esp. pp. 83-187, where the true Israelite of the seed of Abraham can even forgo circumcision.

12. Jean Doresse, *The Secret Books of the Egyptian Gnostics* (New York: Viking Press, 1960).

13. Tertullian, *Contra Valentinianos,* 4.

14. Most fully set forth by Irenaeus, *Adversus haereses,* 1.8-9; 2, 3 ff., and by Hippolytus, *Refutation,* 6.24-32.

15. Epiphanius, *Panarion,* hueresis 37.7. On *apolytrōsis,* see Elaine H. Pagels, "A Valentinian Interpretation of Baptism and Eucharist—and Its Critique of 'Orthodox' Sacramental Theology and Practice," *Harvard Theological Review* LXV:3 (1972), pp. 153 ff.

16. Irenaeus held the same view as Justin, *Adversus haereses,* 5.31.

17. His *Memoirs* survive only in fragments in Eusebius, *Historia ecclesiastica,* 4.21-25.

18. *Liber Pontificales;* Irenaeus, *Adversus haereses,* 3.3; Eusebius, *Historia ecclesiastica,* 4.11, 14, 19; 22; 5.6, 24.

19. Martin Elze, *Tatian und seine Theologie* (Göttingen: Vandenhoeck and Ruprecht, 1960).

20. Eusebius, *Historia ecclesiastica,* iv. 29.

21. Tatian, *Oratio ad Graecos,* 18-19.

22. Donald Dudley, *A History of Cynicism* (London: Methuen, 1937), pp. 143-144.

23. Epictetus, *op. cit.,* iii, 22; *Entrétiens,* text and translation by Joseph Souilhé, III, pp. 70-86.

24. *Oratio ad Graecos,* 19.

25. *Historia ecclesiastica,* iv. 16. 1.

26. F. H. Hayward, *Marcus Aurelius, A Saviour of Men* (London: G. Allen and Unwin, 1935), p. 295; A.D. 167; *The Meditations of the Emperor Marcus Aurelius Antoninus,* ed. Arthur S. L. Farquharson, 2 vols. (Oxford: Clarendon Press, 1944), I, p. 272; A.D. 168.

27. Farquharson, ed., *op. cit.,* I, pp. 260, 272. For more on Rusticus and the prefecture, see further *idem, Marcus Aurelius, His Life and His World* (Oxford, 1951), pp. 52-54, 60-61, 67-68.

28. M. Cornelius Frontonis, *Epistulae,* ed. M. P. J. van den Hout (Leiden: Lugduni Batavorum, 1954), p. 90, line 12.

29. Karl Hubik, *Die Apologien des heiligen Justins* (Vienna: Mayer and Co., 1912).

30. The fragment from the attack is preserved, along with other disagreeable charges by others, in the *Octavius* of Minucius Felix, 9: "id etiam Cirtensis nostri testatur oration," followed by the selection quoted above. See also ch. 31. M. Dorothy Brock, *Studies in Fronto and His Age* (Cambridge: University Press, 1911), p. 93.

31. The *elocutio novella* so much esteemed by Fronto; Farquharson, *op. cit.,* I, p. 272.

32. Domitia Lucilla, long widowed.

33. *Meditations,* i, 7, i, 17; Farquharson, ed., *op. cit.,* I, pp. 5-6. The reference must be to notes on Arrian's *Discourses* of Epictetus; Farquharson, *Marcus Aurelius,* pp. 53, 60.

34. *Acta,* ed. Otto, II, p. i; *Ante-Nicene Fathers,* I, p. 306.

35. Pliny, *Epistle* X, 3.

36. J. F. Gillian, "The Plague under Marcus Aurelius," *American Journal of Philology,* LXXXII (1961), pp. 225-251; for the persecution in 177, see Paul Keresztes, "The Massacre at Lugdunum in 177 A.D.," *Historie,* XVI (1967), 75-86, and *idem,* "Marcus Aurelius a Persecutor?" *HThR,* LXI (1968), pp. 321-341.

37. Hayward, *Marcus Aurelius,* pp. 140-141.

38. *Meditations,* ii, 16; Farquharson, ed., I, p. 49. C. R. Haines, *The Communings with Himself* (Loeb series), p. 381, construes the passage as referring to Christians and as evidence of the Emperor's being favorable to the infant church. Cf. his "Composition and Chronology of the Thoughts of Marcus Aurelius," *Journal of Philology,* XXXIII (1914), p. 288. Farquharson, in contrast, doubts whether the reference to locked doors is specifically to Christians, *op. cit.,* II, p. 307.

39. *Meditations,* xi, 3; Farquharson, ed., Vol. I, p. 217; Vol. II, p. 859.

40. D. R. Dudley, *op. cit.,* p. 143, says A.D. 167; see further pp. 170-175.

41. So Haines (Loeb series); Farquharson, ed., *op. cit.,* regards it as original, II, p. 859.

42. These fragments come to us from Arabic translations of otherwise lost works of Galen, collected by Richard Walzer, *Galen on Jews and Christians* (Oxford: Clarendon, 1949).

43. Reference 5; *ibid.,* p. 15.

44. Reference 6; *ibid.,* p. 15. The passage is embedded in an Arabic summary of Galen's own lost summary of Plato's *Republic,* c. 180. The material in brackets may be from Galen or from the Arab quoting him.

45. Per Beskow has an extensive discussion of the political theology of Justin Martyr in *Rex Gloriae* (Stockholm: Almqvist and Wiksell, 1962), pp. 92-105, 198 *passim.*

46. Here Justin is talking disparagingly about the Samaritan Simon Magus, which makes his identification with the Samaritans all the more unexpected.

47. *Apud* Irenaeus, *Adversus haereses,* iv. 6.2. The remainder of the passage, though formerly ascribed to Justin, has been withdrawn. J. A. Robinson, *Journal of Theological Studies,* Vol. XXXI (1929-30), pp. 374-378. Cf. Robert Grant, "The Fragments of the Greek Apologists and Irenaeus," *Biblical and Patristic Studies in Memory of Robert Pierce Casey,* ed. James Neville Birdsall and W. Robert Thomson (Freiburg: Walter de Gruyter and Co., 1963), on Justin, pp. 182-183.

48. See Paul Winter, *On the Trial of Jesus* (Berlin: Walter de Gruyter and Co., 1961).

49. G. Q. Reijners, O.S.C., *The Terminology of the Holy Cross in Early Christian Literature as Based upon Old Testament Typology* (Nijmegen: Dekker and Van de Vegt, 1965), esp. pp. 35, 41.

50. Demetrius Trakatellis, "The Preexistence of Christ in the Writings

of Justin Martyr: An Exegetical Study with Reference to the Humiliation and Exaltation Christology," Harvard Th.D. Thesis, Cambridge,
1971.

51. Robert McQueen Grant notes how tragically and ironically close
Christians and noble pagans were in the common concern for true
*Romanitas* in *The Sword and the Cross* (New York: Macmillan,
1955).

52. The reference to rule from the cross is from what Justin regarded as
the final verse of Psalm 96—"The Lord hath reigned from a tree"
(not extant in the Septuagint or Hebrew text)—and held by him to
have been excised by the Jews. *Dial.* 73; cf. *I Apol.* 41.

# Liberation in the Light of Hope *

**JÜRGEN MOLTMANN**

## I

### The Cry for Freedom [1]

The cry for freedom is going through the whole world today. The signs of a "revolution of rising expectations" are found everywhere and they are accompanied by an ever deeper sense of suffering. The closer freedom comes, the more the chains hurt. When some men actually free themselves from centuries-long oppression, others recognize that the limits and denials which they have accepted and borne are not necessary and can be overcome. What men once considered impossible becomes possible. They begin to hunger for freedom. But this hunger for liberation first appears in the changing of mute suffering into cries of pain. Quiet apathy changes into loud protest.

Men suffer from the economic exploitation of man by man and cry out for social justice. Men suffer from political oppression and struggle for the recognition of their human dignity and rights. Men suffer from the cultural alienation of man from man through racism and sexism and seek the fullness of true human life in solidarity with one another. Men suffer from the emptiness of their

---

* Translated by M. Douglas Meeks, Eden Theological Seminary, St. Louis. Mo.

personal life, which vanishes so meaninglessly in the structures of a technocratic and bureaucratic society, and seek personal identity. In, with, and under capitalism, dictatorship, racism, sexism, and nihilism, men suffer finally from the deep-set primal anxiety which makes them so inhumane and aggressive. The messianic secret was originally kept by the name "Man" ("Son of Man"), but in our situation "Man" has become a symbol of evil. We suffer not so much from the death of God as from the death of man.[2]

But the cry for freedom goes up not only from an exploited, oppressed, alienated, divided, and anxious mankind. The creation destroyed by man also shouts for deliverance. Nature, including our bodies, has become alien to us. We have denigrated the body (*Leib*) which we are, to the body (*Körper*), which we have and so we condemn both to death. "The creation" also wants to become free from the slavery of "decaying being" and "waits with eager longing for the revealing of the free children of God." (Rom. 8:19 ff.) Nature waits for its "true resurrection" in the human kingdom of man, said Karl Marx. The body waits for its liberation from the sublimation of the spirit and the repression of morality, said Sigmund Freud. Matter in us and around us hungers for the power of the new creation. The cry for freedom thus brings together man and nature in *one* hope. They will be destroyed in their dissension and enmity or will survive in a new community as partners.[3] But the cry for freedom goes up not only from humanity and nature. It is also *God's own cry*. In the groaning of the starving, in the agony of the imprisoned, in the senseless dying of nature, the Spirit of God himself groans, hungers, and sighs.

The messianic traditions of Judaism and Christianity do not speak of an apathetic God, who is enthroned in undisturbed holiness in heaven. They show us the God who suffers with his forsaken creation because he loves it.[4] He suffers with his people in exile; he suffers with a mankind which has become inhuman; he suffers with an enslaved creation condemned to death. He suffers with them, he suffers because of them, and he suffers for them. His suffering is his messianic mystery. For he has created man for freedom—in his image. He has created nature for joy—as the play of his good pleasure. Through his spirit of creation, then, God is involved in the world's history of suffering and through his pain is implicated in it. His Spirit hungers, yearns and cries out for freedom. His Spirit intercedes for those who have been struck dumb. He intercedes with "sighs too deep for words" (Rom. 8:26) and not with a glorious shout of victory. Only in this way does he keep the hope of the creation alive.

The cry for freedom is, therefore, *universal*. It is the hunger of men. It is the longing of nature. It is the passion of God, as it was revealed in the crucified Christ. So long as all men are not free, those who now call themselves free are also fettered. So long as men have not been reconciled to nature and nature to men, there is no complete happiness. So long as God himself suffers in his passion and has not yet come to his rest in a new creation corresponding to him, everything is living in hope and is not yet in a fulfilled joy. The struggle goes on; the victory is not complete.

A *theology of liberation* views all individual sufferings and denials of the world against the background of the patient suffering of God. It thus views all partial liberation movements as on the horizon of God's total and final history of liberation. A theology of liberation which witnesses to God's suffering and God's freedom can be deeply significant for individual liberation movements in at least three ways.[5]

First, we may not think trivially about the issues of freedom. We must dissolve our egoism and begin to think in terms of others, even the enemies of our own freedom. It is understandable that in its daily struggles every liberation movement is somewhat determined by its opposition. As a result it begins to follow the law of reciprocity and even revenge. But this corrupts the very freedom and humanity for which it struggles. The alienations which coercively emerge in such struggles must again be overcome if one wants to remain credible and demonstrate a "better justice."

"Is this necessary revolutionary [rigidity] to be eliminated in the confrontation or is it actually to be eliminated only after the revolution?" Herbert Marcuse answered this question of a Berlin student in 1967 with genuine sensitivity for the disquiet occasioned by Jesus' teaching: "Nothing is more atrocious than sermonizing about love—'do not hate your enemy'—in a world in which hate is thoroughly institutionalized." [6] Marcuse called hate against exploitation and oppression itself a humane and humanistic principle. But if justified hate against exploitation is not accompanied by hope for the birth of humanity within the exploiter, revolution increasingly resembles repression. Therefore, "revolutionary rigidity" must be eliminated in the confrontation itself. A liberated humanity cannot be eschatologically postponed to a date "after the revolution." A Christian theology of liberation lives by anticipating humanness in the midst of inhumanity and by stimulating reconciliation in the midst of the struggle for the redemption of this as yet unredeemed world. [7]

Second, when it comes to the issues of liberation we must overcome our ideological fixation on our own interests. It is regrettable that a conflict has broken out between the various liberation movements over what constitutes the "root of all evil." Socialists maintain that capitalism is the source of all evil and would view racism and sexism merely as capitalistic epiphenomena. Others consider the primary distress to be racial humiliation. Representatives of women's liberation view sexual oppression as the beginning of all oppressions. Ecologists find the pattern of all exploitation in the exploitation of nature.

This conflict reminds one of the philosophical debate of the pre-Socratics over primal matter and whether it is to be found in water, air, or fire. A kind of negative metaphysics has resulted from such ideological fixation. Only occasionally is the question asked why and how men come to capitalistic, racial and sexist aggression. In most situations they are trapped in mutual conditioning. Everywhere we find oppressed oppressors who aggressively pass on to others the suffering which they themselves have experienced. It is like a chain without an end or a beginning.

A Christian theology of liberation sees at work in, with, and under the various oppressions a primal cosmic, transpersonal anxiety. This primal anxiety is constantly and ubiquitously changed into aggression. With this perspective, a Christian liberation theology will not denigrate actual liberation movements. Rather, it will seek to eliminate ideological fixation and it will press for cooperation. The struggle for liberation is always a self-critical struggle. Only a few can say they are totally oppressed persons and not, in other connections, themselves oppressors. The anti-capitalistic struggle does not lead to a new humanity if it is not simultaneously a struggle against dictatorship, against racism, and against sexism. It does not lead to a new humanity if it does not emerge out of experienced liberation from primal anxiety and aggression. Today the vicious circles of oppression have many links in the chain. Without an alliance of the liberating powers these circles cannot be broken.

Third, freedom is an extraordinary blessing—but also a dangerous one. Even as we cry out for freedom, it causes us anxiety. The risk of freedom in an unjust world is tremendous. In order to enter into freedom we need an unbending hope which would rather be disappointed than disappoint others and a strong confidence which would rather let itself be wounded than wound others. "Whoever helps those who are lost is himself lost," said Berthold Brecht. Indeed, whoever is ready for freedom must be ready for the cross. Freedom in the cross—that is the gospel. For Christ is not the regulator of the world but our "deadly freedom" (Reinhold Schneider).

Many enthusiastic liberation movements have been ruined by their superficial optimism. Without that "hope against hope," which is born out of the readiness for suffering and the cross, resistance and confidence do not gain any firm ground. Franz Kafka expressed this quite cleverly and yet hopefully in his depiction of the "world without man." "It is no refutation of the expectation of an ultimate liberation if on the next day the prison remains still unchanged or actually becomes tighter, or even if it is expressly declared that it is never to be dismantled. All this can rather be the necessary presupposition for the ultimate liberation." The visage of Job has characterized the Exodus people of Israel for centuries. It remains the orientation point for all liberation movements which in the depths of their hope come upon the messianic kingdom of "man." [8] The freedom of the resurrection which was revealed through the forsaken, oppressed, and crucified Son of Man remains the sign of hope for the hopeless.

## II

### Freedom in the Light of Hope

Christian faith understands itself primarily as the beginning of a freedom such as the world has not yet seen. The Christian does not believe *in* freedom. His faith *is* his liberation from anxiety into hope, from self-seeking into love, and from the slavery of evil into resistance against evil. "For freedom Christ has set us free," says Paul in Galatians 5:1. "Stand fast, therefore, and do not submit again to a yoke of slavery." [9] Whenever a person believes, he experiences his resurrection into the freedom of eternal life in the midst of this life which leads to death.

From the Christian perspective, freedom no longer means, as from the Greek point-of-view, "insight into necessity." Freedom also no longer means the independent control of individuals or of political bodies over themselves. Christian freedom is born out of the resurrection of Christ and is alive in resistance against the vicious circle of law, sin, and death. Christian faith participates in the inexhaustible possibilities of the God for whom "all things are possible." This inexhaustible abundance of God's possibility reveals itself in the creative act of the resurrection of the crucified Christ. Faith, therefore, means participation in the process of the new creation of the world by God. Resurrection is the revelation of this new, creative freedom of God. Faith means to be resurrected into this creative freedom of God and to act out of its possibilities. "God is no longer the emperor of the Romans and just as little is he man in his beauty and strength, as with the Greeks. He is no promise of power. He is the certainty that one can create a qualitatively new future only if he identifies with those who in this world are most miserable and marginal, if he joins his lot with their destiny to the extent that he can envision no other true victory except theirs." [10]

Such a faith is the power "to move mountains," according

to biblical language. This language also speaks of the mountains being made low and the valleys being exalted so that all men together shall see the glory of the Lord. In other words, Christian faith is the resurrection faith of the prisoners, the blind, the guilty, the oppressed, and the misused. It is faith which leads to creative life precisely where death is ruling.

Christian freedom is, therefore, no religious or merely internal freedom which would distinguish and separate itself from the universal cry for freedom in the world. It also does not exhaust itself in the "free practice of religion" in the "church of your choice." Christian freedom understands itself rather as the beginning and foretaste of that all-encompassing freedom which will bless all men and all things. The Christian faith does not separate men from the world but moves them to solidarity with it. "Their very faith makes them one with unredeemed creation, insofar as faith is in its very nature hope and therefore a looking for the redemption of the body." [11]

Christianity in the European evolutions of the nineteenth century was, therefore, rightly called "the religion of freedom" (by Hegel, Heine, and Weidling). If that were not the core of Christianity, then liberation from this religion would afford man more freedom than would living in it. Whenever the church does not liberate man to this creative faith but rather spreads religious, moral, and political oppression, one must oppose it for the sake of Christ.

It is of course possible to conceive of freedom also as the free choice of the will (*liberum arbitrium*). Then one undergirds man with an absolute sovereignty and provides him with divine predicates. Since Immanuel Kant, German idealism has pondered the problem of autonomy. In its analysis and reflection it never arrived at the autonomous *I* itself but only the "process of autonomy." Thus Fichte said, "One should never have presumed to say 'man is free,' but 'man necessarily struggles, hopes, assumes he will be free.' " [12] For man, the free will emerges only out of the underlying and comprehensive process of freedom. Without free space there is no freedom; without liberation, no free life.

But freedom in the light of messianic hope is something

other than freedom of choice. It is *passion for the possible*. It happens where the chains which bind us to the past and the passing are broken. Liberation happens where the new creation of all things which will be fulfilled in Christ is anticipatorily experienced. "Man has his free being in no other way than in continually becoming free." [13] *Freedom* as the fulfilled process of *liberation* is for Christian hope the eschatological goal of the new creation of God. In Christ and in the work of the Spirit, however, this future throws its shadows forward into history. The *reality* of freedom is the eschatologically new and free world, but the *effects* of this freedom are present in experiences and actions of liberation. One does not have freedom only in the "promised land," but first in the "exodus" and the "long march" through the desert. This means that we should no longer reason deductively from a presupposed subject of freedom to the effects of freedom. Rather we should inductively infer from the concretely experienced effects of liberation the freedom to come. With this reversal, eschatological theology becomes concrete and forsakes idealism's illusions about freedom.

Liberation in the light of the hope for freedom has two sides. It lives in the category of "nevertheless" and in the category of "all the more." [14] Against whom does its *nevertheless* place itself? Because resurrection is a resurrection from the dead, liberating hope sets itself against death. It loves life, not death. Only "life as the good life, wholly snatched away from death, the wholly active life is *peace*." [15]

In this perspective death is not only the physical end of human life. Death is a personal and political power in the midst of life. Many with viable bodies have surrendered to the death drive (Freud). Out of doubt and cynicism other men make a "pact with death" and the threat of death. Whole cultures become necrophile (Fromm) when the possession of dead things suffocates living human relationships. Death begins with the spread of anxiety about freedom. Liberation, on the other hand, begins when we are delivered from anxiety and placed in a free space.

All liberation movements begin when a few people fearlessly resist the demands of their oppressors or their surroundings.

Every oppression employs the threat of death, is built on death, and is bound up with death. Liberation in the light of hope negates anxiety, the death urge, and the threat of death. It negates the loud death of bombs and the quiet death of the soul. This negation is one side of liberation. We come to know liberation when we experience such a negation, but the future of liberation is the *other* side and its hope is greater.

When Paul speaks about a "liberation for," rather than a "liberation from," he often exclaims "how much more . . . !" (e.g., Rom. 5:15-20) How much more is God's grace than the sin of man, how much more is his future than the misery of the present, how much more is his freedom than simply liberation from man's enslavement of man. With Paul Ricoeur that "more" can be called the "economy of undeserved abundance." To express this theologically, we might say that the liberating God is himself on the way and open for the future which lies before him.[16] The liberating God is on the way to his kingdom in which he will be all in all.

This "plus extra" of hope for freedom is at the basis of all liberation movements. The oppressed peoples of Africa and Asia began with the national struggle for liberation from colonial rule, and must now liberate themselves from class and caste dominion. One needs liberation as independence, then liberation as social justice, then liberation as human dignity, and then liberation as the full development of the human person. Liberation is like a train racing through history into an even greater future. It cannot allow itself to be detained. It cannot be complacent about any success, because there is always a "plus extra" of hope in the process of liberation. Therefore, what freedom is cannot be exactly defined. Definitions make rigid what is fluid. They are acts of dominion; they bind, but they do not loose. Freedom is what we actually experience in internal and external liberations, and our language must correspond to that experience if it is to enliven, and not deaden, our understanding.[17]

The *nevertheless* with which liberation negates oppression is only the dark reverse side of the confident *how much more* of its hope. This necessary negation must be grounded in this "more" if it is not to degenerate into mere reaction and end in disappointment, just as hope for freedom must lead to negation if it is not to become illusory.

## III

### The Church in the Liberation Process of God

It is not easy today to speak of the role of the church in the liberation process of God. Many who commit themselves to liberation in one area or another no longer expect anything from the church. Many others who live in the church no longer see the divine necessity of the liberation of the oppressed because they do not want to see it. Without the salvation of the churches from their captivity to the ruling classes, races, and nations, there can scarcely be a saving church. Nor can there be a church for the poor unless the churches are freed from their ties to particular social classes. The church, with its religious symbols, morality, public institutions, and money is, in many countries, bound to a social system which spreads strife and injustice in the world. Therefore, social criticism which focuses on the victims of that oppression will always criticize the religion of that society. Such criticism will focus on the church whenever it represents this civil religion.

Who can liberate the church from its new Babylonian captivity? The church cannot be renewed by social and political criticism from the outside. Basically, we do not need an accommodation of the church to the modern world and its socio-political movements. We need the renewal of the church from within. The nerve of the church is Jesus himself, for every church calls itself by his name and appeals to him. We must take the church radically at its word. *Jesus is the criticism of the church from inside.* He is the criticism of its untruthfulness, for he alone is the origin of its truth and its freedom. Whether a church or a Christian community in a divided, oppressive, and alienated society has a divisive, alienating, and oppressive effect depends ultimately on whether Jesus has become alien to it or whether he is the Lord who determined its existence. The social crisis of the church in the contemporary world is precisely its identity crisis. The problem of its credibility in the world stems from its faith crisis. The church will be renewed and will become a bearer of the freedom of Christ to the extent that it remembers Christ and him alone and hears no other voice but his.[18]

How does this happen? According to the Scriptures, Christ encounters the church as the *crucified liberator*. He came into this world, as Luke says, "to preach good news to the poor. . . . to proclaim release to the captives and recovering of sight to the blind, to set at liberty those who are oppressed, to proclaim the acceptable year of the Lord." (Luke 4:18) Because of this unheard-of messianic mission, he was repudiated by the ruling class of his time and finally was crucified on Golgotha. A church which follows him and does not glance furtively to the left or the right will participate with all its powers and possibilities in his messianic work. His mission is also its mission. But the more it brings the gospel to the poor, liberation to the imprisoned, and sight to the blind, the more it will be involved in his destiny and become a *church under the cross*. It will encounter misunderstanding, opposition, and, finally, persecution. Whoever helps the lost must reckon with becoming lost himself. Yet one will recognize the true church of Christ from the powers of liberation which are alive in it and which proceed from it, and often enough also from the signs of the cross which it must bear because of its resistance. The Reformers were right in counting first word and sacrament, but then suffering, also, as the *notae ecclesiae*.

Christ encounters the church, according to the witness of the Scriptures, as the *resurrected one*. He is the one who has been raised from the death of humiliation into the glorious freedom of God. In him God has broken through the power of death, the constraint of anxiety, and the chains of oppression. In him, the crucified one, the world of death is already overcome and the invincible life has already appeared. A church which is grasped by this resurrected liberator is reborn and sent into the dying world with a living hope. With its confidence it will strengthen small, limited, and tentative hopes and will free them from pride and resignation. In the resurrection of Christ, the ultimate boundary of freedom, the boundary of death, is broken through. A church which lives from this breakthrough can no longer recognize the boundaries of death's rule in economic, political, and cultural life. Rather it seeks to overcome the deadening powers of the negative in these dimensions of life.

And how could one who from Easter is filled with such a hope be able to despair over the disappointments in life? "The resurrected Christ makes life a constant celebration," said Athanasius. Christ makes life a celebration of freedom.[19] And because this resurrected one has experienced all aspects of suffering and forsakenness in his humiliation on the cross, finally death itself belongs in this celebration of freedom.[20] Only in community with the crucified Christ can the Spirit of the resurrection make life a "constant" celebration.

The church of the resurrected Christ is the *exodus community*. It is the community of those who have been brought out of slavery in Egypt and have set out through the desert to the promised land. Israel's journey through the desert was geographically a way from one land to another. The long march of Christians does not proceed from one land to another but from the past into the future. It is to be understood historically, not geographically. It is the long march through the institutions of society, out of oppressions and into new liberated forms of life in the expectation of that life which swallows up death (1 Cor. 15:55 ff.).

Christ encounters the church according to the witness of the Scriptures *in the Spirit*.[21] This is the Spirit of God, who, as Joel and Luke say, "shall come upon all flesh" to make it eternally alive. According to Paul, it is the Spirit of the resurrection which gives the mortal body life. We can understand this Spirit neither idealistically as if it were something intellectual nor romantically as if it were something emotional. The Spirit is God's power of creation which makes possible what is not possible and which calls into being what does not exist (Rom. 4:17). A church which is filled with the Spirit becomes a charismatic congregation. It becomes the place of the "revelation of the Spirit" in the abundance of its gifts (1 Cor. 12:7).

Every *charisma* is both gift (*Gabe*) and task (*Aufgabe*).

Every *charisma* is a power of the new creation. The Spirit activates our capacities and possibilities for the Kingdom of God, for the liberation of the world. According to Paul, this is as true for the preacher as for the widow, for the bishop as for the deacon. The whole of life, its vocations, political responsibilities, family relationships, and even religions (circumsized and uncircumsized, 1 Cor. 7:18 ff.) is grasped by Christ and activated for the liberation of the world. For this reason there are as many and as varied *charismata* as there are many and varied men. But there is only one Spirit and one common future. The abundance of *charismata* is as colorful as the creation itself. Nothing is repressed or oppressed by the Spirit but everything is fulfilled. For the Spirit comes upon all flesh to make it alive. In a charismatic congregation, therefore, there is no fundamental distinction between clergy and laity. Charismatically the whole people of God is embodied religiously, personally, politically, and socially in God's all-encompassing liberation movement.

The more the church remembers *Christ alone* and witnesses exclusively to his messianic mission in the world, the less it is merely a religious image of society. It is a *church under the cross,* an *exodus community,* and a *charismatic community* demonstrating the powers of the new creation and the liberating signs of the coming free world. Only when it grasps its own role in God's process of liberation can it "test the spirits" without anxiety and without accommodation, and thereby enter into an open and critical relationship with contemporary liberation movements.[22]

## IV

### Liberation in Five Dimensions

Man is not a one-dimensional being. He lives and suffers in many dimensions at once. Therefore the process of liberation cannot proceed one-dimensionally. Rather it must work in many different ways simultaneously and coordinate its efforts in the various areas of life. The process of liberation must be catholic in that it deals with the freedom of the whole and not the freedom of the individual at the cost of others. One cannot intend liberation in one area while building dictatorship in another. Hence, we seek the traces of the liberation of man in a series of dimensions. We shall treat only those dimensions of life which cannot be assimilated to others. It is true that in concrete situations these dimensions mutually affect each other and together constitute the negative and positive fullness of life. But distinguishing between them can give us direction for concrete action.

If we begin with liberation in the economic dimension and end with liberation in the religious dimension this does not mean that freedom from hunger (which in one sense is primary) is of primary importance. For it is true that, "Man does not live by bread alone." Religious liberation is the most important insofar as without such liberation (from apathy, anxiety, and aggressiveness) there can be no liberations in the other dimensions. Only those who are liberated can liberate. Just as the mission of Jesus comprehended the messianic liberation of everything, from daily bread to the forgiveness of sins, and just as the charismatic "revelation of the Spirit" extends to all zones of oppressed life because it is the power of new creation, so also liberating action must be present today in all areas of life.

Liberation happens today (1) in the struggle for economic justice against the exploitation of man, (2) in the struggle for human dignity and human rights against the political oppression of man, (3) in the struggle for human solidarity against the alienation of man from man, (4) in the struggle for peace with nature against the industrial destruction of the environment, and (5) in the struggle of hope against apathy for a meaningful personal life.

Exploitation, oppression, alienation, the destruction of nature, and inner despair constitute today the vicious circles in which we are delivering ourselves and our world over to death. Their mutual effect on each other is so great that many people no longer see any way out. In this vicious circle, individual good also works for evil because we often achieve liberation in one sphere by building repressions in another. In this way we do not overcome suffering, but magnify it. One cannot exorcise the devil with another devil. Therefore, everything depends on how well and openly liberation movements cooperate on strategy.

Economic and political liberation are inseparable. To the extent that "socialism" means economic justice and "democracy" means freedom on the basis of human rights, there is no socialism without democracy, and no democracy without socialism (Rosa Luxemburg).[23] If we overcome economic need through a political dictatorship we only exorcise one devil with another. Freedom would not have come one step closer. Conversely, if we establish a political democracy at the cost of social justice, we are in the same vicious circle. Indeed we find in many countries today "socialism" with party dictatorship but no democracy.[24] We find countries in which rapid industrial development is paid for with political oppression, suspension of constitutional rule, and martial law. We know other lands in which economic imperialism has been coupled with political "democracy." In political democracies people have to press for social justice and economic freedom. In socialist dictatorships, people must press for political freedom and the realization of fundamental human rights. Otherwise, liberation is achieved in neither of these dimensions of life.

If we consider the alienation of man from man through racism, nationalism, and sexism, the parameters of mutually interdependent relationships are widened.[25] As long as the alienation of man from man is not broken through, neither economic liberation from hunger nor political liberation from oppression can be achieved, for one group of men will always view other groups merely as enemies in the "struggle for existence." On the other hand, racism, nationalism, and sexism remain in force so long as the economic and political conditions which produce them are not eliminated.

The overcoming of racist, nationalist, and sexist alienation of man from his fellow human beings may be characterized as "solidarity." We do not mean by this an elimination of the differences among races, peoples, and sexes. We mean, rather, *identity through mutual recognition*. The man who is different is not necessarily a competitor in the struggle for power. The fullness of humanity shows itself in a colorful variety of capabilities and gifts. Men can realize "humanness" only with one another, not without or against one another. Liberation from social roles which are determined by ancient struggles for power does not result automatically from economic or political liberation. As a complement to such liberation it has its own worth and difficulties. Black Power cannot fulfill its own intentions in isolation from socialism, nor can women's liberation be successful in isolation from the democratic movement.[26] Thinking in reductionist terms here means the betrayal of freedom.

The building of a human society which genuinely deserves this name will advance through *freedom with nature*. Starvation cannot be overcome with forced industrial development (capitalist or socialist) if we are simultaneously leading the world to an ecological death. Exploited nature protests the "limits of growth" through its own mute and senseless death. With regard to these limits, the conflict between socialism and capitalism becomes relative. After the long phase of man's liberation from nature there must appear today a new phase of nature's liberation from man. For this, a radical transformation of the value systems of progress, profit, and increase of power is necessary. Such a value transformation will have a significant effect on the liberation movements in other dimensions of life. All our efforts at overcoming exploitation, oppression, and alienation will be in vain if we lose sight of nature's suffering.

Without the inner liberation of persons from the primal anxiety which makes them aggressive or apathetic, there can be no improvement of life. One must realize that the improvement of conditions of life on the economic, political, cultural, and natural levels does not automatically produce better men. That would be a materialistic illusion. In the underground of personal and public consciousness today there is a growing perplexity, uncertainty, and despair. People see quite clearly what they can create and what they must do for liberation—but they do not move on to concrete action. This inner poisoning of the interest in life is expanding not only in societies of misery but also in societies of affluence. Anxiety and apathy are not overcome through the elimination of economic need, political oppression, and cultural alienation. They are a peculiar suffering which cannot be reduced to other dimensions.

Aeschylus said that man loses half of his virtue in slavery— but he did *not* say that man gains half of his virtue in freedom. In other words, while exploited, oppressed and alienated men are often the result of bad conditions, liberated men are *not* the result of better conditions. Bad conditions force man to evil, since they leave him without possibilities. But good conditions do not force man to the good, since whether or not he realizes his free possibilities depends entirely on him. Therefore, the meaningless-ness or meaningfulness of life in the personal—and religious— dimension is of the highest significance. There will be neither economic, political, cultural, nor natural liberation without con-version from anxiety and discouragement to what Paul Tillich called the "courage to be."

In the situation of general discouragement with all its known forms of escapism, Christian faith is called upon to give *an account of hope*. This account demonstrates itself through liberation from panic, apathy, and from the fear of (and desire for) death. Without the *hope of faith* in the messianic future of God, there is no hope in action which can stand firm; without *hope in action,* the hope of faith becomes ineffective and irresponsible.

When it comes to the varieties of action called for, we must take seriously the diversity of gifts within liberation movements. The interdependence of oppressions demands the cooperation of these movements. No one can do everything at once. There are various gifts and tasks, but the *freedom* which we seek is *one*. With his treatment of the charismatic community in Romans 12 and 1 Corinthians 12, Paul wanted to overcome the narrow-minded divisions in his congregations. This image seems to me helpful for the church's posture in the various situations of the world as well as for the powers which work toward world libera-tion. There are churches which live only in liturgy and prayer be-cause they have no other possibilities. There are congregations which emphasize preaching or sacraments. There are action groups, shalom groups, and many more. All have their peculiar charismata and possibilities. If they were mutually to recognize and allow their different approaches they could complement each other. They could also awaken the slumbering possibilities in their midst.

If we compare the action reports of groups which work for liberations, we are continually faced with the five dimensions which we have discussed. The points of entry are different and must be different according to their various contexts. There are historically different ways of liberation, but there is only one goal of freedom. Without cooperation among the powers of liberation and a willingness to learn from each other, we will not come to see the kingdom of freedom. We hear the divine call of freedom only when we hear the universal cry for freedom and make it wholly, and not merely partially, our own.

1. This is the revised form of a lecture which I gave in 1972 in Singapore, Manila, Kyoto, and Tokyo. It takes up again the theme which I had worked through in connection with the last Christian-Marxist dialogue in Marienbad, Czechloslovakia, during 1968 under the title "The Revolution of Freedom." See *Religion, Revolution, and the Future,* translated by M. Douglas Meeks (New York: Charles Scribner's Sons, 1969), pp. 63–82.

2. Cf. Margaret Susman, *Das Buch Hiob und das Schicksal des judischen Volkes,* 2nd ed. (Basel: Reinhardt Verlag, 1948), p. 223.

3. That such a partnership is possible in terms of scientific theory can be seen in *Humanokologie und Umweltschutz,* "Studien zur Friedensforschung," No. 8 (Munich: Kleft Verlag, 1972).

4. I have further pursued these reflections in my book *Der gekreuzigte Gott* (2nd ed., Munich: Christian Kaiser Verlag, 1972) because I have the impression that there can be no liberating "theology of liberation" without a new doctrine of God. It is essentially a matter of overcoming the classical doctrine of the *apatheia* of God.

5. For this see M. M. Thomas, "Die Bedeutung des Heils Heute," in *Das Heil der Welt. Dokumente der Weltmissionskonferenz Bangkok 1973* (Stuttgart: Kreuz Verlag, 1973), pp. 31-44.

6. See Herbert Marcuse, *Das Ende der Utopie* (Berlin: Maikowski Verlag, 1967), p. 38.

7. From the Christian perspective, reconciliation and liberation are not in opposition. Reconciliation with the God of liberation means struggle against oppression in the world just as peace with God means discord with a world without peace.

8. Cf. M. Susman, *op. cit.,* p. 238.

9. I am following here the New Testament studies of K. Niederwimmer, *Der Begriff der Freiheit in Neuen Testament* (Berlin: Alfred Töpelmann, 1966); H. Schlier, "Über das vollkommene Gesetz der Freiheit," in *Die Zeit der Kirche* (Freiburg: Herder, 1966), pp. 193-206; and Ernst Käsemann, "The Cry for Liberty in the Worship of the Church," in *Perspectives on Paul*, trans. by Margaret Kohl (Philadelphia: Fortress Press, 1971), pp. 122-137.

10. Roger Garaudy magnificently expressed this in appropriating the "theology of hope." *Die Alternative* (Vienna: Europa Verlag, 1972), pp. 115 ff.

11. Käsemann, *op. cit.*, p. 135.

12. Quoted according to the *Akademieausgabe*, II, 3, p. 183.

13. Rudolf Bultmann, *Das Evangelium des Johannes,* 12th ed. (Göttingen: Vandenhoek and Ruprecht, 1952), p. 335.

14. I am taking up here some reflections which Paul Ricoeur developed in connection with the "theology of hope" in his book *Le conflit des interpretations. Essais d'hermenuetique* (Paris: Edition du Cerf, 1969), pp. 395 ff.

15. M. Susman, *op. cit.*, p. 223.

16. K. Niederwimmer, *op. cit.*, p. 78.

17. Cf. J. Moltmann, *The Gospel of Liberation* (Waco, Texas: Word Books, 1973).

18. The Confessing Church in Germany demonstrated this through the Barmen Theological Declaration of 1934.

19. Cf. to this R. Schutz, *Ta fe soit sans fin* (Taize: Les Presses de Taize, 1971).

20. Dietrich Bonhoeffer, "Stationen auf dem Wege zur Freiheit," in *Widerstand und Ergebung* (Munich: Christian Kaiser Verlag, 1951), p. 250.

21. Cf. Ernst Käsemann, "Ministry and Community in the New Testament," in *Essays on New Testament Themes,* trans. by W. J. Montague (London: SCM Press, 1964), pp. 63-64; Eduard Schweizer, "Zur Ekklesiologie des Neuen Testaments," in *Neotestamentica* (Zurich: Zwingli-Verlag, 1963), pp. 239 ff; Anna Marie Aagaard, *Hellganden sendt til Verden* (Aarhus: Forlaget Aros, 1973); and Hendrikus Berkhof, *The Doctrine of the Holy Spirit* (Richmond: John Knox Press, 1964).

22. In this I am completely in agreement with Frederick Herzog, *Liberation Theology* (New York: The Seabury Press, 1972). The power of this book lies in the way it teaches us to understand anew liberation in light of the Bible and the Bible in the light of liberation.

23. As a Marxist humanist Ernst Bloch has always stood fast on this point. See *Naturrecht und menschliche Wurde* (Frankfurt: Suhrkamp Verlag, 1961).

24. Cf. Gustavo Gutierrez, *A Theology of Liberation* (Maryknoll, N. Y.: Orbis Books, 1973). It seems to me that Gutierrez deemphasizes the

democratic side of socialism which, of course, in his situation is conceivable but fundamentally not possible.

25. James Cone, *Black Theology and Black Power* (New York: The Seabury Press, 1969) presents the best foundation for liberation from racism. Yet his problem seems to lie in the economic differentiation within the self-conscious black community. The interdependence between racism and capitalism will have to be more exactly analyzed.

26. Women's liberation has found a solid theological articulation in Rosemary Reuther, *Liberation Theology* (New York: Paulist Press, 1973). Yet here, as indeed everywhere in liberation movements, there is a threat of ideological fixation. Her vision of a transformation of Christianity from a *Constantinian* to a *prophetic* religion is a demand which is placed upon Christianity from all contemporary liberation movements and which is everywhere shared by the theologians who were open to the fundamental change of consciousness in the sixties.

# Judgment and Mercy

## KRISTER STENDAHL

Judgment and mercy is one of those familiar themes which has always sustained, puzzled, and irritated us. It is one of those handy pairings of words liked by theologians who have many words and are clever at putting them into pairs, having them balance off one another. Learned men lately have even begun to speak about dialectics. This can be a bad method because it is one of those ways in which words are neutralized by one another, although theologians claim that they are not.

Judgment and mercy is a classical pairing of words, pre-Christian, well grounded in the Jewish tradition. It is a pairing found in the Old Testament and in the thought of the rabbis and the sages as they spoke about the two measures, the measurement of judgment and the measurement of mercy. They spoke about it as the two hands of God. The hand of mercy was the right one, and the hand of judgment the left. They even tried to assign, as did Philo, the names of God in the Good Book to these two measurements or aspects of God's work.

In the Christian tradition, judgment and mercy have penetrated deeply into our spiritual wisdom, as we have played the "soul game," transforming practically all of the immense and ferocious drama of history that we read about in the Bible into pastoral counseling and consolation where mercy overcomes the fear of judgment. This means of plowing down these words into the intricacies of the soul has been one of the ways in which we receive what Bonhoeffer rightly called "Cheap grace" and what Marx and others rightly recognized as the "opiate of the people."

There is, however, a totally different way of reading and understanding the relationship between judgment and mercy in the Bible and in the Christian experience. Let me take my point of departure from the 40th chapter of Isaiah, which begins, "Comfort, comfort, my people." Here is the key to the understanding of judgment and mercy. To the oppressed, the suppressed, and the repressed, there is no message with more comfort than to know that all flesh is grass and all the powers that lord it over them are passing away. The message of comfort is the downfall of the "haves," the downfall of the powerful. There is little comfort or no comfort at all for the comfortable. The comfort consists in the announcement of the revolution, of the change of crew, of the leveling, of the fact that those who hunger and thirst for justice are finally going to be satisfied.

There is no comfort for the comfortable, but where do the comfortable fit into a scheme like that? Where do *we* fit into a scheme like that? Does that not mean that the kingdom is closer, the will of God more manifest, when we lose and when things are taken away from us? Does it not mean that we need not fear this, because when comfort comes to those who need it, the will of God is manifest? Few are those who are willing to give, but the truly believing man is one who rejoices when God takes away that which he thought was his, and gives it to another. Consider what this means. Judgment and mercy are not balanced over against each other in a scheme in which the last judgment is tempered and adjusted by God's grace, or Christ, or the Blood of the Cross, or the intercession of the Saints. That is not the way it is. Mercy, salvation, liberation are parts of God's judgment. Judgment is mercy for those who need mercy. Judgment is justice for those who hunger and thirst after it, since they do not have it. In God's act of judgment he puts things right and establishes justice.

The English language is a "docetic" language. It has an unusual ability of dividing up words into a more spiritual and a less spiritual connotation. The English language distinguishes between "justice" and "righteousness." In the world one speaks about justice, and in the church one speaks about righteousness. But Hebrew, Greek, and Latin do not offer that distinction.

When God puts things right, it often happens that the first become the last and the last become the first. That is the glorious mercy to "the last," the mercy of which the Bible speaks. Jesus spent little time in convincing the Pharisees that they were sinners at heart. He went straight to the publicans and the sinners and thereby changed the constituency of the kingdom. The basic point is that we should not think of judgment and mercy as two different things, but rather that the *one thing* that a believer, in his prayer, in his hope, in his reflection, in his faith, ponders is God's judgment.

Then comes the question: for whom does that judgment mean mercy and for whom does it mean condemnation? The Day of Judgment has been the major theme through the ages. This day is the last Sunday of the church year, the Sunday before the first of Advent (which in our country often follows the Day of Thanksgiving). It is the day in which one meditates on the last things, mainly under the image of judgment. In times of trouble this has been a day of hope for the little flock, the oppressed, the suppressed, the repressed. To them there is no other hope than the hope expressed in the early Christian prayer of the Didache: "O Lord, let this dirty earth go to pieces and let Thy kingdom come." This anarchistic-sounding, hopeful note of early Christian piety is like the one expressed in Luke 21:9-28, which might be summarized to read: "Now when you hear about all these terrible things and wars and rumors of wars and worse, then lift up your heads and rejoice because the moment of your liberation is at hand." Judgment is the day looked forward to in which God will finally vindicate his faithful and establish justice. On the other hand, in the big national churches, which are increasingly involved with the affairs of state, it becomes apparent that the day of judgment, the Day of the Lord, is—as understood by Amos and the other prophets of doom—darkness rather than light.

Judgment in any case is the time when God comes through.

The question is not how one balances off mercy and judgment but for whom judgment is mercy and for whom it is threatening doom. For God's people, God's judgment is salvation. And who are God's people? Is it not consistently true that in the Bible the only time that "God's-people" language really functions without the lambasting of the prophets is when it stands for the little ones, the oppressed, suppressed, and repressed? Is it not true that the whole language about a chosen people becomes wrong when applied without the principle of weakness? By other means and in other ways, and on a very personal level, this was Paul's great lesson to the triumphalist and sunshine Christians of his time, to the super-apostles who, in his judgment, were overconfident. To them Paul said, "His grace is sufficient for me because when I am weak, I am strong." (2 Cor. 12:9) The exploding of the concept of strength and the image of strength is perhaps the simplest and most overarching message from the life and death of Jesus.

One observes interesting changes always occurring in language. You may have noticed that one of the changes now taking place is that those who are sensitive to the situation today speak less and less about freedom and more and more about liberation. What is the difference? It is the same difference to which I am pointing. Freedom is something that people think that they have. Freedom might even be something in the name of which they go out and conquer other people—that has happened. Freedom is very different from liberation, a term that is really meaningful only when you do not have freedom or when you have just gained it. Liberation is like the manna in the wilderness. It does not keep very well; it has to be won again and again. It is striking to hear Paul say that for freedom Christ has liberated us, and that we must carry on that liberation (Gal. 5:1). Judgment is the moment in which God liberates, but he can only liberate those who need liberation. Mercy and forgiveness are not a motif, not a counter-force that softens the blows of God's judgment, a kind of bumper or protection, or a kind of asbestos against the heat of judgment. When God's judgment falls, it is mercy to those wronged and doom for those who have done wrong or perpetuated and profited from the wrong of others.

However, there is one more inch of mercy, which the Jewish sages acknowledged in their speaking of how God's measure of mercy was greater than his measure of judgment. There is the great mercy given to us in the possibility of repentance, for conversion, for *metanoia,* turning around. That is perhaps the mercy of the Gospel: that there is still a little time for repentance. This does not seem to be very much mercy, but it is an enormous amount of mercy for him who understands the situation. In the texts connected with Yom Kippur (the Day of Atonement) and in the sayings of Jesus in the Sermon on the Mount, repentance presupposes acts of mending and amending. "So if you are offering your gift at the altar, and there remember that your brother has something against you, leave your gift there before the altar and go; first be reconciled to your brother. . . ." (Matt. 5: 23-24) We should note, by the way, that it is not that you have something against your brother. That hopelessly introverted, self-occupied Western man with whom we have to deal always reads it that way. He would not even feel very guilty before God in the mighty I-thou relationship, if the other person has something against him. He would say: that is his business. But if he has little, or evil, feeling toward his brother, he will feel responsible for that and be anxious to do something about it. Jesus has it the other way around: "and you remember that your brother has something against you." That has to be cleared up first. Repentance means action.

This opportunity for repentance might seem a small thing to all except those who have the slightest notion of the magnitude of their sin. Any who have a knowledge of the evil which they or their culture or their country or their participation in wealth has caused, know the meaning of mercy.

In the preaching tradition of my church, we were very clever in the various ingenious examples used to illustrate the forgiveness of sins. One I remember is the story about the author of hard core pornography who went to church and during the sermon had a genuine conversion experience. He promised the Lord never to write pornography again, and started to write meditations instead. His books of meditations, however, never sold very well, but his pornography kept on selling. That suggests how insignificant it is when little man repents, because his actions move on. If that is true about such things as pornography, how gruesomely true it is about our collective acts, our responsibilities as a nation, and our responsibility as human beings who dirty up this earth. If the consequences last, is it really that important that the individual or even the people repent? Yes, it is, important for the future. But the guilt lies heavy now.

Mercy is the opportunity for repentance. Protestants are critical of Roman Catholic ideas of penance, and much Protestant theology insists that what Christ has done for us is enough. As we say in Sweden, it is pathetic to hear mosquitoes cough. These little acts of penance, Hail Marys, pilgrimages, and the like, are, considering the magnitude of the drama, like mosquitoes' coughs. But perhaps it is helpful to mosquitoes to cough. The point, however, is that repentance calls for action—and I would prefer reparations to pilgrimages—and that is important. It is through mercy that we are invited to repent and do penance imaginatively and constructively. God's judgment allows this mercy. It is through mercy that we are stripped, as justice and liberation come to those to whom they have been denied. This is a heavy message for the comfortable and for those of us who try, though unsuccessfully, to sever ourselves from the comfortable. This message can produce a kind of nonproductive self-hatred and self-pity. Then one understands something of what Cain meant when he said, "My guilt is heavier than I can bear." And one understands why Paul said that we should not be so hard on a man, for it might be that he could be swallowed up by his contrition. And that would be to play into the hands of Satan (2 Cor. 2:5-11).

The mercy of the invitation to repentance includes the invitation to repent for things done for good reasons. Nobody can come to grips with the drama of history unless he recognizes that most of the evil in this world is done by people who do it for good purposes. Evil as such is not that popular. The real evil in this world happens when Satan disguises himself as an angel of light (2 Cor. 11:14). The real evil is done for good, for humanity, for freedom, for ideology, or for any of the other pseudo-gods of human life. That is why guilt is so deceptive and has to be unmasked.

Thus the question is not to balance these two, judgment and mercy. Whenever one reads the Bible or theology, what I would call the "who-is-who" question always arises. Who speaks to whom and for whom? The mighty message of God has been misunderstood usually because men hear the wrong thing. There are many examples of this. Jesus did say that man does not live by bread alone, but he never said that to a hungry person. When he was faced with hungry persons, he fed them (even 4,000 out in the wilderness). He mass-produced wine in Cana in Galilee just to keep the feast from turning sour. But speaking for himself, he said to Satan, "Man does not live by bread alone." The church, however, often quotes this in the wrong context.

Who speaks to whom? For whom is judgment mercy? That is the question, and unless one understands that, even the most gloriously dialectical theological understanding and message become not only counterproductive but evil. Consider the most beautiful of all messages that one perhaps could read in the New Testament—the message of reconciliation. What a beautiful word! But it is a dangerous word for the comfortable, for the "haves" to use. All of us remember well that evening in March when we learned that Martin Luther King had been killed. I remember vividly that after only a few minutes, all the networks, independently of one another (having learned from Homer presumably that everybody has to have his standing epithet), named Martin Luther King "the apostle of nonviolence." All of those white newscasters were chewing on that glorious phrase, "the apostle of nonviolence." Obviously King was the apostle of nonviolence —to his own, and at tremendous risk. That, however, was not his message to *us* who are white and comfortable. Of course, in the name of religion—and it was after all the *Reverend* Dr. Martin Luther King—one wanted to speak religious language, and in the presence of death it came over well, too. "The apostle of nonviolence" sounded wonderful. But his message to us was, "Shape up, or else!"

That turns me back to where we began. Of course, for him who has and for him who is comfortable, reconciliation is very attractive—the sooner the better so that we need to give up as little as possible. That is what reconciliation has come to mean, in stark contrast to the sign of reconciliation in the Christian tradition, the cross, where Christ gave his all that reconciliation might occur. The hermeneutical trick, if you want, the hermeneutical method, is to withstand the homogenizing, neutralizing, dialecticizing, and balancing acts with the terms judgment and mercy.

There is little mercy except the chance of repentance for us who sit in judgment; but when judgment comes to us, there is much mercy for the oppressed. So what shall I cry but the words of Joel, the prophet: "Therefore also now, says the Lord, turn ye even to me with all your heart, with fasting and weeping and mourning; rend your heart and not your garments. Return unto the Lord your God, for he is gracious and merciful, slow to anger and abounding in steadfast love, and repents of evil . . . Blow the trumpet in Zion; sanctify the congregation, assemble the elders, gather the children, even nursing infants. Let the bridegroom leave his room and the bride her chamber. Let the priests, the ministers of the Lord weep between the porch and the altar. . . ." (Joel 2:12-16) And let those rejoice for whom the judgment that goes over us is liberation.

# social science
# and theology

# Theology in the Context
of the Social Sciences

**BRUCE MORGAN**

Discussing the ecclesiastical ethic of the High Middle Ages
and its relation to politics, economics, and social doctrine, Ernst
Troeltsch made this observation:

> . . . this ethic proves that neither in theory nor in practice has
> it any conception of the possibility of the independent develop-
> ment of all these sciences and tracts of human life from within,
> out of their own sense of inner necessity and fundamental psy-
> chological aptitude. . . . when these questions are discussed the
> moral judgment which is passed upon them is always based
> solely upon a comparison with a purely ideal standard. A social
> order which had reached a higher practical stage of development
> would not have allowed itself to be so completely dominated by
> ethics.[1]

With the background of Troeltsch's comment, let us look at
a few lines from a standard work, *The American Experience*
by Henry Bamford Parkes, a synthesis of social science work in
the field of American studies:

> . . . when one examines the religious development of the Ameri-
> cans one can discover reflected in it the same psychic tendencies
> that are so apparent in their political evolution. Projected into
> theological symbolism are to be found the same repudiation of
> external authority, the same confidence in the average man, the
> same exaltation of the will and the same belief that evil can be
> overcome. Franklin and Edwards, in spite of the irreconcilable

differences in the beliefs they consciously held and explicitly taught, are representatives of the same basic American character and it can be argued that that character was reflected more completely and more truly in theology than it was in political and economic theory. . . . A theology is a kind of collective poem or work of art that records the secret emotional history of a community, and that drive of the American will, which was the ultimate reason for the failure of the social ideals of eighteenth century liberalism was very manifest in the evolution of American religion.[2]

And, after a discussion of the contribution of Edwards, Parkes writes:

In the twentieth century, when Edwards' theology is no longer regarded as literally true, it is possible to interpret it as a symbolic expression of the deep psychic forces that pervaded the culture that produced it; to consider it in other words not as theology but as poetry. . . . As a poet Edwards foreshadowed the two major themes that occupy the great American writers of the following century. On the one hand his doctrine of "a spiritual and divine light immediately imparted to the soul" pointed toward Emerson and Whitman. On the other hand his intoxication with the idea of omnipotence, the cruelty that is implied, and the overweening pride of logic with which he set out to explain the entire universe, represented tendencies that pervaded the writings of Poe and of Melville. If Edwards is judged as an American poet, then only Melville can be said to have surpassed him in depth and intensity of spiritual experience. . . . That drive of the will, both American and Calvinist, which is so conspicuous in Edwards, had its most complete aesthetic embodiment in Melville's Captain Ahab.[3]

Parkes represents an advanced position along the line plotted by Troeltsch, indicating the liberation of the social sciences as they have "developed from within, out of their own sense of inner necessity and fundamental psychological aptitude." In fact—and this could be said as easily of other such interpreters of American civilization as Richard Hofstadter, Henry Nash Smith, Leo Marx and J. W. Ward—Parkes displays the confidence of some social scientists that they can control their ancient inhibiting master, theology, itself. To be sure not all social scientists are so reductive in their analysis of theology; many are simply reportorial. But quite rare is the social scientist who is willing to take theology seriously as a bona fide contributor to the social sciences' examination of the world.

Thus some Christian intellectuals live and work in an anomalous context. They share with many of their intellectual colleagues a lively interest in social analysis and a deep concern for the social good. Together with others they seek "the human meaning of the social sciences." For them the ancient symbolic structure of Christian theology is still personally viable, if not as mere "tradition," still as what they believe to be more than mere projection. But they live and work in a world of disciplined social analysis where, for the majority, the Christian symbolic structure is no longer workable, and they find it at times the object of a kind of antiquarian interest and reductive analysis. Such Christians converse with colleagues about social reality in their own specialized languages. At least in moments of secret awareness they wonder whether or where the symbolic structure to which they are committed really has any bite in their own intellectual world. It is not simply that they have given up all yearnings for a *corpus christianum*. More crucially they are less than clear as to the long-term intellectual relevance of the Christian message itself. They are aware that a great deal of the time they are working and thinking in a way not discernibly different from the ways practiced by non-Christian colleagues.

At a meeting of the Catholic Theological Society of America in the mid-sixties, its president, Monsignor Richard T. Doherty, said that the newer disciplines such as sociology, anthropology, psychology, and social philosophy could give theologians insight into the "process of bringing our theology down from the lofty heights of abstraction and fitting it into the concrete situation of contemporary man." The social sciences, he said, "could prove of similar service to contemporary theologians as Greek philosophy became the ancilla of St. Thomas Aquinas." He went on to say that the new sciences give scholars "an insight into the concrete situation that is twentieth century man such as theologians of bygone days dared not even dream." [4] What Monsignor Doherty did not mention is the difference in relative positions of the church in the thirteenth and the twentieth centuries. In the thirteenth century the church needed a language to help articulate the superior hierarchical position it, as faith and institution, largely occupied. Today the church must learn the alien languages of sciences it has long since ceased to dominate.

In all of this one is reminded of Bonhoeffer's statement that the world has come of age. Regardless of what he actually intended by that phrase, social scientists feel that they have come of age, and no longer see themselves as adolescents under tutelage. In Bonhoeffer's terms, they feel their adulthood and look to a maturity still ahead. Their sense of themselves come of age is not a claim of omnicompetence or of an accomplished cognitive grasp of the whole of social reality. It is rather a confidence in their methodologies, into which they believe they have increasingly incorporated the processes of refinement and correction. This confidence is coupled with a lack of confidence in, or even interest in, other sources of illumination. The pragmatic American social scientist seems content to leave all kinds of questions at loose ends, to proceed open-endedly, eclectically, and with modest proximate goals. Whenever a particular line of investigation runs out, or a particular model fails to apply, or a particular social scheme misfires, he, like John Dewey, goes back to the drawing board.

Several years ago Daniel Bell raised the question as to whether intellectuals in the West had come to the end of ideology.[5] Though he noted the rise of all manner of new ideologies, he described the played-out character of social and political ideologies in the West, as well as the crises of ideology in the Soviet-dominated part of the Communist world. He asked whether we must not go on without ideologies. Those who had attacked the apathy of the university, the often attacked or apathetic students of the early fifties and mid-sixties, were perhaps more aware than their teachers of the failure of ideology. They were willing to proceed in an open-ended fashion, with large measures of uncertainty, to work out, step by step, the implications of the possibilities that were presented to them.

Now most if not all who have lived with university students

and faculty are quite sure that ideology was not utterly dissipated, even before the ferment of the latter half of the recent decade. We must not forget how furiously ideological was the attack on the "end of ideology." It is my own view that this irony constitutes a healthy reminder of the incompleteness of the social sciences' quest for maturity. It has, for example, precipitated a long overdue break up of the ideologies of the "consensus school" of American history. But even the most serious among the "radical" scholars display their own inability to escape the dominant methodological canons of their disciplines. Thus Jesse Lemisch usefully initiates studies of the American Revolution from the standpoint of the urban workers [6]—but he gains credence because of the thoroughly "traditional" way he uses his materials.

To paraphrase Paul Lehmann, the social sciences, in deriving prescriptions from descriptions, in deriving imperatives from the indicatives of case studies, operate ethically, whether wittingly or not. For example, at the University of Michigan there is now an institute for the study of conflict resolution (complete with its own journal). Daniel Lerner has argued that social research of a decent sort is uniquely a democratic discipline, possible only "in a society that places a high value upon continuous self-improvement through self-study." Citing Lerner, an Amherst College publication argues that the social sciences are a significant part of the liberal arts "because they are concerned with the freedom of man: freedom not only from the harshness of external nature and the despotism of tyrants, but also from ignorance, superstition, and a lack of self-awareness. In dealing with all forms of human restraint on freedom, and in trying to establish connections among them—in showing, for example, that dictators thrive on social and psychological frustration—the social sciences occupy a place at the very center of the liberal arts program. They help to teach us not only who we are, but who we might be." [7]

We may indeed suspect that the end of ideology has not come, even in the West. Moreover we are surely not prepared to say that the end of ideology has come even within the methodology and practice of the social sciences. A subtle ideology hiding behind an "end of ideology" or "beyond ideology" mask, though doubtless overstated in some of the last half-decade's ideological frenzy, is surely there for the perceptive to see. Of course, if we were sure that we had learned to proceed in the social sciences without ideological deflection or impairment, and that we had really learned to move forward without the propulsive power of ideology, then we could say that the social sciences had come of age.

## II

For the Christian there are several possible interpretations of the present situation and appropriate procedures flowing from them.

1. If the social sciences have truly come of age, or at least approach this elusive goal, then the following questions seem in order: Has not theology so become the servant of others that she must cease to be, in order to further the skills of those professions which need no theological reference? Has not theology before it a final act of involvement in the world, namely, not to strive to hand down a theological tradition to subsequent generations but, as theology, to withdraw from the scene in such a way that human and not inhuman alternatives will fill the vacuum created by the queen of the sciences' obedient abdication?

2. If we think that the coming of age of the social sciences is an illusion, in effect, a new symptom of ancient sin, we can preach the gospel to the social sciences, calling for intellectual repentance and extending the invitation to a new life of greater intellectual wholeness.

3. If we think the coming of age of the social sciences is an illusion, we can see it as a new form of man's ancient self-assertiveness and alienation from his ground, whereby an exhibition of confidence at one level cloaks a gnawing suspicion that man can never come of age when confined to that level. We can then analyze man's projective activities, his artistic creations, his intellectual social constructs and visions and his projected social schemes, his "poetry," seeing his projective life as anchored, however obscurely, in a metaphysical substratum of being itself. We must then continually seek to lead man into the depth and wholeness of adulthood out of the adolescent one-dimensional fragmentariness that poses as adulthood already achieved. The

technical reason of the social sciences is thus led to seek its ultimate meaning in the wholeness of ontological reason.

4. If we believe that the social sciences, though maturing, have not yet fully come of age, we may not feel sure whether this is due only to a temporary delay, a generation perhaps, or to an eternal barrier across the path. In other words, we may believe the problem to be one of remaining gaps that will inexorably be filled, or to be one of an irreducible difference of dimension, whereby theology must forever complement the social sciences in giving a whole understanding of man.

I think we genuinely do not know at this moment if this is our condition. But if it is—and this is obviously my choice among the four alternatives posed—then we must live in a style appropriate to this quandary. It would be a style appropriate to the man who realizes that in the near future he may be going out of business, but who for the time being is very much in business indeed. We are at that strange point where we are becoming aware that it is presumptuous to predict either the demise of theology's relevance, or its long-continued usefulness; but we know we need "a new frame of heart fit for our new estate." In such a new estate we can make our contributions with a light and joyful heart, hoping that, should full adulthood be achieved by the social sciences, we, or our children, will be given the grace to depart at the appropriate season, the role of theology in the economy of God having been played out.

If and when the intellectual world of the social sciences comes of age it would be an occasion for rejoicing and not for lament. For surely at the heart of our biblical heritage there is the sense of God's purpose that ultimately all the walls between the sacred and the secular, between church and world, and between clergy and laity, will be cut away. Even today some continue to think of the institutional structure of the church as the instrument through which God's purposes on earth are chiefly to be fulfilled. But it is surely necessary in the contemporary scene for us to think of the Holy Spirit as the implementer of God's purposes in the world.

If we feel that the coming of age of the social sciences has *not* yet been fully achieved and are uncertain as to when or whether it will, we must make our contributions out of the reality of who we are as Christians and members of the body of Christ, not as possessors of ready-made syntheses and systems. Our contributions must be genuinely made in service, not in grandeur or majesty. We will recognize that the social sciences are unwilling in principle to admit their need for illumination from outside. Meeting their need in terms of their own discourse is a genuinely self-sacrificing and self-effacing servant role for Christians and the church. This is fulfilling our concern for man, as servants of man, even when men may be confident that they have no need of such service. This is being "the man for others."

Here we should enter an important caveat. Christians must be as clear as possible as to whether they have a genuine contribution to make to the life of the social sciences, or are simply engaged in translating the categories of the social sciences into the categories of traditional theology and ethics. I suspect that much now being done in books like the "Christian meaning of such-and-such," or "Christianity and Oo-ology," is little more than translation and often not very good translation at that, since it is often less than sophisticated about that from which or into which it is translating. The apologetic motif has been so strong in the motivation of many of these attempts that frequently, especially in the area of psychology, as earlier in the natural sciences, they result in the falsification of science as well as of theology.

Of course, for the education of the church's constituency, there may be some justification for giving theological meanings to non-theological languages and non-theological meanings to theological language. It may be that the churches' agencies of popular education have actually produced a higher level of sociological or psychological sophistication among their rank-and-file than among the non-churched.

We have traditionally thought that Christian theology and ethics could make contributions to social analysis at three points: (1) Human nature and motivation. Clearly here psychology and anthropology, with some assistance from sociology, are well on the way to preempting the field. It could be argued, I think, that

Marx and Freud were the last of the great universalists, and that in a sense their descendants in the non-Communist world, and even somewhat within the Communist world, have tended to work toward the deuniversalization and deideologization of both figures, and toward a description of man more sensitive to man's diversity and the subtle nuances of his selfhood, though perhaps getting closer to what may be "pan-human" elements. (2) The nature of the good and responsible society. And here of course political science, economics, social psychology, and even sociology are at work. Many of these disciplines eschew the task of ethical prescription and claim that they are simply describing alternative courses to reach ends which must be chosen from outside their own disciplines. I think, however, that this is beginning to have a more and more hollow ring and some psychologists, some political scientists, and some sociologists—and not only the "activist scholars" of the last half decade—are beginning to admit that they must deal with the problem of ethical prescription, since they are trying to deal with all the materials out of which prescription can arise. (3) The movement of history and its interpretation. Historians seem less confident, though sometimes more dogmatic, than any of the other social scientists. This may be partially explained by their insecurity in calling themselves social scientists at all. In some institutions they are considered as belonging to the humanities. Many of them indeed assert that they are artists, and that history is more of an art than a science. However, one suspects that history is going to be increasingly enriched by and assimilated to the social and even the behavioral sciences.

### III

The style most appropriate for the relation between theology and social science as described above might be called "intra-mundane anonymity." But it will always be a relative and partial anonymity so long as Christians and churches continue to be visible. Even when we are hard at work in the social sciences, people will often know we are Christians, or they will be curious enough about the background of certain suggestions we make to ask the question which elicits the identifying answer. An anonymity that is unwilling to disclose its identity is an exercise in duplicity. I take my model here from Karl Barth who wrote in his famous essay "Christian Community and Civil Community" that "in the political sphere the Christian community can draw attention to the gospel only indirectly, as reflected in its political decisions, and those decisions can be made intelligible and brought to victory not because they are based on Christian premises but only because they are politically better and more calculated to preserve and develop the common life . . . in the political sphere Christians can only bring in their Christianity anonymously." [8] I think this is the best charter we have for our procedures with respect now not to politics itself but to the social sciences.

There is a peculiar affinity both between Christian theology and politics and between Christian theology and the social sciences, an affinity arising out of the analogous relationship that human communities bear to the Kingdom of God. This is a different kind of affinity from that between theology and the natural sciences. For both Christian theology and the social sciences deal with society and community. At their best neither theology nor social science thinks it is dealing with ideal forms or stereotypes, but with what they find to be the actual facts and circumstances of human existence, with realistic assessments of what man, society, and community are like. Both see in the human situation community-creating forces on the one hand, community-destroying forces on the other. Christian theology describes God as being political, establishing community with and among men—men who are mutually estranged, aggressive, hostile, and warring, but who labor at developing institutions and ordering the common life. Christian theology, as Barth has put it, sees the Kingdom as "the politics of God," [9] reconciling the estranged people and establishing community. God has been man with man so that man can be man with men before God. Christian theology thus has a natural and urgent concern for social experimentation, innovation, and invention. The Christian and the church are able to contribute to social analysis and policy.

In addition, in the area of the social sciences today the

Christian can often play a gadfly role, without any necessity of announcing "I am a Christian gadfly." He is not the only person who can play this role, but in many cases he may be the only person who will. Of course, he may play this role because of a continued involvement in another ideology, as Professor Lehmann has suggested,[10] but he will be attempting to unfreeze that which is beginning to be frozen in a fixed ideological position. At those points where the social sciences have developed an artificial isolation from each other, and from social reality itself, the Christian will try to be concerned, to breach the walls and ventilate the possibilities of communication among the disciplines—and with the outside world. Where too early and too superficial syntheses have occurred among the social sciences, he will sort out or redefine the disciplines so they can probe more deeply their own methodologies, resources, and tasks, hoping for later reintegration at a more profound level. In a variety of ways he will seek to deuniversalize the conclusions of the social scientists except where universal statement is clearly warranted. But such criticism may be considered since traditional Christianity's intellectual behavior has often been characterized by universal statements about man and society. Then the Christian must be most careful to subject every incipiently universalistic Christian statement to the test of the most sophisticated findings of the social sciences.

The Christian will help to stir up the analytic waters of human motivation, expressed, for example, in economic theory. Here the Christian will throw his weight behind those in the field of the psychology of economic behavior who are attempting to force a reconsideration of the complexity, variety, unmanageability, and unpredictability of human motivation. The Christian will be among those in the field of international relations who insist that national self-interest is rarely the sole motivating force for a nation in its economic or political relations with other nations. Here, too, there are varieties of motivational patterns that must be recognized. The Christian will not accept, without more evidence than is now adduced, the conclusion that forgiveness and reconciliation can have nothing to do with the naked struggle for power between nation states, and will encourage experimentation with those theoretical formulations that attempt to allow for these possibilities in international relations.

The Christian will listen attentively to an economist like Gunnar Myrdal, who approaches the question of economic development from the viewpoint of the interests of the underdeveloped countries [11] rather than the interests of the developed countries. The latter approach tends to universalize the interests of the developed countries and ignores other approaches, which results in policies and practices that are unrealistic and unjust. The Christian will, I think, respond immediately to the social policy of George Kennan, who says, "We are not the avenging angel of all humanity. We have more modest and immediate problems of our own. We must leave something to the Almighty whose justice may be supposed in any case to be superior to ours." Speaking of the hopes held by many for the ultimate destruction or disappearance of Communist power, he continues, "It is the beginning of all wisdom in our encounter with world Communism generally, to recognize that frustrating and annoying and perhaps even morally unjust as this may be, this is a problem to which there is no immediate and total solution." Speaking of the ugliness of the attitudes of Communist leadership, he says, "We must not make the mistake of taking any of this as absolute and unchangeable. These too are only men. They once had mothers and childhood and affection. They are today what circumstances have made of them. It is circumstances which will determine what they or their successors will be in ten or twenty years' time. It is up to us to try to shape their circumstances in such a way that the fruitlessness of some of their undertakings will become apparent to them." Or this, "A triumph of the Communists in certain of those outlying countries [around China] might be the beginning of a long night, but it would not necessarily be an endless night. History shows that people, and particularly I think people in Asia, are very inventive in finding ways to frustrate foreign rule and to develop bargaining power in the end, vis-à-vis a foreign conqueror or an over-shadowing neighbor. So while we have every reason to take this encounter with the utmost seriousness and do all in our power to avoid reverses, we should be careful not to proclaim ourselves in advance defeated and undone by eventualities which were they to mature we would have to live with and would probably succeed in living with. . . ." [12]

These are examples of real contributions, and are not simply translations. If the day were to come when the social sciences had reached such a point of true sophistication that all such contributions and others like them were easily compassable within their resources and their methodologies, then it seems to me the social sciences would truly have come of age and any on-going labor of Christian theology and ethics in this realm would be superfluous. If that day never comes, then the obligations of Christians will evolve as the changing situation demands. We are tempted to say that, for the time being at least, it may be the function of Christian theology to keep alive and urgent the questions of human wholeness. Such a commission is full of the temptation to seek a new and pretentious heteronomy. But for the time being that risk must be accepted.

Our major concern, then, as Christians is not Christian identification but better social sciences, better practitioners thereof, and a better society. As Christians we may well take as expressing the proper spirit of our approach to the social sciences and social reality the words of Walter Lippmann in one of his first books, "All we can do is to search the world as we find it, extricate the forces that seem to move it, and surround them with criticism and suggestion." [13]

## IV

Finally, as those who are sure that theology has a present if perhaps not a long future, we are also responsible to theology. In the present groping of theology for its identity we must be open to all those possibilities for a reconstruction of theology close to the center of human life. That we cannot now see the way to such a theology in no way obviates our responsibility to theology's future, whether that future holds a rich new flowering of symbols and myths capable of moving modern men, or simply a timely, responsible, and humane journey into silence.

1. Ernst Troeltsch, *The Social Teaching of the Christian Churches*, trans. Olive Wyon (London: George Allen and Unwin, 1931), Vol. I, p. 257.
2. Henry Bamford Parkes, *The American Experience* (New York: Vintage 1947, 1959), pp. 64-65.
3. *Ibid.*, pp. 86-87.
4. *New York Times*, June 24, 1964.
5. Daniel Bell, *The End of Ideology: On the Exhaustion of Political Ideas in the Fifties* (New York: Free Press, 1960).
6. See, for example, his "The American Revolution as Seen from the Bottom Up," in *Towards a New Past*, ed. Barton J. Bernstein (New York: Pantheon, 1967). Also Staughton Lynd, "The Mechanics in New York Politics, 1774-1788," *Labor History* V (Fall, 1964).
7. Peter Schrag, "The Social Sciences," *Amherst Reports* (Amherst: College Press, 1964), pp. 19-20.
8. Karl Barth, "The Christian Community and Civil Community," 1946, tr. Stanley Godman, in *Against the Stream* (London: SCM Press, 1954), pp. 45-46.
9. *Ibid.*, p. 34.
10. Paul L. Lehmann, "The Context of Theological Inquiry," Convocation Address, Harvard Divinity School, Sept. 26, 1956.
11. Gunnar Myrdal, *An International Economy* (London: Routledge and Kegan Paul, 1956), p. 289.
12. George Kennan, "A Fresh Look at Our China Policy," *New York Times* Magazine, Nov. 22, 1964.
13. Walter Lippmann, *Drift and Mastery* (Englewood Cliffs: Prentice-Hall 1914, 1961), introduction, p. 18.

# Beyond Ideological Theology

## BENJAMIN A. REIST

When one reflects on Paul Lehmann's *Ethics in a Christian Context* in the light of the sociology of knowledge, the most far-reaching challenge of his work comes into view. There is a trail to the future in this work. It is exciting but dangerous to consider, for its destination surely lies beyond our present horizons in terrain no Caleb has yet surveyed. Theology is always faced with the question, Where do we go from here? If Lehmann is right, we must go up the trail which will lead us beyond ideological theology.

Theology has been slow to take up the issues raised by the sociology of knowledge and sharply focused in one of its central concepts, *ideology*. Indeed, Lehmann himself does not make specific reference to it, though his argument is in fact an excellent portent of what will happen as soon as the theological enterprise is structured in terms of this decisive dimension. The roots of this concern lie far back in the thought of the nineteenth century with the dawning emergence of the social sciences. The first theologian to attempt to work with this in mind was Ernst Troeltsch. Accordingly, it is of more than minimal significance that Lehmann's insistence on the *hermeneutical problem* as central for theological ethics turns on the insight of Troeltsch.[1] Context is the fundamental issue for theological ethics. In the categories of contemporary theological conversation, this is the entrée of the hermeneutical problem. In categories which have a broader currency, intelligible in conversations alongside theology, one not only can but must say that the hermeneutical problem is, *mutatis mutandis,* theology's way of dealing with the problem of ideology as this operates in its own struggles. For the hermeneutical problem—the problem of explicitly disciplining the interpretation of the texts central to Christian faith—necessarily involves the equally disciplined explication of the conditioning relativities that shape both the questions and the answers comprising Christian thought, and this can hardly be achieved without close attention to the sociology of knowledge.

We may borrow the succinct early phraseology of Peter Berger to delineate what lies behind this contention. Crystallizing the complex insights of Max Scheler and Karl Mannheim, behind whose efforts lie the struggles of Marx, Nietzsche, and German historicism, Berger notes simply that "the sociology of knowledge concerns itself with the social location of ideas." [2] This concern is rooted in an important assumption, namely that "society predefines for us that fundamental symbolic apparatus with which we grasp the world, order our experience and interpret our own existence." [3] The problem of ideology thus emerges (though it must be noted that the sociology of knowledge is not exhausted by this problem [4]): "We speak of an ideology when a certain idea serves a vested interest in society." [5]

The question is, what is the social location of Christian ideas —what society shapes the symbolic apparatus with which Christians come to terms with the world? One who is sensitive to the demands of the sociology of knowledge cannot answer this question too hastily. It is, of course, immediately evident that there is only one possible response: *the Church.* But the depths of the implications of this answer are not at all self-evident. Lehmann's argument lends itself to analysis from the standpoint of the sociology of knowledge precisely because of its constructive recognition of just this fact. The choice of the term *koinonia* for the central concept of *Ethics in a Christian Context* reflects Lehmann's sensitivity to the fluidity which has marked the Christian community from the time of the New Testament forward. [6] *The* problem for ethics in a *Christian* context is generated by the dynamic character of that context. Now if one tries to build *theologically* an insight into ethics which is so conditioned, both the limits and the potentiality of theology considered in the light of the sociology of knowledge are exposed. To take this seriously is the first step in the attempt to construct a contextual method for the theological enterprise.

## I

There is a necessary ambiguity to the term "ideology." It refers to the socially-conditioned and therefore limited character of all thought. To be sensitive to these limits is to be sensitive to the inherent pretension of any grappling with ultimate realities. Since all thought is socially conditioned, the context within which any such attempt takes its rise provides the indispensable clues for understanding its insights. But this understanding has a price. For wherever these insights are perceived specifically in the light of the matrix whence they come, their limits become patently clear: without the context, the cogency of the insights is drastically undermined. Pretension enters the scene as the effort to compensate for this. Indeed, the farther a point of view moves from its conditioning context, the more pretentious its proponents are likely to become.

To see this, however, is not to entertain the cynical rejection of all man's efforts to state the grand visions that inform his sense of meaning. Rather, what is involved is the healthy recognition of that relativism which marks all things human. To think as a human being is to think relativistically. Recognition, then, of the ideological character of all thought is the doorway to authenticity, maturity, and freedom. It is the *sine qua non* of what Berger, in a rare phrase, once called "the curious ability to look around the corners of one's own *Weltanschauung*." [7]

To know that one thinks ideologically, if one thinks at all, is a liberation. It is a liberation from the debilitating pretension that evokes only cynical reaction or inauthentic agreement, and it is a liberation for involvement in that pluralism which at once constitutes the freedom and the openness to the new possibilities that always generate the creativity of man. To move beyond ideological theology is to welcome involvement in the pluralism of human thought about ultimate realities. It is to anticipate eagerly the new possibilities yet awaiting the statement of the ancient gospel— possibilities that cannot even be envisioned without just this involvement.

In its deepest meaning, then, the concept of ideology has a positive as well as a negative overtone. The basic issue is whether one knows one thinks ideologically, not only in the sense that one's ideas are subsumed into one's vested interests, but also in the sense that one grasps the social conditioning of one's own thought. Accordingly, one could color the very term *ideology* positively and mean by it this latter dimension with its depth of self-awareness. It is better not to do this, however. For the sake of clarity it is preferable to leave in place, as the decisive connotation, the pejorative meaning of the term. Thus an ideological theology is a theology which either does not know or refused to recognize its social conditioning.

What, then, is the opposite of ideological theology? Is it too much to assert that it is *contextual* theology? Ideological theology refuses to recognize its conditioning matrix. Contextual theology has this recognition as its beginning point. This is the decisive import of Lehmann's insistence that the *koinonia* is both the central fact and the central concept for the exploration of ethics in a Christian context. It is the *decisive* import of Lehmann's effort because to grapple with ethics in his way involves more than ethics. It presupposes the entire theological enterprise, and this itself is drastically transmuted in the process. To put the matter as concisely as possible, this effort demands that theology as a whole be colored with a rich social hue.

## II

There is a necessary ambivalence to Lehmann's concept of the *koinonia*. This is the clue to the significance of his *Ethics in a Christian Context* for the wider task of theology as a whole. At the outset, however, one must insist on an absolutely basic differentiation, that between *ambiguity* and *ambivalence*. Lehmann's concept is not ambiguous; it is ambivalent. He is not trying to say two things at once. He is trying to say something that necessarily has two dimensions.

We can see why this is crucial by pondering briefly a critique of Lehmann's point which has arisen on several fronts, but nowhere more caustically than in the opening phases of Joseph Fletcher's *Situation Ethics*:

> . . . I should make clear at the outset what is meant by "contextual" in this book. Paul Lehmann muddies the water with his use of the term because he attaches to it two different but often confused meanings. Sometimes he means that Christian action is to be carried out without a theological frame of reference, in the *koinonia,* in the context of *faith.* Sometimes he means that Christian action should be tailored to fit objective circumstances, the *situation.* It is in this second sense that I use it. (After all, *all* Christian ethics is "contextual" in the first sense, but that deprives the term of any discrete meaning in theological ethics!) Properly used, the word is applicable to *any* situation-sensitive decision-making, whether its ideology is theological or nontheological—e.g., either Christian or Marxist.[8]

There is more than meets the eye here. To be sure, Lehmann's statement of the contextual ethic raises many problems, not the least of which are stylistic in character. The work *is* hard to read. But is the real problem where Fletcher sees it? Is ideology really capable of being neutralized? Is there *no* difference between one situationist and another? Is the issue only a formal one?

Fletcher has to answer each of these with an emphatic affirmation, for the oft-reiterated core of his case is that

> . . . love is not a substantive—nothing of the kind. It is a principle, a "formal" principle, expressing what type of real actions Christians are to call good.[9]

Now it is an open question as to whether he is successful in maintaining this view. However that may be, the point here is that this is Fletcher's way of making room for the relativism and fluidity which he rightly regards to be decisive for any valid articulation of Christian ethics. Thus, for him the only constant is a formal principle. This is precisely why he is critical of Lehmann. Moreover, it is the reason behind the fact that his critique is wide of the mark. He sees in Lehmann's concept only a confusing ambiguity.

Lehmann sees something that Fletcher does not—that contextualism is the only option for Christians, *both* the form *and* the content of the Christian ethic are fluid, for both are alive. The task is not to immobilize one (either one!) so that the other may be plugged into the relativistic dynamic of human existence. It is rather to see, as Barth long ago saw,[10] that for Christian thought there is no basic distinction between form and content. Each follows the other, and the lead oscillates indiscriminantly between the two. Thus for Lehmann,

> The fact is that the dynamics of the divine behavior in the world exclude both an abstract and a preceptual apprehension of the will of God. There is no formal principle of Christian behavior because Christian behavior cannot be generalized. And Christian behavior cannot be generalized because the will of God cannot be generalized.[11]

This is the root of the ambivalence of the concept of the *koinonia*. The *koinonia* refers both to the theologically-ordered context of faith and to the broader, humanistic context of man's involvements with other men whether they are Christian or not. This is the fluidity and this is the relativism which Lehmann brings to the center of the stage. The *koinonia* is ambivalent because it must somehow simultaneously embrace both theological and humanistic reflection and the exchange between the two.

The contrast between theology and humanism is misleading unless it is grasped in the mode of the sociology of knowledge. Suppose the terms are read phenomenologically. Suppose "theology" refers to the reflection of the explicit community of Christian faith, and "humanism" refers to that thinking in any community that celebrates, while seeking to understand, man. What is then involved is not a polarity but an overlapping of not quite congruent spheres—spheres, however, which are not simply tangential but in fact intersect in the broad segment of common concern, man.

The *koinonia* as Lehmann conceives it is ambivalent because of this intersection. It does not refer to the whole church, but to "the *ecclesiola in ecclesia,* the little church within the church." [12]

Nor does it refer to all non-Christian reflection about ultimate realities, but only the humanistic ones. It is ambivalent because it is only discernible in that intersection where two kinds of language are current in mutually and beneficially exchangeable ways. To change the metaphor, what Tillich used to call "the boundary" has become for Lehmann a broad region, one which is capable of vast expansion in both directions.

## III

*Koinonia* is a theological word. As Lehmann uses it, it is ambivalent. But its double valences are not equally weighted. It would be a mistake to think that they should be. Indeed, to strive to *equate* them would be not a move beyond ideological theology but a reduplication of its impasse at a deeper level. Lehmann's argument will always outrage Christian ideologists. They will find his discussion annoying and frustrating because without making an explicit observation in this connection (perhaps without realizing it) he has sought to clarify the ambivalence of the *koinonia* without allowing it to deteriorate into mere ambiguity.

There are several examples of this in *Ethics in a Christian Context*. The most important will serve our purposes well. This is Lehmann's use of the thought of Freud for the articulation of his own point regarding conscience.

Lehmann makes common cause with Freud against Thomas and Kant. His discussion of the latter turns on two characterizations: For Thomas, "Conscience is . . . the bond between law and responsibility"; for Kant, "Conscience is the bond between duty and obligation." [13] To refute both, but particularly Kant, Lehmann insists with approval that

> . . . what Freud had discovered clinically was that the conscience did not, as Kant had claimed, express and facilitate the moralization of man. On the contrary, the net effect of the Kantian account of conscience was the dehumanization of man.[14]

With this step the crucial maneuver culminating Lehmann's argument as a whole is completely in the open. At the conclusion of the second of the three parts comprising *Ethics in a Christian*

*Context,* Lehmann crystallizes his juxtaposition of Schleiermacher and Barth regarding "Christian and Philosophical Thinking about Ethics" [15] by moving beyond Barth as follows:

> The issue of humanization is the decisive ethical issue, and a Christian ethic that understands its proper task will not seek to have it otherwise.[16]

Only in the midst of the ambivalent *koinonia* could it be put this way (which is why it is a move beyond Barth). And if in the *koinonia* what is going on is a conversation about conscience, this necessarily means siding with Freud against Thomas and Kant. But more than that, it means a head-on collision with Freud over the issue of humanization. From the standpoint of contextual theology, Freud is both right and wrong. He is right with his questions; he is wrong with his answers. For, as Lehmann contends, with Freud "the sensitivity to what it takes to make and to keep human life human is severely restricted to an attainable adjustment between self-conscious self-awareness and the relevant limits imposed by external environment." And this will never do since it turns on a humanity that settles for "the precarious tranquillity of the measurably uninvolved life." [17]

So to debate with Freud evokes the new possibility of a long ignored opening. Nothing less than Calvin's equation, ". . . a good conscience is nothing other than inward integrity of heart," [18] is germane. This calls into the fray yet another reason for clarifying the drastic difference between Calvin and Luther on the central importance of justification by faith. It also reminds us of the fact that for the Hebraic thought of the Old Testament, indelibly coloring the New Testament which emerges from it, *conscience* and *heart* are intimately relatable terms.

By now Lehmann's argument is spent, and in the process the debate with Freud has fallen far to the rear. This always happens in the *koinonia,* for the very term is theology's word for the region in which its concern and that of the humanists intersect. What is decisive is to note that the new theological possibility could have arisen only in the midst of just this intersection. An *ideological* theology would be predisposed to stack the deck in favor of

Thomas and, curiously enough, Kant. Contextual theology knows how to wager its blue chips when the humanist deals. When it wins it wins more than blue chips—it wins the right to deal itself!

Lehmann's conversation with and beyond Freud regarding conscience illustrates the most basic mark of contextual theology, its fluidity. The context of contextual theology—what in its own language it calls the *koinonia*—is alive, and therefore defies control. If then contexual theology is *contextual* in its own sense of the term, it must be theology beyond ideology, since it eschews that attempt to control the situation which is absolutely fundamental to the success of an ideological masquerade. Contextual theology must be ready to move beyond its own formulations whenever the ideological limits of these are discerned. This restless sense of movement may be recognized by the following operational characteristics.

1. Contextual theology is consciously involved *qua* theology in the pluralism of man's search for meaning. This is the relentless thrust of Lehmann's insistence that the issue of humanization is central for Christian ethics. The fact is that it is central for theology at large. The mark of the integrity with which this is held is precisely locatable: Provisional alliances with other voices in the intersection are not options but necessities. For the test case for theology vis-à-vis humanization will always be not whether others will accept a specifically Christian point but whether they will find it intelligible. Contextual theology is dependent on this exchange. It is here, and nowhere else, that the source of its imaginative impulse is to be found.

2. The second characteristic follows immediately. Involvement in pluralism carries with it a decisive element of *risk*. More is at stake here than simply the observation that anything creative is shot full of risk since the new always shatters the old. What is crucial is the fact that contextual theology's risks are always twofold.

On the one hand there is the risk of lack of recognition by fellow Christians. Contextual theology will always be plagued by the necessity of rearguard action. Christian ideologists can be expected to turn to terror in the face of what they must regard as pointless iconoclasm. The icons are valued highly by the vested interest group.

On the other hand, and far more important though not more persistent, there is the risk of drastic change in the form of new concreteness. For example, the conversation with and beyond Freud forces Lehmann down a path he dare not resist—not if he is really going to be contextual. It forces him to a substantive claim which ultimately involves his opposition to Christians who oppose any men of conscience. This simultaneously enlarges (in the *koinonia*) and constricts (for the ideologists) the Christian doctrine of man. For if Lehmann is right then one must have more in common with non-Christian men of conscience than with Christians who minimize conscience to the distortion of the freedom and potentiality of man. This risk of concreteness is decisive for any contextual theology worthy of the name. Apart from this it is not valid in its own eyes as theology.

3. Thirdly, for contextual theology the *koinonia* is the locus of the oscillation between dogmatics and ethics. It is no accident that Emil Brunner, Reinhold Niebuhr, Karl Barth, and Dietrich Bonhoeffer provide the background against which Lehmann's work takes shape. These four by no means exhaust that spectrum, of course, but they do suggest how insistently Lehmann presupposes the inseparability of dogmatics and ethics. In Lehmann's argument, however, this connection is reversible. This is not to say that ethics *replaces* dogmatics. But it is to say that theological inquiry moves into unexpected realms when it is carried on under the pressure of the ethical problem.

The conversation beyond Freud regarding conscience yields for Lehmann a striking formulation: "Conscience is the focal instance of theonomous behavior." [19] If this is true, then the struggle to clarify conscience necessarily involves far more than the term itself can ever disclose. Just how broad is the spectrum that this struggle must presuppose?

It is significant that with this point the broader reaches of Lehmann's discussion must be explicitly, though briefly, adduced. The formulation just noted emerges along the path of the *heteronomy/autonomy/theonomy* differentiation so familiar to this theological generation as a result of the work of Paul Tillich. Tillich sees theonomous man as man authentically grounded in the ground of being, God. The difference between Tillich and Lehmann in this connection is crucial. For Lehmann God cannot be symbolized in ontological terms; he can only be described in ethical terms. Now given, for example, the argument of *The Courage to Be,* one can never assume that for Tillich the onto-logical and the ethical may be separated. Nor are they separable for Lehmann. But for Lehmann one gets at the ontological only from the ethical side. The ultimate reality is understandable for him not in terms of the ground of being but in terms of "the politics of God," [20] and nothing less than this is at stake in the assertion that conscience is the *focal* instance of theonomous be-havior. This language is by no means minimal. More than the doctrine of man is clarified. For if Lehmann's argument holds, then man as conscience in the context of the *koinonia* is the focus —not the content but the focus—of the doctrine of God.

4. Finally, for contextual theology the theological task is one of *description,* not *definition.* Lehmann states this early in his argument as follows:

> The scriptural preoccupation with a God who speaks, who is known in and through "his Word," points to a power of imagina-tive apprehension which rejects definition but does not forswear description as man's way of responding to and reflecting upon what God is doing in the world.[21]

As material for a definition the phrase "the politics of God" will never do, but as the animating heart of a description it is capable of directing theological imagination along paths that are as old as the Hebraic understanding of the covenant between Yahweh and Israel and as new as the seething problems of modern, secular man. A descriptive theology is free to utilize its heritage in untried ways. In an incisive observation, Lehmann notes that modern biblical scholarship has brought us to just this exciting possibility.

> Perhaps the most enduring fruit of the higher criticism of the Scriptures will be the liberation of biblical images. Biblical in-vestigation from Wellhausen to Bultmann may be credited,

among its many achievements, with having set the biblical images free. . . .[22]

To be sure, this is not the first argument to notice the centrality of words such as "covenant," "Lord," "messiah," and "new age" for a biblically-ordered theology. However, there *is* something distinctive about the following claim:

> . . . the formative biblical images which point to and describe the divine activity in the world are *political* images, both in    the phenomenological and in the fundamental sense of the word.[23]

For contextual theology the coincidence of the *phenomenological* and the *fundamental* is not accidental. It is the heart of the gospel itself. The definitions with which theology descriptively works are always open to change. There is no final theological formulation, not because other men or later men will derive new definitions, but because the substance of theological reflection is dynamic. Not reduction to the all-controlling definition but expansion to the all-encompassing description is the test to which the rich heritage of the language of the Bible and the manifold tradition emerging from it is put by theology in the midst of the ambivalent *koinonia*.

Operating in each of these four ways simultaneously, contextual theology is theology beyond ideology in the sense that it is ill-suited to restrict its service to the vested interests that spawn it. There are others in that intersection called the *koinonia*. What is involved is an overlapping, double community—a community which will be constituted sometimes by friendly dialogue, and sometimes by polemical confrontation, but in either case a community about which only one thing may be predicted with certainty, namely its permanence. Contextual theology cannot do its tasks without dealing with insights which may be useful to others on their own terms. The ambivalence of its operation is in fact the *sine qua non* of its work. This ambivalence may itself be described in terms of a differentiation between Christians who are struggling to state the *kerygma* humanistically and humanists who do not yet know, or who could not care less, that something of the center of their concerns coincides with something of the depths of genuinely Christian conviction and affirmation. By its own criteria, however, contextual theology deteriorates into mere ideology whenever and wherever it understands and articulates this differentiation at the expense of the humanity of the other. It earns the accolade of theology beyond ideology only when and if it recognizes that this is a differentiation that will never disappear.

## V

A passion for concreteness pervades the operation of contextual theology. Arising as it does as the far-reaching implication of contextual ethics, contextual theology is at the same time the presupposition of such an ethic. Without a fluid theology a fluid ethic will deteriorate into the very legalism it initially opposed. But such a theology will be able to maintain its dynamic character only if it is continually in touch with reality. It is the multiplex character of reality itself that delivers theology from its most pernicious temptation, viz, its willingness to retreat from the demands of any given present time into the art of interpreting abstractions encased in definitions. And it is contextual ethics that provides both the recognition of and the involvement in the wild plurality of reality itself. Such ethical involvement always demands the radical opening of the theological presuppositions informing it—*radical* opening, because none of these presuppositions can be considered beyond the reach of severely critical re-examination and drastic extrapolation in the face of and in response to the multiplex reality in which involvement must continually unfold. Any theological stance which is not capable of such an opening will invariably be one that manifests all the rigidity of an ideology. That is, it will be thought in the service of vested interests, though that seeks only to buttress a given status quo. But what happens when theology does become genuinely contextual because of the contextual ethic it necessarily generates?

It is striking that within ten years of the publication of *Ethics in a Christian Context* there should be such clear indications of the beginnings of the answer to the question just posed. One of these is close at hand, and it has already reached decisive proportions. It unfolds in the American scene and has to do with the ethnic revolutions now dominant within it. Just as Lehmann's book was being published the civil rights movement was shifting into high gear. Before the decade of the 1960's was finished this movement deepened—it did not collapse, as is so often mistakenly asserted—into the full scale black revolution. This in turn triggered the ethnic revolutions across the entire spectrum of the ethnic mosaic that is humanity. Those sensitive to the demands of the contextual ethic, as articulated by Lehmann, found themselves immediately drawn into this entire development.

In the process of this involvement, however, what has transpired is the posing of more than an ethical question. What has transpired is a *theological* question that must drive beyond the consolidated theological positions of all involved, including Lehmann himself. One has only to mention the forceful, polemical, intensely creative work of Lehmann's younger black colleague at Union Seminary, James Cone, in order to bring this to mind. And when one adds to Cone's voice that of the equally forceful, polemical, intensely creative Sioux activist, Vine Deloria, Jr., the issue at hand is even more compelling. Cone, in all of his writings, radically rejects the view that the black revolution can be simply inserted into the already elaborated agenda of theological reflection. In the midst of one of his most cogent arguments, Cone insists on the following:

> Because sin is a concept that is meaningful only for an oppressed community as it reflects upon its liberation, it is not possible to make a universal analysis that is meaningful for both black and white people. . . . No white theologian has been able to relate sin to the black and white encounter in America. . . . Invariably, white theologians analyze sin as if blacks and whites represent one community.[24]

Similarly, at a crucial turning point in the first of the four books he has published, Deloria observes:

> I believe that an Indian version of Christianity could do much for our society. But there is little chance for such a melding of cards. Everyone in the religious sphere wants his trump to play on the last trick.[25]

Theological, not just ethical, labor is at hand in each of these remarks, and precisely this is what marks the deepening of the civil rights movement into the irreversible ethnic revolutions. The price of involvement in the struggles which these revolutions entail is the price of reckoning with the new theological agenda that figures such as Cone and Deloria are shaping.

In such crucibles will be forged the real implications of contextual theology's move beyond the ideological limits of all theology as we now know it. For central to the enterprise is the challenging of the social contexts in which ideas live by authentic, total involvement in just these contexts. The lasting contribution of Lehmann's theological creativity is that he has put us on the way toward the fulfillment of this task, and he has done so with a rigor that admits no turning back.

1. Paul Lehmann, *Ethics in a Christian Context* (New York: Harper and Row, 1963), p. 27.
2. Peter L. Berger, *Invitation to Sociology: A Humanistic Perspective* (Garden City, New York: Anchor Books, Doubleday & Co., Inc., 1963), p. 110.
3. *Ibid.,* p. 117.
4. *Ibid.,* p. 114.
5. *Ibid.,* p. 111.
6. Lehmann, *op. cit.,* pp. 45 ff.
7. Peter L. Berger, *The Precarious Vision: A Sociologist Looks at Social Fictions and Christian Faith* (Garden City, New York: Doubleday & Co., Inc., 1961), p. 17.
8. Joseph Fletcher, *Situation Ethics: The New Morality* (Philadelphia: The Westminster Press, 1966), p. 14.
9. *Ibid.,* p. 60.
10. Karl Barth, *Church Dogmatics,* I/1 (Edinburgh: T & T Clark, 1936), p. 351 (cf. *Die kirchliche Dogmatik,* I/1, Evangelischer Verlag AG, Zollikon-Zürich, 1932, p. 323).
11. Lehmann, *op. cit.,* p. 77.
12. *Ibid.,* p. 50.
13. *Ibid.,* pp. 330 and 333 respectively.
14. *Ibid.,* p. 337.
15. This is the title of Part Two of Lehmann's work.
16. Lehmann, *op. cit.,* p. 283.
17. *Ibid.,* p. 343.
18. Ibid., p. 366, quoting Calvin, *Institutes of the Christian Religion,* III, xix, 16. Lehmann's case is even stronger in the light of Calvin's

reiteration of precisely this terminology in connection with his doctrine of the church. Cf. IV, x, 4.

19. Lehmann, *op. cit.*, p. 351.
20. *Ibid.*, pp. 86 ff.
21. *Ibid.*, p. 89.
22. *Ibid.*, p. 90.
23. *Ibid.*, p. 90 (Lehmann's italics).
24. James H. Cone, *A Black Theology of Liberation* (Philadelphia and New York: J. B. Lippincott Company, 1970), pp. 190-191.
25. Vine Deloria, Jr., *Custer Died For Your Sins: An Indian Manifesto* (New York: Avon Books, by arrangement with The Macmillan Company, 1970), p. 127.

# The Fashioning of Power:
## A Christian Perspective on
## the Life-Style Phenomenon

**JAMES LODER**

### I

"Style" as I mean it here is neither fashion nor fad. It is centrally a matter of personal, social, and cultural integration based on a formal pattern which pervades and interrelates the registers of behavior, shaping and directing a personality through scores of varied activities and extremities. Over the course of a lifetime a composition emerges whose parts derive their significance from their relation to the whole. As Whitehead said, "style is the fashioning of power."

What follows is a study of "the fashioning" of well-adjusted, socially acceptable patterns of self-destruction. It is also a study of the nature of the structural shift implied by setting such patterns in the context of Christian conviction, thought, and action. Because the emphasis here is upon structure rather than dynamics, it might be more accurate to speak of "the power of fashioning"; but the overall aim is to describe structural continuities which fashion the total energy of a lifetime.

### II

The central unity of style in relation to the parts which comprise it can be briefly illustrated. Gardner Murphy records that Max Wertheimer [1] used to ask a group of friends to gather around the piano while he played a series of compositions

187

revealing the personality of each one present. Each would then indicate privately the name of the individual described in the composition. But Wertheimer noted that to say a composition represents "Herr Schmidt" because of the heavy tread was a poor response because the composition was non-analytical, designed to catch one's style of personal comportment on an "intuitive" or global level. The core of the personality—analogous to the essence of a literary or musical style—was a basic synthesis capable of embodiment in several modalities yet consistent through various adaptions. The composition caught the core, not its manifestations, in this or that modality.

This example in stressing synthesis suggests the first step in the analysis of a life-style. From the standpoint of human development, there is a core, a central structure; out of it develops a characteristic pattern around which all subsequent modalities of experience are composed. To be more specific, we must attempt to set forth a typical style. There are many individual variations on any style, but this example will illustrate how a style may be understood as the expansion of a basic structural pattern.

Following is a study of structures which support "the spirit of Hermes." [2] Accordingly, the theme of this illustrative style is achievement." One may see this style beginning during the early years of development in homes which stress "independence training." [3] Although there is not a perfect correlation between independence training and the achievement motive, it is highly probable that mothers who want early independence for their sons[4] and who, among other techniques, reward their successful performances with hugs and kisses will have sons whose achievement motivation is high. It is as if there were operative during the early years (perhaps the first three years) of life a reaction formation in which the child learns to do just the opposite of what he wants most. Before the years in which competition becomes important, he wants most the hugs and kisses which ascribe to him an unconditional worth, but they are withheld until he performs well. So he throws himself into performing well and does so with all the passion with which he desires to be affirmed for who he *is,* a child of worth. He eventually learns to repress spontaneous affect and convert that energy into high performance activity and successful competitive ventures. This is the core structure of the achievement-oriented life-style.

As the years pass, this structure expands and becomes more complex by assimilating and accommodating to its changing environment. In recent history it has been shown that an increase in maternal dominance of the American middle-class home, "matriarchy," tends to favor achievement-orientation for sons.[5] Moreover, if the family situation is conducted in the typical middle-class fashion of "cold democracy" under female leadership, the motive to achieve is strongly augmented.[6] There is, in effect, a family pattern—the original primary group—which reinforces, enables, and encourages the young achiever to generalize from his core experience to the rest of the world. Talcott Parsons and others [7] have claimed that the pattern which works at home transfers effectively to primary group patterns which are developed beyond the family. Moreover, cold democracy administered under female leadership in the public school context builds up achievement in the students. In a study by Ackerman, teachers most effective in raising the achievement scores for their pupils were judged "least considerate," which those thought to be friendly and congenial were least effective.[8] The style of achievement-orientation received immense re-enforcement several years ago when Sputnik threw American technological self-confidence into a state of anxiety. Out of this anxiety came invidious comparisons between Ivan and Johnny, and the result was a vigorous emphasis upon "excellence" in public education. This meant "excellence" in academic achievement and especially in convergent thinking so essential to the hard dry sciences. Ability grouping and the guidance counselor came into their own, and the competition aspect of the achievement-orientation became a major motivational force.

One can only estimate the effect of this surge toward "excellence" upon recent youth movements in the United States. But in an article writen in 1961, Bronfenbrenner, reflecting upon these trends toward re-enforcement of the achievement-orientation, came to some very disturbing conclusions. Citing studies by

Baldwin, Kalhorn, Breese, and Haggard, he concluded that these patterns of child rearing, peer group development, and the public school emphasis upon excellence tended to produce a person who is purposeful, but who is also more aggressive, tense, domineering, and cruel.[9]

One can easily argue that in a highly mobile, differentiated, industrialized, technocratic society such as ours, a person must be educated to a high level of purposeful competence. One study to come forth in support of socialization of the child for an achievement-oriented society was *Education and the New America* by Kimball and McClelland. The aim of public education, as these writers saw it, was to cultivate a disciplined mind which would be committed to the performance and furtherance of what must be called the achievement-oriented society. The authors and like-minded sympathizers have had their influence particularly upon the several interlocking spheres of professional education. But critics of this trend in education—not the least of whom are the responsible but restless students—are increasingly aware of the self-destructive impact which Bronfenbrenner predicted as the outcome of our obsessions with achievement in the socialization agencies of our society.

Thus, the style of achievement-orientation is at all levels of socialization. It has its central structural core, its family and primary group context, and, in spite of humanistic and "romantic" critics, its fertile milieu in public education. Moreover, a self-consciously technocratic society awaits the achiever and his competencies, ready to put him into any number of training programs and "teams" of experts whose success depends upon planned, purposeful, and aggressive action.

Beyond these psychological and social dimensions, every style has its "culture," its public symbols and forms of celebration by which it creates, sustains, and extends its value system and by which it defines and purges itself of alien values. For the Western achiever, this is the Protestant Ethic.

In a society of abundance, the "Protestant Ethic" has become a popular whipping boy, but too often its roots in developmental and socialization experience, i.e., in the entire achievement-oriented style, are totally ignored. It is decried as a value system celebrated by old style "agrarian capitalism," a set of values handed down from the past now to be changed by force of choice. It is not so easily compartmentalized and changed. Rather, the value system associated with the Protestant Ethic must be seen as merely one dimension of a pervasive style of American life.

This value system, rooted in the Protestant reformation and embedded in American culture, is practiced by Protestant, Catholic, and Jew. It is celebrated and entrenched wherever there is simple self-denial, devotion to duty, and the pious expectation that worldly benefits will come to reward the economically "righteous" man. Wherever savings are plowed back into the firm even to reap benefits which the present generation cannot expect to enjoy, the so-called Protestant Ethic is being advanced. Moreover, every childhood pattern marked by independence training, "cold democracy," and education for "excellence" is both an expression and an extension of this value system. Attacking the value dimension of a life-style may make good polemics but it changes nothing. A style, to be changed, must be confronted at its core and with a sense for its totality.[10]

Ironically, self-destruction (destruction of the self-potential) is the ultimate outcome of a repressive, planned, purposeful existence at the center of achievement-orientation. Bronfenbrenner's warnings of doom are not to be taken lightly. The central tendency of achievement-orientation is repressive of a deep human cry for assurance of ascriptive (not achieved) worth. The outcome is aggression, tension, domineering control, and cruelty. Those who sense that this is not really a *life*-style, but a death style, are thrown to an opposite extreme by the funereal odor which gathers over the achiever's world. Obviously a "radical" youth movement which asserts that in an achieving society of abundance man ought to live as if "bread is!" can do nothing but polarize the achievement-oriented style. Youth here claims precisely what age has denied itself in the central tendency of achievement-oriented style—namely, ascriptive worth.

This polarization of the generations into a neurotic cycle could be developed at some length, but the point here is that achievement-orientation appears to be self-destructive. It repressively belittles the achiever's latent wish for ascriptive worth, forcing him into self-justifying behavior. If it fails, it leaves him with nothing but his aggression, tension, domineering tendencies, and cruelty. If it succeeds, it creates an environment in which those around him are not only enabled but feel compelled to make the affirmations he has denied himself. This leaves his "asceticism" unappreciated, and his "sociological hugs and kisses" may only stand to condemn rather than reward him.

Perhaps the deepest confusion of all comes when one tries to educate the achiever in a Christian context without actually confronting his style of life. The achiever will take only "appropriate" and therefore probably only "successful" educational risks, learn the "winning" answers, interpret them to justify his style and assume—perhaps not erroneously—that the church is celebrating his way of life. It is poignantly evident that if the educational work of the church, from its education of the public to the education of its professionals, cannot deal with the solidarity and pervasiveness of such a style, then it cannot teach in any way which is commensurate with the claims of the gospel it teaches.

Achievement-orientation, although it is potentially destructive to the self, is the style I have chosen for illustration because its basic points of reference are generally common knowledge. Yet it is not as obviously self-destructive in our society as is, say, the authoritarian personality. Newer styles of equally pervasive significance will subsequently be developed along similar lines,[11] but the style I have just described is sufficient to show the interplay of several forces. These forces are developmental and social-institutional. Moving developmentally through the list, the major behavioral determinants of style are the following. First, a central structural integration which comes to its earliest form of consolidation by approximately the third year of life. This consolidation is rewarded as an "identity" at adolescence, again during the middle years, and finally in "old age" (as distinct from "senescence"). Second, an originating primary group, usually the nuclear family or its functional analogue, works to reenforce the earliest integration. Third, an educational system hastens the transition of the central structure from the family to the social role system. Fourth, a social role system rewards the central integrative tendency and its educational expression with adequate sociological surrogates for those hugs and kisses that first reenforced the development of that tendency. Fifth, a cherished symbol system with some religious significance in a shared "philosophy of life" ritually purges guilt feelings and justifies the accumulation of temporarily satisfying rewards.

Having stated these behavioral factors, I am aware that a major influence is still unnamed. How are these factors incorporated, integrated and transformed for individuality? How is any type of style made personal? This occurs, I believe, by dominant images, by the imagination. Emerging out of the earliest, most rudimentary forms of physiological organization is the capacity of the psyche to transform physical forms into psychic ones and to produce meaningful integration in the place of the fragmentation of sensory experience. Out of this symbolic operation of the psyche are produced earliest intuitions, identifications, self-images, personal and public myths.

The "logic" of imagination in its creation of the personal myth is probably far more fundamental to style—and more elusive—than any single influence we have mentioned thus far. Every individual whose style conforms generally to the achievement-oriented types has his own version of it, based on his imaginatively constructed self-image and his personal myth about the origin and destiny of his life. Within this imaginatively constructed universe he lives out his version of the style. He feels on the one hand, that he meets or does not meet the demands of the achieving society very well; on the other hand, he feels he is always a perfectly unique individual. Thus we may say that a certain ineffability of a person's style lies concealed in his imaginative synthesis of interpersonal and public influences which are otherwise shared by those who are cast in the mold of his same style. Further consideration of this aspect would take us into the dynamics of style or the empowering of imagination, a matter beyond the scope of this essay. At this point we must turn to a comparative study of the formal aspects of achievement-orientation and the Christian style of life.

## Life-Style: A Christian Perspective

### I

In the achievement-oriented style the theological culture characteristic of the Protestant reformed tradition serves to sacralize a distinctively self-destructive pattern. Christian symbols are important to other styles as well.[12] To speak of a Christian style of life is not simply to speak of a particular symbol system which may be cast like a sacred canopy over a variety of dynamic patterns. Rather it is to point to a particular alteration of the core structure which changes the total pattern. Under such conditions, the core structure of style is so similar to the structure of Christian symbolism and action that I may call this an isomorphic relationship. This claim will require some elaboration.

The Christian life-style is grounded in a conviction not ultimately reducible to a socially-constructed web of values and behavior. To be sure, any such socially-constructed web continues even after an experience of conversion, since very often the behavior involved has acquired a functional autonomy.[13] But the significant fact for conviction is that such functional autonomy becomes subject to re-direction and choice, to a conscience-free negation or affirmation.

Thus when a person raised in an achievement-oriented home becomes Christian—whether in a blinding, burning moment or over a sustained period of time—he does not lose his tendency to be oriented toward achievement. Rather it becomes startlingly or increasingly clear to him that his life is relentlessly driven from within by the obsessive need to achieve. Since the obsessive character of this style is widespread and socially acceptable, apart from such conversion, the obsession easily goes unnoticed. He himself will only gradually and with difficulty see that his

relation to achievement is very much like an addiction for which
he may have a temporary solution (more achievement). But he
is also never satisfied, since cessation of achievement means
cessation of worth. To become conscious of such an addiction is
often not enough to shake its grip, so Christian conviction is more
than awareness. It is the act of God which does not alter the
achieving potential so much as it restores the freedom to choose
for or against achieving. In Christian conversion the achieving ego
does not collapse, but latent patterns such as those demanding
achievement lose their compulsive tendency and their power to
suppress choice.

The definitive core of the Christian style is conviction.
There is no definite age level when such conviction is most likely
to appear, but it rarely becomes stabilized before adolescence.
The basic elements of the structure of conviction can be generally
described as an antithesis-in-synthesis. I have attempted to put
this into the following formula: $+(I/not\text{-}I)+$. The reason I put it
in this form is that the elements represented do not exist in some
sequence; they coexist and compose an organic system in which a
change in one term influences the equilibrium of the whole. Such
a view is, of course, only a *model* of conviction, not the conviction itself. Now to the elements of the model.

The "I" refers to the subjective source of choice and to the
symbolically based, socially constructed patterns which have
given shape to the self throughout the individual's personal history. This "I," to take the previous case, refers to the function-
ally autonomous, achievement-oriented ego discussed above.

The "not-I" is more difficult to explain. As we may say it is
the primal sense of what I will call "absence" which accompanies
birth. It is concealed by repression, as in the reaction formation
dynamic which is at the core of the achievement-oriented style.
It is the severe pain of recognizing the unyielding silence and
emptiness of "absence" which seals the individual into whatever
personal presence may be available and on whatever terms that
presence demands.

Birth imbues the child simultaneously with a sense of his
separateness as an organism and with the sense of the painful

price he must pay to sustain that separate identity. He has to accept "absence" as the price of his own real presence in the world. But he will accept as little "absence" as possible because from the beginning it is associated with intense pain. This is his condition as an emerging self, an "I." All his choices, by what they negate as well as by what they confirm, serve to remind him that his emerging identity in any form presupposes "absence."

The "I" naturally struggles against "absense" as if it were a mortal enemy. It becomes narcissistic, omnipotent, and omniscient, popular, feared, manipulative, "well-adjusted," "grizzly realistic," etc., in order to fill the "absence" with some fantastic extension of itself. Under conviction, however, the "I" stripped of its narcissism, omnipotence, etc., accepts itself as a carrier of "absence."

I have been speaking of the pervasive phenomenon of "absence," but from the standpoint of the general model it may be better to refer to this phenomenon as the "not-I." Generally, our worlds are populated by legitimate extensions of ourselves. The objects of the world emerge for us out of our symbolic reconstruction of sensory motor experience. But even as we construct the world through extensions of the "I" we simultaneously create and extend the "not-I." Every choice *for* presupposes a choice *against;* every formation of an object before my mind's eye presupposes the functional elimination from my awareness of all other possible objects. The "I" and its extensions are relentlessly pursued by the "not-I." This is the binary structure of being and knowing. Speaking of the "not-I" rather than of absence also stresses a crucial aspect of conviction. Namely, negation is not ultimately prior to being; it exists as Sartre says "on the surface of being." The "Not-I" is ultimately derivative from the "I," but proximately it remains in an incessant tension with the being of the "I."

Conviction may then be seen as the other side of nihilism. Nihilism presupposes the ultimate priority of nothing and that all being and beings are ultimately made into nothing. For conviction, "nothing" is a quality of being and is hence better termed "nothingness" (or as we have called it in reference to personal being, the "not-I").

Ordinarily the "not-I" is associated with negative emotion. Thus, Sartre says "nothingness *haunts* being." [14] But against our primal fears of the "not-I," conviction asserts that the "I/not-I" tension is the ultimate truth about personal existence and that our acceptance of that condition is the very ground of our authenticity as human beings.

The establishment of the priority of being human over against its negation is beyond the power of the "I." Here it is important to remember that under natural conditions nothingness haunts the "I." As in the case of the achievement-oriented person, the "not-I" (in the form of the absence of ascriptive worth) literally haunts him to death because it is always present but never accepted. In a sense, the achievement-oriented personality is a true nihilist. By his refusal to recognize a lived tension with the "not-I," he is gradually destroyed; it makes "nothing" of his best efforts.

For conviction, the "I/not-I" tension is inescapable. Hence conviction is without illusions. Any assertion of the priority of being by the "I" simultaneously asserts its contradiction.

Conviction, characterized by the "I/not-I" tension in which being is ultimate, presupposes the presence and power of a Convictor who, coming from the outside, overcomes our nihilistic uncertainty.[15] Hence, in the structure of conviction, the "I/not-I" tension is bracketed with the signs of affirmation ( + ).

Under conviction one does not ultimately speak for himself but for him by whom he is convicted. The "not-I" is the aspect of conviction which preserves the possibility of choosing authentically for oneself and at the same time preserves contingency upon the Convictor for any such choices. Thus under conviction, "not-I" is integral to freedom and to the power to create and be created. Apart from conviction, the "not-I"—once it is recognized— changes its countenance and becomes haunting and threatening, and the "I" cowers and runs for cover into narcissism, omnipotence, etc. This, let us note *en passant,* is the basic structure underlying the Genesis account of shame.

The "not-I" need not always be accompanied by negative emotion. We need not always be "haunted" by nothingness. We may instead be intrigued by its capacity to contribute to a heightened sense of self not as simply autonomous but as convicted. We may be intrigued by its capacity to provoke creativity which expresses the power which is creating and extending the conviction itself. Agreeing that style is the fashioning of power (Whitehead), I am suggesting that the core of the Christian style of life may be seen as rooted in the foregoing structure of conviction, and that by such a convictional structure the Spirit of God is given human formation.

It was the style of the prophets to speak in the $+(I/not\text{-}I)+$ form. They spoke as themselves but proclaimed that it was not they but Yahweh who was speaking to the people. "Thus says the Lord" is the sign that the prophet is speaking convictionally; it is an $+(I/not\text{-}I)+$ construction. Jesus is also recorded as having spoken in the same construction. The Gospel of John abounds with examples, such as John 8:13-14. In this context Jesus is criticized by the Pharisees for testifying to himself, but faith is a fundamental correction to the religious narcissism of which he was accused. "You judge according to the flesh, I judge no one. Yet even if I do judge, my judgment is true, for it is not I alone that Judge, but I and He who sent me." Again, Romans 7 is an extended Pauline usage of this same convictional construction. Here the "I/not-I" dialectic is elaborated in detail and the ultimately positive $(+)$ assertion is that the Spirit of life in Christ Jesus has set him free. The same construction appears again and again in Philippians both when the author refers to himself and when he refers to his readers (e.g., Phil. 2:12-13).

## II

I hypothesized at the outset of the former section that the structure of the central core of the Christian life-style (conviction) was congruent with structure of Christian symbolism. Since Christian symbolism is a vast field, I will limit myself in this discussion to one critical area, theological semantics. The assumption is that the semantic system of theology deals with the reference and meaning of those words which are peculiarly suited to the expression and construction of Christian conviction. Therefore, more than grammar or pragmatics, a discussion of semantics will get us into the structural basis upon which conviction can be put into meaningful symbolic forms.

In his recent attempt to deal with this, Langdon Gilkey concluded that meaningful religious discussion (1) is "doubly intentional, referring to the finite world and to the sacred and the ultimate that is manifest in and through the finite," (2) is concerned with existential or ultimate issues of life," and (3) "provides crucial models or norms by which life is directed and judged and so by which culture as a whole is itself guided and assessed." [16] Although I am generally in agreement with Gilkey's helpful discussion, a seriatim comment on each of his conclusions will bring this discussion of theological semantics into focus.

By "doubly intentional" Gilkey is actually suggesting that there are three dimensions of theological symbols: those which point to the ultimate, to the finite, and to the symbol in its totality. A careful, more extensive, analysis similar to this was made by Ian Ramsey [17] under the notion of theological language (semantics in particular) as logically "odd." His point is that under conviction we try to express in symbolic form the odd situation that God has revealed himself. The result is a set of logically improper word pictures which, by their very impropriety, are designed to awaken conviction. An example would be the phrase "heavenly father." "Father" is proper, ordinary semantics meaning literally pastoral kinship. But when we speak of God we do not have ordinary fathers in mind, so we must simultaneously negate ordinary usage of the term and at the same time magnify its reference to ultimate proportions. This we accomplish by adding the adjective "heavenly." These three steps are widely applied. Take almost any theological term like love, grace, or faith. Each is an ordinary term, negated and magnified. Magnification can take place with capital letters as with Paul Tillich's reference to "The Unconditioned" or with prefixes such as "omni-" or "super-."

The point is that this study by Ramsey suggests that there is a further consideration—namely, the negative relationships between theological semantics and ordinary language. Austin Farrar once referred to this as the "negative analogical dialectic."

I prefer to call it the negative meaning embedded in theological semantics. This negative meaning is the symbolic transformation and expression of the "not-I" dimension of conviction. It is as crucial to theological semantics as the "not-I" factor is in the structure of conviction. This negative meaning is embraced by theological semantics as the "not-I" factor is embraced by conviction.

If we keep Gilkey's discussion in mind, we can conclude that theological semantics has only one aim,[18] the systematic integration of three symbolic dimensions: finite reference, its negation, and ultimate reference. Such semantic structure provides a linguistic congruence with the structural model of conviction as discussed above.

Gilkey's concern that religious language arise from and speak to the existential conditions of man may be seen as another way of saying that religious language to be true to its nature must be convictional. However, having specified above what seems to be the essential structure of conviction, it seems necessary to say that not just any so-called existential situation will do. Theological semantics as discussed above calls forth and expresses a particular formation at the core of human being. It is true that this formation is existential in the sense that it is to be lived simultaneously in its ambiguity and in its integrity.

This, of course, is an "odd" situation in the very sense in which Ramsey used the term. It is this very oddity in both its convictional and linguistic forms which gives rise almost automatically to a critique of current society and culture. In relation to this discussion it implies a critique of achievement-orientation from the standpoint of conviction and convictional language. But I want to relate this dimension of theological discourse to the overall picture of the Christian life-style and to Paul Lehmann in particular. This will lead us into the third consideration mentioned in the introduction to this section on Christian life-style, namely, action.

### III

Paul Lehmann has often been criticized for the polymorphous

complexity of his prose. However, it seems to me that one rarely makes such a criticism without at the same time acknowledging that something important seems to be going on when he speaks and writes. He embodies a combination of factors very like the elements of conviction and theological semantics which have been discussed above. Paul Lehmann's style is convictional. The articulation he gives it reflects his patient struggle to weave language around the structure of conviction so as to have it finally emerge as an expression of—and expansion upon—the elements of that conviction.

Assuming that conviction is the core of the Christian's life-style, it may now be possible, using Lehmann's terminology, to describe the fuller dimensions of that style of life. We said in section I that, beyond the core, the next important dimension was the primary group in which that core received reenforcement, challenge, and expansion. The *koinonia* provides this dimension. We must hasten to say that the *koinonia*, "the fellowship creating reality of Jesus Christ," is a convictional operation which is fundamentally transcendent and therefore free to be solidly social. This sort of statement only makes sense in an "odd" way because of course the term *koinonia* is an "odd" word. It is theological semantics reminding us all at once that it is a fellowship, but no ordinary fellowship. However, the magnification in Lehmann's prose is actually carried by preserving the Greek form in an ordinary English word context.

Now we are beginning to see how the critique of current society and culture springs automatically from conviction. If we move into the wider circles of influence related to the Christian life-style, we find Lehmann speaking of "the politics of God," and "What God is doing to make and to keep human life human." Notice again the language is "odd." It depends upon conviction to give it a felt meaning, a basis in life. On the other hand, conviction depends upon just such language to give itself expression over against a one-dimensional social existence. This implies a critique of the entire picture of socially-constructed reality from education through social and institutional behavior into the socialized functions of theological language.

Lehmann's claim is consistently convictional. It seems to me what he wants to describe is a type of conscientious action which matches the structural pattern of conviction and theological semantics. The three dimensions of that action are (a) acceptance of the ordinary; that is, the environment of humanization, an ordinary knowledge (experience and cognition) of good and evil; (b) negation of that environment; and (c) obedience and theonomous behavior through which to negate that environment. The systematic integration of the three dimensions into a single purpose Lehmann calls "conscience." Conscience then is convictional action. In his words,

> Conscience is the act . . . which expresses and exposes the connection between the knowledge of good and evil as the environment of humanization and the obedient response to this environment.[19]

To act according to conscience is to participate in what God is doing in the world and is to be truly human. Given the systematic structure of conviction and action commensurate with that structure, the hope of that humanity will change from context to context, but consistently will preserve and equalize the elements of that structure.

The Christian style, like any other style, is governed throughout by a central structure, conviction. This convictional structure is supported and extended in the *koinonia*. The *koinonia*, reflecting as it does in its structure the oddity of convictional forms, moves both within and beyond the social system, including the institutional church. Such "odd" interpersonal formation automatically gives rise to social and cultural criticism. The *koinonia* provides the context for convictional action, or "conscience." The semantic system by which existence within and action expressive of conviction is pressed into symbolic forms is structurally congruent with conviction itself. Thus that semantic structure has the potentiality both for expression and for calling forth a conviction not yet fully recognized—as when one names the shadowy forms of the psyche they take on meaning and provide a lived or felt basis for the symbolic terms by which they are named.

The Christian life-style shapes power in a self-consistent fashion, yet in its very core it creates the reality of choice—hence freedom and future—by grounding identity in theonomous dependence. Thus the Christian style opens all achievement-orientations to the repeated reformation of conviction, action, and symbol.

For Lehmann, then, ethics is at least in part a matter of convictional style, a style of life. Style, as it has been analyzed here, may be the thematic unity running through Lehmann's writings which persists through the variegated analyses and moments of inspiration for which he is well known. In any case, the integration of conviction, convictional speech, and "conscience" constitutes a nearly full outline of the formal aspects of a Christian life-style.

With the Christian style, as with others, one feels his is uniquely his own even as he recognizes others who share the same style structure. Here Lehmann stresses as I did in the preceding section the central role of the imagination. As he says, "the parabolic image juxtaposes . . . the ways of God and the ways of man . . . consequently they are the stuff of authentic reflection upon and description of the activity of God."

What is missing in Lehmann's view, and what remains to be understood in the context of this structure of life-style, is the dynamics of imagination. By some future understanding of this dynamics we may be able to discern how it is that revelation and the spirit of the pious imagination complement each other not exclusively in the formation of biblical literature—which is certainly a major concern—but also in formation of the convicted person.

---

1. Gardner Murphy, *Personality: A Bio-Social Approach* (New York: Harpers, 1947), p. 646.
2. The basic research from which the following description of life-style is drawn has been performed under the inspiration and leadership of David McClelland. Writings on achievement-orientation by McClelland and others are voluminous. Reference here is to McClelland's *The Achieving Society* (Princeton: Van Nostrand Co., 1961). Hermes provides the mythological type for this life-style when he appears in the

*Homeric Hymn to Hermes* as the patron of the upwardly mobile Athenian merchant entrepreneur.

3. A correlation of various studies related to achievement and human development is made by Roger Brown, *Social Psychology* (New York: Free Press, 1965), Chapter 9, pp. 423 f.

4. In American society women characteristically exhibit a strong motivation to achieve in relation to the goals of "popularity" and "social acceptance." Their goals differ from those of men whose achievement motivation is aroused by talk of "intelligence" and "leadership." Thus, the pattern of achievement orientation to which I am pointing varies in particular characteristics between men and women, but its underlying structure is constant.

5. Urie Bronfenbrenner, "The Effects of Social and Cultural Change on Personality," in *Personality and Social Systems,* ed. Neil J. Smelser and William T. Smelser (New York: Wiley, 1963), pp. 347-356. This was confirmed more recently (1969) in a personal conversation with Bronfenbrenner.

6. *Ibid.*

7. Talcott Parsons, "The Genesis of Motivational Patterns," in *Personality and Social Systems,* pp. 136-149.

8. W. I. Ackerman, "Teacher Competence and Pupil Change," *Harvard Educational Review,* 1954, 24, pp. 273-289.

9. Bronfenbrenner, *op. cit.*

10. A strong and currently popular plea against a major aspect of this style comes from Ivan Illich whose call for the de-schooling of society cuts well into the educational aspect of this style, but he too tends to overlook the force of the central structure. If it cannot find expression one way, it will seek out another and end in a contradictory state—well-schooled or de-schooled.

11. Other examples of styles which have the same structural characteristics as well as a built-in self-destructive dimension are: "Protean man," "therapeutic man," "revolutionary personality." Although others are numerous, these terms may suffice to suggest to the reader the range of possibilities.

12. For example, the theological culture characteristic of a rigid fundamentalism frequently socializes the authoritarian pattern. Accordingly, the authoritarian life-style can create and support a sort of Christian fascism.

13. Here is a crucial structural distinction between the Christian and the secular style of life and so it should be underlined. The Christian style is a re-working of a socialized self from the foundation up; nevertheless the "stuff" of the personality and its particular social and cultural context remain a constant in the fashioning of the Christian style. As a brief example, take the case of St. Paul's paradigmatic

conversion. It seems apparent that his vigorous determination to chasten the Christians was still present as "vigorous determination," but now it was redirected toward extending Christianity to the Gentiles and not incidentally chastening from time to time those who showed themselves to be the enemies of that mission.

14. J. P. Sartre, *Being and Nothingness* (New York: Philosophical Library, 1956), p. 16; *The Ego and the Id* (N.Y.: W. W. Norton and Co., 1960), p. 69, fn. 1.

15. The Latin root of "convict" means "to overcome," "to conquer."

16. Langdon Gilkey, *Naming the Whirlwind* (Indianapolis: Bobbs-Merrill Co., 1969), p. 295. Obviously syntax and pragmatics are also influenced by conviction, but the point will not be treated here.

17. Ian Ramsey, *Religious Language* (New York: Macmillan, 1963).

18. For the use of "intentionality" in this context, see Merleau-Ponty's discussion of the "intentional arc." *Phenomenology of Perception* (London: Routledge and Kegan Paul), p. 136.

19. *Ibid.*, p. 350.

# the future of theology

# Toward a Theology
## of Christological Concentration *

**JAN M. LOCHMAN**

Since the Enlightenment, the Christological center of the Christian message has been sidestepped by modern philosophy and theology in favor of what might be called theologies of the first and third articles. These theologies did not deny that Christianity has "something to do with Jesus Christ," but even in the best instances this "something" was so indirectly and secondarily explicated that not much was left of the actual and original content of New Testament Christology. The motives and aims of the advocates of these two courses of theology were good. Their concern was for a theology and religion which would be more acceptable to modern man. But did they accomplish this? If one poses this question in today's intellectual and ecclesiastical context, then it is impossible in my opinion to answer other than in the negative. Unless I am mistaken, both of these theological paths are in bad repair.

### Theology of the First Article

The attempt was made, especially by the seventeenth and eighteenth century deists, to fight the storm of secular criticism of the church and religion by favoring a theology of the first article and achieving, as far as possible, its independence from

---

* Translated by Julius S. Winkler, Davidson College

Christology. In such a theology what was "natural" and "universal" was appreciated more than what was "revelational" and "historical." Ernst Troeltsch called the formulation of a deistic philosophy of religion the most important event of the entire Enlightenment period. In nineteenth century theology the idea of a philosophy of religion developed which understood that discipline as "a universal historical and phenomenological religious enquiry which traces individual religion back to the universal concept, and evaluates individual religion, and above all Christianity, only on the basis of this concept," (as Troeltsch expresses it in his essay *Deism*).[2] Such universal conceptuality was also employed as a way of understanding the gospel itself, as expressed, for example, in Adolf von Harnack's assertion in his *Wesen des Christentums* that it is not the Son who belongs in the gospel, but rather the Father.

Thus a theology of the first article triumphed over Christology at the beginning of our century. The Czech philosopher, Tomas Masaryk, might be taken as another example. This unique thinker and statesman was not without a deep respect for Jesus (as is true of many other Christian representatives of deism). Indeed, Jesus was significant for him where he was not always taken seriously in orthodox Christianity—namely, in the political and social realm. The way of Jesus was obligatory for Masaryk. It was Jesus, not Caesar, who defined Masaryk's philosophic-political program. But in the actual living of his faith Jesus did not play the decisive role. Not that religion was unimportant for Masaryk. On the contrary, his in-depth analysis of the crisis of modern man emphasized the religious aspects and roots of this crisis, which he understood unambiguously as a crisis of faith. It was in this way that he came into a critical dialogue with positivism and Marxism. But Masaryk understood the realm of religion to involve no Christological ties whatever. He was concerned basically with a life *sub specie aeternitatis*, in the belief in a creator and his providence. Jesus was the witness of this belief, but never its object. For him, only a theology of the first article was really acceptable and actually helpful in the crisis of modern man.

Theological debates of recent years indicate that the theology of the first article is in a state of crisis. In 1963 the Anglican bishop John A. Robinson published *Honest to God,* his broadly aimed attack upon the theistic background of traditional Christian faith and theology. Robinson disputes the capacity of this tradition to sustain either the substance of the Christian message or the spiritual situation of modern man. He claims that traditional theism objectivizes the gospel, mythologizes its joyful message, and alienates it from modern man, to whom all the theistic and mythological presuppositions are completely foreign and unbelievable, and it is high time for the church to get rid of it. To support his criticism, Robinson refers to important accents of modern Protestant theology, especially to Bonhoeffer's concept of a "religionless Christianity," to Bultmann and his struggle for a demythologizing of the New Testament, and to Tillich and his symbolic theology. *Honest to God* aroused a number of younger theologians (among them T. Altizer, W. Hamilton, and with important differences, Paul van Buren) who then established on their own, and with great passion, the "Death of God" theology.

At about the same time the battle was joined against the theology of the first article on German soil. It was mainly Herbert Braun and his friends who, provocatively and radically, put the question of God on the agenda of German theology. They undertook a thorough questioning of traditional theism, not only from the standpoint of the New Testament, but in the interest of a Christian witness to the human situation. For Braun, the New Testament critic, the concept of God is by no means an indispensable ingredient of the authentic New Testament kerygma, which can be presented without even mentioning of the word "God." Of course, the biblical texts speak of God on every page. But that is not the substance of their message. Theistic language and conceptuality were common to Judaism as well as Hellenism, and the New Testament writers simply placed their faith in the linguistic and ideological framework of their time. But what was authentically new was not that framework, but rather a liberating disclosure of human existence in the light of radical demand

and radical grace. Today the world view of our contemporaries is no longer hellenistic, medieval, or even deistic. Thus, for Braun, any attempt to bind theology to such problematical theistic forms, to impose on them such an impossible ideological handicap, means a catastrophic perversion of the liberating message of the New Testament.

Other critical voices have been raised from quite different cultural and social contexts. Efforts on behalf of an "atheistic theology" were undertaken in the socialistic countries, specifically in East Germany, which attempted to answer the challenge of Marxism without being forced into the "ideological positions" of an anti-materialism and an anti-atheism. Such theologies almost embraced atheism in their Marxist interpretation of the world and society. But these attempts met with little success in the church, because often rather clumsy official propaganda had put the church on guard against any form or approximation of atheism. Nor did they have much luck with the Marxist public, where they appeared somewhat ambiguous and equivocal: why not just convert to Marxism in the first place? But they did have a significance in their desire to be a genuine—and not a false—"vexation" to the given social milieu. At any rate, it is noteworthy that a radical critical questioning of deistic theology was raised in this ecumenical area too.

What do these manifold and radical "theological-atheistic" voices mean for a theology of the first article? Looking at the biblical message, it is difficult to claim that the biblical concept of God can be explained away simply by reference to the background of Judaism and Hellenism. Viewing the apostolic and prophetic message, it seems entirely possible to discover an authentic biblical "theism," or better, a message of the living god, who is not a god of the philosophers but rather, as Pascal previously claimed, the god of Abraham, Isaac and Jacob. "Atheistic theology," then, appears in this light to be insufficiently differentiating and an oversimplification of the problem.

From quite a different direction, it is doubtful that the question of God is as dead for modern religion as the atheistic theologians presume. Naturally a mythological theology, be it antique, medieval, or modern, is a burden and a vexation. Demythologizing is a permanent task of the church. But here, too, one should avoid generalization. For not only is there a "transcendence which alienates," that is, a false objectivity which is simply incompatible with the gospel and with the freedom of Christian men, but there is also a "transcendence which liberates." This is the transcendence of grace. The concept of God can still perform substantial service in the desire for dialogue, and it seems that some atheists appreciate this possibility better than some theologians. In Christian-Marxist conversations it was often fascinating to observe the fresh interest with which several Marxists posed the question of transcendence, and even pursued its specifically theological consequences. The title of the book by V. Gardavsky, *God Is Not Quite Dead,* is not just an attractive *bon mot.*[3]

Thus, in my opinion, the theology of the first article is not laid to rest by recent criticism. But it is thoroughly called into question. It is discredited in its traditional claim of representing that form of theological and religious thinking most suited to modern man and of advocating the case of faith more appropriately and believably than a Christological theology. Precisely in this respect has there taken place within the tide of modern scepticism a dramatic intellectual transformation.

For some of us in the thirties and forties, theistic ideals still stood substantially unchallenged, while the specifically Christian confession produced estrangement. In our school days it was not hard for us to accept a theology of the first article which was impressively presented in the best recognized spiritual tradition and which was thus in the existing cultural context "socially acceptable." What did cost us much existential struggle was adopting the second, the Christological, article. That was culturally so foreign that we were able to overcome it only by a venture of faith and by honest and long intellectual effort. Unless I deceive myself, the situation today is different. It is the theses of a universal theism that have become problematical for most people—more so than belief in Christ. This means that the path of a theology

of the first article, in programmatic and often well-intended eva-
sion of the second, has become much more uncertain. The effort
to save the church on this basis has proved illusory.

## Theology of the Third Article

Parallel to this movement of a theology of the first article
(and sometimes with mutual crossovers) ran a related development which one could designate as theology of the third article.
The third article in the Apostles' Creed was originally inseparable
from the Christological article preceding it: The Lord is the Spirit
(2 Cor. 3:17). Modern theology has severed this tie and "liberated" the spirit from its Christological embrace. It has been, like
the concept of God in the first article, reinterpreted and univer-
salized. It is concerned now with "spirit" in general, and finally,
with the "human spirit." In this sense a theology of the third article corresponds to the tendency toward anthropocentrism which
began in the Renaissance and moved into the present via the
Enlightenment and nineteenth century theology. With this term
one could—if somewhat schematically—denote the entire movement from the middle ages to modernity. The medieval theocratic
(or better, ontocratic) view of the world has been superseded
by an interpretation in which man (rather than "God," "orders,"
or "institutions") plays the decisive role. "Man is the measure
of all things" in regard to nature as well as society. Thus man
takes the world into his hands and it becomes—with all its actual
and potential conditions—his world, the "world of man." This
includes the world's religion, which now belongs to man's do-
main. For this religious sphere is only a question of man's spirit,
as it touches on the sacred. Thus a theology of the third article
appears to be the appropriate attitude of religious thinking in
modern times.

The golden age of theology of the third article was probably
the nineteenth century, and began with the father of modern
theology, Friedrich Schleiermacher. In a sense Schleiermacher
could be termed a Christological (or better, Christologizing)
theologian. In his *Glaubenslehre* he advocated what he considered
an intellectually acceptable Christology, but his youthful writings,

which express his romantic disposition, are examples of a resolute theology of the third article. For him, the essence of religion is "feeling and observation of the universe." [4] The actual mediator between God and man is the aroused inwardness of human feeling, the mediating "tertium" of our spirit. For Jesus Christ there is yet no substantial place. In his *Über die Religion* Schleiermacher presents Jesus only as the historical founder of Christianity and does not even mention him by name (although Plato and Spinoza are addressed in apostrophe—and Spinoza is labeled "saint"). When Schleiermacher does attempt to work Jesus into his system, it is only with the painful expenditure of much speculative energy. A good example in his *Weihnachtsfeier* (1806): "What we [in the Christmas celebration] are celebrating is nothing other than ourselves, as we are in toto, our human nature . . . viewed and recognized out of the divine principle. Why, however, we must set up One . . . and why precisely this One . . . will be made clear [in the following]." [5] What follows is rather complicated. Man in himself is nothing other than Earth-Spirit, the cognition of the Earth in its eternal Being and in its constantly changing Becoming. Thus there is in the world no corruption and no waste and no necessity for redemption. The individual, on the other hand, runs afoul of other earthly forms; that is his downfall. Only if he loses his isolated existence and finds it again in the community of mankind—as represented by the Church—will his alienation be overcome. And finally comes the Christological crowning of the argument. This church must have a beginning point, which is in the genuine godly man, Jesus Christ. "In Christ we thus see the earth spirit form itself into self-consciousness in the individual." [6]

I should emphasize that this theology of the third article was not intended as an infiltration or an undermining of the Christian faith. On the contrary, most advocates of this direction, certainly Schleiermacher (and one would have to add Kant and Hegel for that matter), regarded themselves as advocates of the best interpretation of the Christian message. They did not intend the destruction of faith, but rather its construction within a changed intellectual climate. In this respect Schleiermacher is especially exemplary. From the beginning to the end he fought for the cause of the Christian religion. But it was clear to him, as to the others, that there was no more reliable path to this positive goal than a theology of the third article. The second article had to be sacrificed (in terms of its original content) in order to be saved; it had to discover a stronger basis in the third. Despite all attacks by sceptics and critics and atheists, the saving *ceterum autem* of these remarkable thinkers continued to be expressed in the thesis: religion is the affair of man.

This theology of the third article had scarcely been formulated before it was disputed—first by individual radicals, but soon thereafter by the broad current of secular history. The first man to pose the radical question was Ludwig Feuerbach. His criticism was effective because he accepted the presuppositions of such a theology but then drew opposing conclusions. That "religion is man's affair" is also Feuerbach's thesis. But whereas the theologians of the third article hoped by means of this thesis to save religion by proving its indisputable place in man's spirit, Feuerbach planned to use the same thesis to uproot and dispatch religion. Religion is the affair of man—yes indeed! It is a human affair and nothing more. The reasonable nucleus of all theological mystery is anthropology. In his religious ideas and longings, man projects himself into illusionary dimensions. Such projection is understandable but dangerous, for man thus becomes alienated. Feuerbach maintained that it was possible to look through the mist of religion and overcome religious alienation only when the theology of the spirit is recognized for what it is, namely, the phenomenology of the human spirit. That is the logic of his undertaking. Tirelessly he analyzed the world of religion and, with special prejudice, Christology, and he pursued this method to the bitter end. In his relatively unknown "Preliminary Theses toward the Reform of Philosophy," he states

> The Christian religion has bound the name of man and the name of God into the one name of God-Man—has raised the name man so that it is an attribute of the highest being. Conforming to this truth recent philosophy has turned this attribute into the substantive, the predicate into the subject—the new philosophy is the realized Idea—the truth (actuality) of Christianity. But

precisely because it has the essence of Christianity in it, it gives up the name. Christianity has pronounced the truth. This unarguable, pure, unsullied truth is a new truth—a new autonomous deed of mankind.[7]

Feuerbach's criticism was taken up and pursued by other thinkers of the nineteenth and twentieth centuries: by Marx and Engels and their assessment of religion as the opiate of the masses; by Nietzsche with his thesis that religion enslaves and endangers mankind; by Freud and his analysis of religion and the strategies of the unconscious; by other thinkers too numerous to mention; and above all by the anonymous effects of progressing secularization. It would definitely be an unfair oversimplification to say that the case of religion had thus been settled. Beside these voices stand others, which point to the anthropological relevance of religion. One should not ignore the likes of Karl Jaspers, the Aemrican process philosophy, or indeed certain developments within Marxism itself. But it has become clear in all this that a universal theology of the third article, a theology of the spirit, in which "religion is man's affair" is a deeply ambiguous matter. To build a church upon such a theology seems less possible today than ever before.

### Christological Concentration

The preceding reflections render a relatively negative assessment of theologies of the first and third articles. These two paths have failed to accomplish their goal of a more believable form of theology and the Christian message for modern man. Their ideological presumptions—the idea of a universal theism and the idea of a religious humanity—appear to be, for contemporary theology, more a burden than a mitigation. Now, what does this mean, positively, for the path of evangelical theology today?

Perhaps one positive meaning might be lurking in just the failure of the first two options. How would it be if we were to consider again the fact that "Christianity has something to do with Jesus Christ"? Or—to add an apostolic word to that of a modern atheist—that the church and theology not even today "can lay down any other foundation than that which is laid, which is

Jesus Christ"? (1 Cor. 3:11) How would it be if we recognized those other two paths as well intended detours and turned again to the real path? In the sense of the New Testament that would certainly mean to take the path of a Christological theology with new concentration. Would that not be an open possibility? Open when viewed from the unequivocal position of the New Testament, but perhaps also open when viewed from the contemporary situation.

Contemporary evangelical theology, however weak and ill-advised it sometimes appears to be, has certainly entered upon the path of a Christological concentration. The concept of "Christological concentration" stems from Karl Barth, who, in his report on "How my mind has changed" wrote the following concerning the years 1929 to 1939: "I had to learn in these years that Christian doctrine exclusively, logically, and comprehensively has to be directly or indirectly the doctrine of Jesus Christ as the promised living word of God in order to earn its name and in order to build up the Christian church in the world in the way the Christian church needs to be built up." [8] And thirteen years later, on Christmas eve of 1952, he wrote in a significant letter to Bultmann about his understanding of the New Testament: "At the risk of further head-shaking and displeasure I still venture to whisper to you only this one thing, that I have become more and more a Zinzendorfian to the extent that in the New Testament I began to be occupied more and more only with the central figure as such—which is to say with any and everything only in the light and evidence of this central figure." [9] The decisive thing is that in this program of a "Christological concentration," Barth was operating in a wide-ranging and profound effort to think through the entire area of church dogma rigorously and consistently. One can accurately say that there has been no other theologian in our time, and not really in the entire age since the Reformation, who could have approached and realized the program of a Christological theology so clear-sightedly. The entire system of orthodox theology was reconstructed, every stone tapped and tested, and then reset in a new, dynamic Christological context. For some, Karl Barth is considered almost forgotten. Yet precisely in this basic desire and basic execution of his theological path he remains very much alive as one of the most relevant theologians ever.

Barth may be the most significant theologian of "Christological concentration," but it is important to note that he was by no means alone. I am thinking not only of his "school," but rather of other contemporary theologians who traveled their own paths, sometimes in expressed discord with Barth. This is true of that other heavyweight of present day theology, Barth's pathmate or antipode, Bultmann (which relationship Barth described as "Like a whale . . . and an elephant meeting each other in boundless astonishment on some oceanic shore . . .").[10] Naturally Bultmann's Christology is quite different from the Christology of church dogma. And naturally from the Barthian standpoint— as well as from other standpoints—it has its problematical features. And yet it would be wrong to absolutize what Barth said about mutual boundless astonishment. No matter how different the two theologians are, in one decisive tendency they are close, namely, in the program (if not the realization) of a Christological theology. Bultmann considers himself a "Christocentric theologian." The occurrence of Christ is, for him too, the unsurrenderable center of the New Testament. Their paths part in the explication of, but not in their programmatic fidelity to, this occurrence.

The third "Big B" of German theology, Bonhoeffer, can also be designated an example of a theology of Christological concentration. This is true to the very depths of his personal experience and his martyrdom. His lectures on Christology, which have been preserved by others, show a strict Christological dimension, and his letters from prison express the practical, historical, theological, and socio-ethical consequences of this concentration. It is significant that the great theme which appears to him to be both theologically decisive and loaded with future importance is defined in the words "Christ and the World Come of Age." This phrase is placed in conscious contrast to themes of metaphysics and inwardness found in theologies of the first and third articles. Thus Bonhoeffer prepared the way for evangelical theology of the postwar period, which was to be the path of Christological concentration.

But it is not just the big names in European theology of the last generation that can be mentioned as examples of a Christocentric reorientation of evangelical theology. Should not in this connection—so to speak, in the same breath with the name Bonhoeffer—the name Paul Lehmann be mentioned? Has he not for a lifetime persistently and independently advocated a theology of Christological concentration?

And there are others. It is noteworthy that even the sharply critical and skeptical among the contemporary theologians—those, for example, who utterly reject any theology of the first or third article—very often disclose Christological motives. This is true of Robinson, von Braun, and a few of the "Death of God" theologians. When, for example, Paul van Buren sums up his complete dismantling of Christian thought, it is Jesus of Nazareth who stands out for him on the ruins of tradition as an open and fruitful path. Of course, some of these thinkers advocate only a "mini-Christology," in which the reduction of Christological motifs is ruthlessly carried out, so that the Christological consensus in today's theology becomes thereby rather narrow and ambiguous. One could also say that it is not easy to build a church here either. And yet, as variable and disputable as this direction of contemporary theology is in its content and motifs, the astonishing consensus as far as basic direction is concerned is a datum of significance and, in all the weakness and helplessness of our present theological existence, a hopeful datum at that.

Why a hopeful sign?

It seems to me that, from both the perspective of the New Testament and the perspective of the contemporary situation, a theology of Christological concentration brings with it two fundamental possibilities, two "openings," which could be liberating forces for theology and the church.

As far as the New Testament is concerned, there is no doubt that a "Christological concentration" appears not just as one of many possible concentrations, as one experiment among others, but rather as *the* concentration. Christian theology is reflection on the *centrum securitas,* on the actual middle, on the *Fundamentum Christus.* (To cite once again the key apostolic sentence: "No one can lay a foundation other than the one that is laid.") Thus, from the point of view of the kerygma, a concentration in this direction is to be viewed as a positive possibility, provided it is not understood as a one-sided and "sectarian" christomonism, but in its broad trinitarian context.

At the same time a theology of Christological concentration offers a better chance of fruitful dialogue with modern man, and thus a better chance of fulfilling the promise made by theologians of the other two paths. I say nothing more than a chance. There is no universal guarantee, no patent solution. This is true especially with respect to the second article. As the word of the cross and of resurrection, the Christological word is still today a *skandalon,* and it will remain so throughout history. A Christological theology, however, offers the clear-cut path to this genuine, central, kerygmatic *skandalon.*

But above all, it is from the Christological standpoint that precisely those dimensions of life such as history and society, alienation and reconciliation, which are so tremendously important for the development of a true humanity, become accessible. And in this sense Paul Lehmann's affirmation of an ethic and a politics in "a Christian context" appears both correct and possible. It is this noteworthy convergence of a new comprehension of the apostolic message with our intellectual-historical experience that seems hopeful. The result should be a theology which is simultaneously biblical and relevant to the intellectual situation of the times, faithful to the kerygma, and faithful to our contemporaries in the Church and in the world.

I close with a personal observation. For me, Christological concentration is not just an academic-theological phenomenon but an ecumenical and ecclesiastical occurrence. Would the ecumenical advances in our time, for example in new encounters with the Catholic church, even be thinkable, let alone fruitful, without a "Christological concentration"? Above all, I think of the experience of theological and ecclesiastical existence in the socialist countries, for it was this Christological reorientation which helped us to withstand the crisis into which the church was thrown "at the end of the Constantinian era."

What does the "end of the Constantinian era" mean in this connection? In terms of intellectual history, it means an understanding of universal religious and theistic elements as the climate of public life. In contemporary socialist society this is done by means of programmatic secularization through education and propaganda with an anti-theistic and anti-religious bias, as well as by means of *de facto* secularization of cultural and social life. In this atmosphere a universal theistic or religious theology may find many individual sympathizers who desire to express their resentment against the changing tide of history. But this motivation is exposed to the same criticism Bonhoeffer leveled against an existentially and "methodistically" oriented theology: it is a way of staying in the ghetto, a way of forming a sect within a changed culture and society.

By contrast, Christological concentration helps the church surmount this ghetto temptation and helps theology overcome intellectual "Constantinianism." It is not bound to dead-and-gone views of the world and of man, to theistic-religious elements of a "Christian civilization," or "Christian culture." It attempts with Bonhoeffer to draw its theme from the real center of faith and to present it in a hopeful way: Christ and the world come of age. Here the path is open wide even for the unchurched of our post-Constantinian world. As a theology of evangelical solidarity and not of patronage, a theology of dialogue and not of religious encapsulation, a theology of hope and not of conserving, this Christocentric theology helps even in times of deepest convulsions to guide and comfort the congregations of Jesus Christ.

---

1. Translated by Julius S. Winkler, Davidson College. For an expanded development of the argument in this abbreviated essay, the reader is directed to Professor Lochman's book, *Christus oder Prometheus* (Hamburg: Furche Verlag, 1972).
2. Ernst Troeltsch, *Gesammelte Schriften*, Vol. 4 (=*Aufsätze zur Geistesgeschichte und Religionssoziologie*), ed. Hans Baron (Tübingen: J. C. B. Mohr, 1925), p. 845.

3. Vitezslav Gardavský, *Gott ist nicht ganz tot* (Munich: Kaiser Verlag, 1968).

4. Friedrich Schleiermacher, *Ueber die Religion*, ed. Martin Rade (Berlin: Deutsche Bibliothek, n.d.), p. 37.

5. Friedrich Schleiermacher, *Kleine Schriften und Predigten 1800-1820*, Vol. 1, ed. Hayo Gerdes and Emanuel Hirsch (Berlin: De Gruyter Verlag, 1970), pp. 271 f.

6. *Ibid.*, p. 273.

7. Ludwig Feuerbach, *Kleine Philosophische Schriften (1842-1845)*, ed. Max Gustav Lange (Leipzig: Verlag Felix Meiner, 1950), p. 78.

8. Karl Barth, *Der Götze Wackelt*, ed. Karl Kupisch (Berlin: Käthe Vogt Verlag, 1961), p. 185. Cf. *Christian Century*, Vol. 56 (1939), p. 1132.

9. *Karl Barth—Rudolf Bultmann Briefwechsel 1922-1966*, ed. Bernd Jaspert (Zürich: Theologischer Verlag, 1971), p. 199.

10. *Ibid.*, p. 196.

# Reorientation in Theology: Listening to Black Theology

The situation of American Protestantism today requires that theology "conjecture" its own frame of church reference. This may appear as an appeal to an *ecclesiola in ecclesia,* but ought actually to be an appeal to Christ as head of the church. For while Christ is always the Christ *for* the church he is also the Christ *against* the church, and he is the latter especially in times when the church loses its proper self-understanding. Today we are in such an emergency situation. The church has become subject to the powers that be. It is no longer free. There is considerable justification for talking about *the political captivity* of the church in the United States.[1]

Thus, political theology, as a response to this situation, is the appropriate form of dogmatic prolegomena today. Political theology is not at all a matter of making theology political. It is a serious attempt to analyze the emergency situation within the church. The major concern of contemporary theology must be the liberation of the church from the powers and principalities that seek to destroy it. So the theology of the church that appears to be developing in terms of *doctrinal content* is not just a political theology, but a liberation theology.

## Liberation as a Theological Issue

Neo-liberal theology in the sixties in America sought to

find a common ground between the modern mind and Christian thought, but in so doing it disregarded significant factors that were perverting the church. It disregarded—at least on the level of significant theological construction—the fact that the Christian church was split into black and white camps. It took black theology—which made its appearance at the end of the sixties—to dramatize that split. Now we realize that there had been a conflict over the nature of the church for a long time. The black-white split is not the only theme of the conflict, but it plays a crucial role. Black theologians are now asking: how could the white church develop a theology without taking into account black suffering under white oppression?

Black theology has raised an issue in the church that might otherwise have been by-passed. It is the question of how the Christian self evolves. The challenge to think black or to become black is not an invitation to become neurotic.[2] It is, as best as we can understand it, a challenge to view the evolution of the self from the perspective of the wretched of the earth, the contemporary slaves. Obviously contemporary consciousness also evolves in reference to the modern world view. But in my opinion the development of individual selfhood today is less dependent on how a person sizes up the world at large than on how he regards his relationships to his fellows.

The issues regarding the development of the self are complex, and much can be learned from various analyses of the social fabric. A brief appeal to Hegel, however, might be instructive insofar as his assessment became influential through the Marxist critique of society. In the *Phenomenology of the Spirit*, Hegel begins his analysis of the master-servant relationship with the thesis that self-consciousness exists only when it is acknowledged or recognized. Self-consciousness on a primal level must come out of itself and find itself in another being, seeing its own self in the other. But then again it must return to itself, giving the otherness "back again to the other self-consciousness."[3] At this point one has to understand that for Hegel the action of the self has a double significance in that it is "its own action and the action of the other as well." The logic here implied is that action from one side only would be useless, "because what is to happen can only be brought about by means of both."

All of this leads Hegel to say that "an individual makes his appearance in antithesis to an individual." We thus arrive at two self-consciousnesses which "prove themselves and each other through a life-and-death struggle." They cannot avoid the struggle, "for they must bring their certainty of themselves, the certainty of being for themselves, to the level of objective truth, and make this a fact both in the case of the other and in their own case as well. And it is solely by risking life that freedom is obtained; only thus is it tried and proved that the essential nature of self-consciousness is not bare existence, is not the immediate form in which it at first makes its appearance, is not its mere absorption in the expanse of life."

The relationship between master and servant is for Hegel a particular instance of what he is talking about. Here the life-and-death struggle between selves is concretely experienced in the different development of the servant and the master. "The master relates himself to the servant mediately through independent existence, for that is precisely what keeps the servant in bond; it is his chain, from which he could not, in the struggle, get away, and for that reason he proves himself dependent, shows that his independence consists in being a thing. . . . In the master, the self-existence is felt to be an other, is only external; in fear, the self-existence is present implicitly; in fashioning the thing, self-existence comes to be felt explicitly as its own proper being, and it attains the consciousness that itself exists in its own right and on its own account."

It is impossible in this brief essay to interpret the whole of Hegel's view of the master-servant relationship. The major point is that even philosophically, and entirely apart from the contemporary struggle, that relationship can be seen as much more determinative of self-consciousness than appears on the surface. This pinpoints some of the difficulties we are facing today. What the emphasis of black theology amounts to in this context is the realization that the black in this country is still largely the servant and mainly develops his self-consciousness as he filters through his mind the wishes of the white master and receives his approval. The other side of the matter is that the white does not have his self-consciousness apart from the black's dependence on him. The master-servant syndrome in the black-white tension is probably more determinative of who a person is in the United States today than any other dimension of our existence. What is more, it is bolstered by political agreements. And political power undergirds the master's position in his determination to control what the servant may do.

Ironically, the church is the last bastion of the superiority of the master. For as long as the white master can go to his communion table without having to share it with the black his sense of superiority remains ultimately undisturbed. It is exactly at this point that liberation becomes a theological issue. The person who uses the church to support his visions of superiority needs to be freed for a new understanding of the self. The church is the community where this freedom can be concretely experienced. And the concrete experience of freedom in community is liberation.

Thinking black, becoming black—something a black also has to learn—probably means no more than becoming aware of the existence of the servant, the oppressed, and to take one's place beside him in order to liberate the church, so that there can be a place where there are brothers and sisters in Christ who mutually acknowledge freedom as the core of human life.

### Christology, Epistemology, and Anthropology

Once this is understood the issues of the theological spectrum become reoriented. Christology speaks of a new selfhood that is not based on the life-and-death struggle between two selves; the emergence of a master-self, or the emergence of a servant-self. Christ is not—as with a large group of neo-liberals—God's "stand-in" who holds the world open for God.[4] He is the liberator who, in identifying with the oppressed, frees man from the powers and principalities that condemn him to the life-and-death struggle between selves. Incarnation on a primal level means that that struggle has already been transcended. In this one man, Jesus Christ, each self is addressed as an equal partner of that *coporate selfhood* which establishes the reality of our individual selves. In Hegel's scheme, the master remains the master, and the slave remains the slave. In other schemes the master-servant syndrome is overcome through struggle. But from the gospel perspective *all* schemes of human self-orientation will be contradicted because they fail to acknowledge the reality of the corporate selfhood that is already real in Christ. Christ functions as the counter-self; he is the contradiction of selfhood as man usually understands it.

This new understanding of Christ is possible only within the church, the community in which corporate selfhood can become the principle of existence, where one self approaches another self on the basis of a new ground. But as long as the church as a whole does not afford the context in which this reality is mutually acknowledged, we need to join in a *collegia libertatis,* a liberation church, that as counter-church appeals to the conscience of the church as a whole by pointing to *the Christ against the church.* We move too quickly into society with our schemes of liberation, never stopping to think what it is that, from the Christian perspective, needs to be liberated. In view of the fact that we may regard Christ as the counter-self, it is first of all the church that needs liberation. In other words, it is pointless to think of a liberation church as a revolutionary cadre for blowing up bridges across the Potomac. A liberation church is concerned first with the liberation of men in those places where *Christians* wield power over their fellowmen. The need is not to elaborate a new ecclesiology, but to stress that a Christology relevant for liberation can only be developed among a people who take the church as the context of life seriously.

A Christology developed within community understands the incarnation as participating in the life-and-death struggle in which the selves clash. Christ *takes sides* in the struggle. He turns to the wretched of the earth, the disadvantaged, and becomes their liberator. He controls the human situation. But we can understand this only from the viewpoint of the oppressed.

At this point we also need to take a new look at theological epistemology. After confrontation with the Christ event and after we have labored at wresting from this event the meaning it will yield, the question of *how* all this makes sense becomes important. The question of theological epistemology is simple: how do we know this event as the Christ event, the event of our liberation? On one level, the immediate answer is that we know it as we take sides with Christ in the battle for survival among the wretched of the earth. It is completely useless to raise the question of theological epistemology as if it were primarily a question for a theological classroom. Christ on the primal level is not an abstract problem for intellectual reflection.

In taking sides with the wretched of the earth, we do not know abstractly why we know, but we know concretely the power that makes us know freedom. In loving the woman of your life, the "epistemology" of your relationship does not precede your falling in love, but as you fall in love you begin to know the liberating power of love. The gift of liberation that faith embraces has many analogies in history.[5] Freedom is freedom wherever we find it. The truth of freedom as freedom in Christ is only "proved" by its stronger resilience, its greater nerve, its tougher steel, and its longer breath. Freedom will recognize freedom whenever it finds it. Theological epistemology here is not primarily concerned with overcoming the nasty subject-object split (which, incidentally, Hegel overcame in his own way a long time ago) or how we might fit religious language into secular language. The issue is how the experience of greater freedom will be embraced by man.

The criteria for knowing transcendent freedom are thus provided by existential knowledge, not abstract knowledge. But it should also be understood that, because of man's sin, there is no immediate access to transcendent freedom. Here the problem of theological epistemology merges with the issues of Christian anthropology. It is especially at this point that the confrontation between black and white theology begins to shape a new American church experience.[6] It is unfortunate that James Cone introduces his view of man as a fallen creature only *after* he has discussed the nature of man on general grounds. We know man only as fallen. And it is exactly the fallenness of man that has again come to our attention in the black-white confrontation. For Cone, sin is a community concept: "To be in sin, then, is to deny the values that make the community what it is." [7] We can agree with him that white American Protestants, whether as liberals, neo-orthodox or fundamentalists, discuss sin too much in the abstract. But it is not clear how much one can learn from such a claim as the following: "Because sin is a concept that is meaningful only for an oppressed community as it reflects upon its liberation, it is not possible to make a universal analysis that is meaningful for both black and white people. Black theology believes that the true nature of sin is perceived only in the moment of oppression and liberation." [8] Taking into consideration such figures of Christian history as Martin Luther or John Wesley, one cannot agree with the principle of Cone's view of sin. The universalizing of sin is a grave problem in that it often results in sin being taken much too lightly. But time and again in the history of the Christian community men have stood up to confess man's self-contradiction as did Anselm: *nondum considerasti quanti ponderis sit peccatum.* ("You have not as yet considered the weight of sin!")

Just as the other tenets of the Christian faith, the doctrine of sin cannot be developed apart from the Christian community. In his emphasis on community, Cone is getting at an important point. But how, within this community, is sin experienced? Is it not in confrontation with God's liberating activity *in Christ?* Sin is man's concealing himself from the openness of God in Christ, a concealment in which he makes himself the center of a make-believe world, like Adam and Eve in the Garden. Sin is man's concealing from himself his true situation, his corporate selfhood in which he is primarily accountable to God. Man is free—

in the openness of God. But he begins to regard himself as autonomous and in doing so hides from himself his true condition (symbolically expressed in the first couple's hiding in the garden). So he chooses to quantify his efforts in terms of the values of good and evil and thereby misuses his freedom.[9]

What is needed in a radically new image of man? Since he has lost his innocence, we cannot imagine what freedom might have been. But we do see in Adam and Eve that sin is the concealment of freedom. Only in Jesus Christ do we get an indication of what openness toward freedom really is. In him we meet the direction of our destiny. And since we remain in our sinful state, even while we believe in him, our use of freedom is always refracted. In the community of faith we might be able to affirm with Cone: "Sin then is the condition of human existence in which man denies the essence of God's liberating activity as revealed in Jesus Christ."[10] But that liberating activity impinges upon the totality of human existence, the infinite ways in which we hide our freedom and hide ourselves from freedom. And in its light we need to become more modest in regard to who we are as persons. The *imago Dei* is not a given, but is at best an "imaging" toward the future, an "imaging" that evolves into true manhood by the liberating work of God.

### The Problem of the Historical Jesus

The confrontation between black and white theology impresses upon us more so than any other contemporary circumstance the need to view man in the light of Jesus Christ. Man without regard to Jesus Christ is an abstraction. He is the real beginning of the creation of man. And for that reason he and man are intimately intertwined. Jesus Christ is the *first* true Adam. What becomes utterly important is to see our manhood in him rather than have our self-understanding determine who he is.

In confrontation with black theology it becomes very clear how much our image of Jesus Christ reflects our white Western values. Says Cone, "The white conservatives and liberals alike present images of a white Christ that are completely alien to the liberation of the black community. Their Christ is a mild, easy-going white American who can afford to mouth luxuries of 'love,' 'mercy,' 'long-suffering,' and other white irrelevancies, because he has a multi-billion-dollar military force to protect him from the encroachments of the ghetto and the 'communist conspiracy.' " [11] Cone tries to tackle the problem by appealing to the historical Jesus: "Black Theology also sees this as the chief error of white American religious thought, which allows the white condition to determine the meaning of Christ. The historical Jesus must be taken seriously if we intend to avoid making Christ into our own images." [12]

Here we encounter perhaps the toughest problem of the black-white confrontation in theology. How are we going to get at the historical Jesus? We must certainly use the tools of historical scholarship—which is a universal enterprise. Thus, the historical Jesus cannot be tied to the black community only. And it has not as yet been clarified what the use of historico-critical tools relative to Jesus by blacks and whites in concert might mean. But as we try to regrasp and retell the gospel stories, it becomes quite clear that we encounter the witness of the church and not, in every respect, the "historical Jesus." [13] And this means that it was not merely that something happened once upon a time in and through a person, an individual called Jesus of Nazareth, but that something also happened to those and among those who believed in him and followed him.

This does not at all eliminate historical research. What the historico-critical method will do time and again is to keep our feet on the ground and make us realize that we are confronted with the possibility of transcendent freedom through a particular historical event. It requires faith, however, to see in this human being, Jesus of Nazareth, God's act of liberation. This is not *gnosis,* which disregards the humanity of the liberating agent, but it respects the offense of that agent. Only in faith can the real point of the historical reality of Jesus of Nazareth be grasped.

Cone's approach, in my view, becomes more complex than necessary at this point when he says:

> Unless we can articulate clearly an image of Christ that is consistent with the essence of the biblical message and at the same time relate it to the struggle for black liberation, Black Theology loses its reason for being. It is thus incumbent upon us to demonstrate the relationship between the historical Jesus and the oppressed, showing that the equation of the contemporary Christ with Black Power arises out of a serious encounter with the biblical revelation.[14]

Is it not sufficient to encounter the biblical Christ and to realize that *he* identifies with the oppressed to the end of liberating man? Why does there have to be an equation of the contemporary Christ with black power? Could it not be misleading to identify Christ with any contemporary power? What of equating Christ with communist power? Don't we move here into a sphere where sauce for the goose is sauce for the gander? Wasn't the communist proletariat always the oppressed people par excellence?

Christ has promised to be wherever wretchedness is, but not so as to permit anyone to control his presence or to pontificate about it. In the parable, it is the righteous who ask: "Lord, when did we see thee hungry and feed thee, or thirsty and give thee drink?" (Matt. 25:37) The mystery of Christ's presence is no justification for a retreat from responsibility for the wretched of the earth. But it points to the need for faith, the difficulty of putting our hands on the truth. We can ultimately find Christ only through himself as he meets us in Jesus of Nazareth. And God only through Christ! At one point of his ministry, Jesus felt constrained to say of himself: "If anyone says to you, 'Lo, here is the Christ!' or 'There he is!' do not believe it." (Matt. 24:23) The Christ cannot be identified *by us* with just any historical particularity. He has his identity in himself. And we must find God's identity in him—even in his blackness. *Christ Jesus is black the way no other man is black*—because in his sovereign way, in radical contingency, God turns his assumption of lowliness into transcendent freedom for man. No other person or event has accomplished that.

### The Language of Liberation

What we encounter in the Gospels is the language of those

who received Jesus Christ. We pointed before to the criteria of
existential language according to which we "know" that the
event of Jesus Christ makes sense. This means that something
is triggered in us that verifies itself. All of us are still influenced
by the view of language as only a report of data in precise,
accurate, and objectifying terms. The question is whether this
use of language is the primary one for grasping the Christian
faith. In the confrontation between black and white the issue
of language becomes especially pressing, since what is at stake
is the communication of freedom. If the material analogy for
understanding the Christian experience is freedom, is there also
an analogy of the language that communicates this freedom?
Can it somehow be grasped by men that Christian language
communicating freedom might function in a peculiar way?

In *The Orphic Voice,* Elizabeth Sewell offers an instance
of such analogy. Language is here conceived of as an activity
rather than an entity: "This means giving up the right to abstract
language into timeless pattern, and making the effort to grasp it
not as a fixed phenomenon but as a moving event, language plus
mind, subject to time and process and change—to try to think
in biological terms, perhaps." [15] In this understanding of language
the word has a peculiar function: "A word means the mental
activity it conjures up, just as much as it means the object to
which it refers and all the past uses to which it has been put.
This activity is an essential part of language's workings, and it
is as much physical as mental. . . ." The major component of
words "is the active response which they call up in the mind.
This is what makes the interpretation of them vary so much
between one mind and another, since human beings vary widely
in the forms of activity of which they are capable." This is a way
of looking at language in which "the universe of discourse
turns out to be a world of action and of individual minds acting
in certain concordant or discordant ways." Underlying all uses of
language is a basic use: "Word-language and poetry are at once
its highest expression and the best key we yet have to it. . . ." The
activity involved in this kind of language underlies also all other
language activity: "Analysis, then—logic, dialectic—rest on a fun-

damental act of confidence and synthesis (or call it faith and love)." Words spoken are thus a total human event. Both body and mind are involved: "In other words, the body thinks. . . . The human organism thinks as a whole, and our division of it into mind and body is the result of overemphasis on logic and intellect in near isolation which has led us into so one-sided a view of the activity of thought, so gross an underestimation of the body's forms of thought and knowledge."

Sewell at one point also draws Christian language into the field of a new understanding of language. "Christian theology in its speculative aspect, mythology or poetry, and science are three disciplines of discovery and learning. They differ in their subject matter; they are unified in their structure and aim. Thought of in this way, they may all three appear less as a body of knowledge, something you possess, than as a particular activity founded in an appropriate set of beliefs," It may not be important at all in the long run for Christian language to have been mentioned in this argument. But it does help us to see one view of language that can function as an analogy to the use of Christian language.

What this analogy of a new understanding of language suggests is that as we appropriate the language of freedom in the Gospels we are appropriating activity, a body-mind unity. And in terms of our subject, the question is in what sense these words can generate an appropriate activity on the level of the black-white confrontation. On this level the issue is not primarily whether or not the adequate image ("photograph") of Jesus is formed in our mind, but whether or not we can "get in" on his activity. Obviously our activity in response cannot be uniform. All of us are individuals reflecting a variety of backgrounds and experiences. But the point is whether or not on a primal level of life we are able to respond in the totality of our being to the totality of being that is packed into this particular language.

Only that view of language is adequate to the concerns of black theology that is able to open man for freedom. The gospel demands a total response, a body-mind or deed-word response in which man grasps the primordial unity of his being in freedom.

To use "personal pronoun language," what is communicated is not something strange to me. Rather, the basic possibility of my own being is challenged to express itself in its most primal way, namely in freedom. Is this experience somewhat analogous to what blacks have in mind when they speak of soul? One would hope so. In any case, definite images are triggered in my mind when I am addressed by the gospel of freedom. But the gospel does not demand of me that I get into particular images like so many straitjackets. It seeks to draw me out of myself. It wants to liberate me. Therefore one is not justified by the intellectual sweep of one's theological ideas or the particular accuracy of one's images of Christ, but by faith—that activity engendered by language that unifies me as a person. The simple street sweeper or garbage collector can come to terms with this language—if he can think black, that is, if he can see himself as a man who needs liberation.

## A New Grasp of Theological Limitations

I am not at all persuaded that from the experience of black-white confrontation in theology miracles of understanding will soon occur. But one thing becomes clear in that confrontation: Christ was meant for the poor and the poor in spirit. "It will be hard for a rich man to enter the kingdom of heaven." (Matt. 19:23) We often fail to consider this fact in our modern theological reflections. Rather, we expect Christ to have something to say to everything we have in our hearts and minds—our epistemological hang-ups, our linguistic dilemmas, psychological downs, or political *cul de sacs.*

What today is vaguely referred to as Christ is not altogether directly and immediately "knowable." It may well be that one needs to be born black—to be born poor, or poor in spirit—to be able to enter God's kingdom. The sin of wealth, the sin of "whiteness," may make it nearly impossible for us to see what is crucially Christian, the *novum,* the new thing, the freedom "which passeth all understanding." It is tremendously difficult to keep one's mind focused on the wretched of the earth, regardless of how we define them. No one identifies with wretchedness "naturally." That is why systematic theology cannot do without the biblical text, which calls it back to that focus time and again.

Only *after* we have discussed the issues of Christology and have seen the problem of theological epistemology can we speak of the basic character of man, his "nature." To put it specifically in regard to Cone, we can speak of man as a free being only *after* we have seen man's freedom in Christ. For it is only in him that we can grasp something of the possibility of transcendent freedom.

Cone speaks of the paradox of human existence: "Freedom is the opposite of oppression, but only the oppressed are truly free." [16] This is the gist of his anthropology. Naturally, then, in his Christology which *follows* his anthropology, he will draw out this line: "The finality of Jesus lies in the totality of his existence in complete freedom as the Oppressed One, who reveals through his death and resurrection that God himself is present in all dimensions of human liberation." [17] Freedom here again is tied to oppression. But why must this be so? First of all, freedom in Jesus Christ is *not* primarily tied to identification with the oppressed, but to identification with God. Because God is free he is able to identify with the oppressed in Jesus Christ. Otherwise God's freedom would depend on oppression, on evil in the world, and consequently also on sin, and God would be captive to his creation and the mistakes it makes. In his unconcealment, God's freedom is his ability to overrule the seemingly ironclad necessities of nature, his ability to overrule man's evil and oppression and to make man new.

If one takes our present theological situation seriously as dominated by the black-white confrontation, one may notice a number of parallels between our situation and that of the New Testament. But one cannot do all things at the same time. The limitations of our situation compel us to focus on the severest political and social strain where man has the least chance to be freed from being a non-person. In a word, the conflict finally takes shape as the conflict between the free man and the state with its subservient "state church." However much the white has wronged the black in this country and is still wronging him, liberation cannot come by merely individual changes of mind. The master has bolstered his psychological and mental attitudes by political power—especially in terms of the state. Today Jesus Christ thus once again may prove himself to be our Lord, especially as power for battle (the whole armor of God) against the all-powerful state.

Theological reflection today is obviously not going to solve all our problems. But we may find that the gospel hands us power to do battle with the powers that seek to control our lives. To some extent we are already living in a totalitarian state. Webster defines "totalitarian" as "relating to a political regime based on subordination of the individual to the state and strict control of all aspects of the life and productive capacity of the nation." But there is no reason why we should condone a power structure that condones the ghettos of our cities or a criminal war in Asia. There is no reason why we should support it by our taxes. There is no reason, for that matter, why we should support any capitalist exploitation, why we should be mere cogs in the system of dehumanization. The issue of liberation here finds its severest challenge and demands that theology reorient its focus with all "deliberate speed, majestic instancy." [18]

1. Broader explorations of this issue are to be found in my essays "Political Theology in the American Context," *Theological Markings,* 1:1 (Spring, 1971), pp. 28-42, and "Political Theology As New Hermeneutical Focus," *Theological Markings,* 3:1 (Spring, 1973), pp. 27-34.

2. See James H. Cone, *A Black Theology of Liberation* (Philadelphia and New York: J. B. Lippincott Company, 1970), p. 120, *passim.*

3. For this and the following quotes see Carl J. Friedrich (ed.), *The Philosophy of Hegel* (New York: The Modern Library, 1953), pp. 400-409.

4. Cf. John A. T. Robinson, "In What Sense is Christ Unique?" *The Christian Century,* 87:47 (November 25, 1970), pp. 1409-12.

5. It has been difficult for me to grasp why Paul Lehmann in an unpublished paper on "The Language of Faith and the Function of Theology," (1970), feels constrained radically to distinguish between analogy and metaphor, in order to claim, as I understand him, that only metaphor is the proper language expression of faith. Does not

metaphor also contain analogy? It appears that there are different types of analogies. And metaphor is *one* type. In any case, Webster describes metaphor as follows: "A figure of speech denoting by a word or phrase usu. one kind of object or idea in place of another to suggest a *likeness or analogy* between them." (*italics mine*) I am not at all seeking to oppose the theological use of metaphor. It is a centrally important one. The point I wish to make is that metaphor is also analogical.

6. In my view it is only now within this context that it becomes inescapable that we begin to examine the relevance of Karl Barth's theology for the American scene. One of the reasons why I felt that the time had not as yet come to relate American Protestant thought to Barth was that the concept of heresy had been made completely innocuous in white theology. Recall, for example, the debate about Bishop Pike's "heretical" stance in the Episcopal church. Barth's whole thought is methodologically centered around a *new* concept of heresy. Only now with black theology's serious reflection on heresy in the American church has an opening been made for an adequate understanding of what Barth was trying to do. I hope this is a partial answer to Paul Lehmann's observation that I had been singularly silent about Barth in my *Understanding God*. See P. L. Lehmann, "Karl Barth and the Future of Theology," *Religious Studies,* 6:2 (June 1970), pp. 105-120.

7. James H. Cone, *op. cit.,* p. 187.

8. *Ibid.,* p. 190.

9. I have tried to clarify the point as regards the black-white context in *"The Political Gospel,"* *The Christian Century,* 87:46 (November 18, 1970), pp. 1380-83.

10. James H. Cone, *op. cit.,* p. 190.

11. *Ibid.,* p. 198.

12. *Ibid.,* p. 202.

13. See my *Understanding God* (New York: Charles Scribner's Sons, 1966), pp. 50-64.

14. James H. Cone, *op. cit.,* pp. 203 f.

15. For this and the following quotes see Elizabeth Sewell, *The Orphic Voice: Poetry and Natural History* (New Haven: Yale University Press, 1960), pp. 23-67. The entire book is an attempt to put into perspective a "new" understanding of language that has deep roots in German romanticism, Shakespeare, Bacon, etc., that is, in that whole tradition which goes as far back as the mythological figure of Orpheus. Cf. my *Understanding God* on the "poetic word" and "poetic proclamation." Quite on purpose I prefaced one of the chapters with a word from the romanticism of Eichendorff which expresses the Orphic character of human language.

16. James H. Cone, *op. cit.*, p. 160.
17. *Ibid.*, p. 210.
18. C. Vann Woodward, *The Strange Career of Jim Crow* (New York: Oxford University Press, 1957), p. 179.

# Love Without Limits

**EBERHARD BETHGE**

> "There was a man who had two sons . . . the younger son gathered all he had and took his journey into a far country . . . he began to be in want. . . . And he would gladly have fed on the pods the swine ate. . . . But when he came to himself he said . . . 'I will arise and go to my father. . . .' But while he was yet at a distance, his father . . . had compassion, and ran and embraced him and kissed him. . . .
>
> "Now his elder son . . . was angry . . . . he answered his father, 'Lo these many years I have served you, and I never disobeyed your command; yet you never gave me a kid . . . . But when this son of yours came, who devoured your living . . . you killed for him the fatted calf!" (Luke 15:11-30 selected)

Though this story never fails to impress me, it always leaves me with some uneasiness. I think it does so for two reasons. First, the happy ending one longs for does not come at the end, but in the middle, so that the story is darkened with a troublesome second half. The tradition of the Church has been to cut off that second half and to call the story just "the parable of the prodigal son." Second, that last half of the narrative presents us with no real conclusion. We would like a final judgment spoken over the elder brother who seemed good but apparently became evil. We are fascinated by final judgment. My children always expected me to forecast a fitting end for the villain when we left a movie. And many believed there should be a kind of final judgment on my native Germany after that chapter of our history which ended in 1945. The Chruch throughout its long history has seldom resisted the urge to indulge in such final grading. And sometimes even the Bible does so, as for instance in the story of the two sons in Matthew 21.

I would suggest that just these two observations, the misplaced happy ending and the absence of final judgment, point to the very essence of this text, hold the story together, and make it contemporaneous for us.

In order to see the point more clearly, let us look again at the well-known story. I see in it three fields of force, almost magnetic fields of feelings and attitudes which are in sharp tension with one another, disturbing and even threatening one another. There is the younger son attracted by the magnetism of total independence and freedom who wants to break down the protecting limitations of his home. There is the father, living in the magnetic field of fatherly compassion, from which he moves across the boundaries and the privileges belonging to the dignity and authority of a patriarch. And there is the elder son, held within the magnetic field of goodness, but unable to cross the border of his own piety and virtue.

The great fields of human achievements—freedom, compassion, and goodness—violate each other when they come into confrontation. The characters of our story experience their boundaries as curse and as blessing and as curse again. That is what is central to this story, that in encounter boundaries change meaning again and again. Boundaries become killing and creative, protective and oppressing, hostile and inviting. And that is what boundaries always become. Germans know what borders mean: overrun and removed, erected and drawn again, encountered and lamented. One cannot bear them, but nevertheless will draw them again and fortify them anew.

In this story, conflict comes at the borders of those beloved fields of freedom, compassion, and goodness, and leaves us bewildered. Excellence clashes with humanity, goodness with forgiveness, justice with generosity, achievement with gift, decency with spontaneity. Order becomes hostile to love! Is the law really checked by the gospel? The introduction to our story lets us feel already how love is threatened: "Now the tax collectors and sinners were all drawing near to hear him. And the Pharisees and the scribes murmured, saying, 'This man receives sinners and eats with them.'" (Luke 15:1-2)

Freedom, compassion, goodness—which has the stronger pull?

## The Younger One

In order to rid himself of all restraints, the younger son trespasses the limitations of the traditional and proper patriarchal father-son relation. He crosses the frontiers of his fatherland and overrides the limitations of his faculties. Finally he transgresses the sanctified walls of his religion, worship, and piety, forgets the sabbath, and participates in the ultimate impurity for a Jew by living with swine.

But then the boundaries which he had overcome suddenly begin to change their meaning. What he had thought he could not bear anymore (authority, sharing, tradition, responsiblity to the past and future, a given form of life)—suddenly becomes a tantalizing dream by day and night. In the moment when all these are beyond his reach, he yearns for them. If only he could be near them or have the smallest share in them! The freedom he had dreamed about has turned into a chaotic hell. The restraining enclosure he had hated seems now to be heavenly liberty itself. Thus the same limitations which had driven him away bring him home, the boundlessness which had promised life, now reveals itself as death. The father in the story says quite accurately: "this my son was dead." The walls which once had suffocated him now give him new life; the father says, "[he] is alive again."

## The Father

The father encounters his limitations too. He suffers them, and he too abandons them. He does not observe those boundaries which are set for him as an oriental patriarch.

It all begins with the painful acknowledgment of the limits which the son had set for him by his actions. The father has to accept his total powerlessness in this moment. Coercion would not change anything, could only make things worse. He cannot reach the heart of his son anymore; he cannot reach him in that far country. Compassion is weak; it has only one capability, a painful one. It can do nothing other than wait. He can do nothing but suffer.

But when the son comes back, it is without any reservation and without any precondition that the father meets him. All dignity is forgotten, all pedagogical reflection has ceased, if it were ever there. Pointedly, the story tells us that the head of the house "ran" to meet the prodigal son, that he interrupts his confession, that he orders, not just any clothing, but the dress of dignity which traditionally was used when the son comes of age and represents his sharing of authority in the estate. We are told that he gives him the ring which is the sign of his majority and authority and shows publicly his total acceptance, that he orders the preparation of not just any of the herd but the fatted calf always preserved for the celebration of the majority of the heir. Then he opens the festivities with music and dancing.

Obviously the provokingly-detailed picture in this part of the text makes clear what forgiveness really is and what it is not. It is not a patriarchal gift given, as it were, from above and out of superior wealth, but rather a limitless giving out of suffering, compassion, and terrible need. It is the father who seems to say, "I cannot live without you, I terribly need you!"

I remember an American friend saying to me that the whole ecumenical effort will be worthless and poisoned by vanity as long as it arises from an attitude in which each tradition offers only its own particular gifts and insights at the common table. The ecumenical movement will be healthy only when we come with an attitude of terrible need, when we admit that we cannot live without each other before God, that we need each other. This is the only successful way to break down boundaries.

Note that the father confronts the elder son with just that absence of precondition and reservation. He does not argue with him. He acknowledges all the son has done to him. But he has only friendly words for him, and he entreats him to grasp this moment of compassion, which has become the moment of resurrection. Why not then add gaiety to grace—for the limitlessness of the father's love has triumphed over the younger son's rejection and limitation.

## The Elder Son

It is exactly this grace which shatters the values of the older brother. The festivities destroy the order of his convictions. What he had lived for suddenly lost all its delight. Work and responsibility now seemed worthless. Had he not renounced so much for the preservation and the protection of this home? "Lo, these many years have I served you"! All that he deserved was devaluated in that moment. How was it possible that the other one received the same, or even more?

Indeed, much was expected of the elder son, maybe too much. It would take too much generosity and too much of a sense of humor for him to rejoice with that lucky young fellow. Elder brothers and sisters have always suffered the much-too-generous treatment of the youngster in the house. What decent human being could be expected to offer such unconditional love to someone who certainly did not deserve it? Were those long years of trouble and discipline just for nothing?

There was nothing to criticize in the conduct of the elder son up to this moment. But this very moment—when the boundlessness of the younger one is outdistanced by the boundlessness of the father—becomes the critical boundary for the elder son. And he fails. In the hour of compassion goodness stumbles into its danger zone. Not before, but now.

In this hour the elder brother descends to the level of objective comparison. The mechanics of equivalents begins to rule his mind. The narrative of Luke has him say, "your son," never, "my brother." He has become a mere object for comparison. That considerate person he once was has suddenly been robbed of all sensitivity and he loses the ability to identify with his brother. The well disciplined and developed identity of the elder brother becomes distorted by this lack of identification, and he succumbs in a spasm of self-isolation.

Virtue, obedience, and piety have themselves become pit-falls. The irreligious one, the younger, has been drawn into the field of forgiving compassion. But the religious one, the elder, has exposed himself in that fatal moment as a man bitterly defending his religion as a special privilege. In the hour of love his religion became legalistic, bitterly balancing the books, putting men in the boxes of its own judgment. It had become exclusively interested in the preservation and consideration of its own limits.

Something really disturbing has happened. Love and goodness, which had been identical, fall apart. Love, it appears, wipes out the difference between good and evil, and that is unbearable. The elder brother is right. There *is* no difference anymore. Good has become evil and evil has become good. And this must not be. "I wish that you, the younger one, did not exist. You are not allowed to be here!" In this way the elder brother misses the moment of boundlessness. Make no mistake, he is not against love, not at all. Rather, he is for love in the proper doses, love with certain conditions attached. That is his religion, a religion which crucifies love by law and order, but finally is itself defeated at the hands of undivided and unlimited love.

Our story began with the wish of the younger brother for a life apart, for, as the South Africans say, "separate development." The story ends with the elder brother standing apart with his own idea of separate development. In each case true love suffers from the self-limiting drive of divisiveness. But it is exactly at this tragic point that this text tells us the story of a triumphant, un-conditioned love which overcomes all divisions.

It is for this reason that the narrative does not end with a summary evaluation and judgment. It cannot end in this way, because divine love does not end in this way. It cannot rest with final judgment. Or we might say that undivided love *is* final judgment. And this means as well that final judgment is undivided love! Both the Old and New Testaments present us with the strange picture of a God who is struggling with himself as to whether he will apportion his love, or grant it without limitation. The true majesty of this love is that he suffers whenever he encounters the self-limiting boundaries of men. Sometimes this love simply acknowledges such limits and obstacles, because it is love and not coercion. But sometimes it overruns all boundaries. It overcomes our knowing all too well who belongs to the father's house and who does not. It overcomes the limits of our virtue and decency. Sometimes this love accepts defeat and waits. At other times, it conquers and calls us to the moment of compassion.

So this is a story of both love and judgment. As judgment the story certainly speaks against us; but just as it speaks against us, it also speaks for us and to us. And what it says to us becomes truly our only raison d'etre. For who can live without experiencing at least once that surprising, abundant, and boundless love of God?

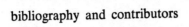

bibliography and contributors

# A Paul Lehmann Bibliography [1]

## ROBERT C. MATHEWSON

The following bibliography lists the writings of Paul L. Lehmann chronologically and includes all of his published work up to January, 1974. The bibliography lists first, the books by or translated by Paul L. Lehmann, and these are followed by a selection of critical reviews relating to these items. The second and major portion of the bibliography lists by year of publication articles and reviews by Paul L. Lehmann. While the compiler hopes that it is complete as of the given date, he is also aware that there may be other articles lurking in journals that he has missed and he would appreciate being informed of such. For those of us who have often wished that more of Professor Lehmann's thought were published, it has been a genuine pleasure to discover the great number of articles that are in print.

This bibliography suggests something of Professor Lehmann's method. Many of his important concepts first appear in articles, and after vigorous debate and clarification, may reappear in somewhat different form in later essays and books. Certain ideas that have become a part of the contemporary theological vocabulary owe their birth to such an early essay. Long before it was the popular thing to do, Lehmann was working in the area of theology's response to the problems of power in society, the freedom of man, and the place of law in the political life of the community.

---

1. Reprinted, with additions, from *Theology Today,* Vol. XXIX, No. 1 (April 1972), pp. 120-132.

## Books

*Forgiveness: Decisive Issue in Protestant Thought,* with a Foreword by Reinhold Niebuhr. Pp. 234. New York, Harper and Brothers, 1940.

*Churchman,* CLIV: 20, A. L. Murray.
*Crozer Quarterly,* XVII: 224, G. W. Davis.
*The Journal of Religion,* XXI, No. 2: 221-24, D. Horton.
*The Review of Religion,* V, No. 2: 220-23, H. W. Schneider.

*Re-educating Germany,* by Werner Richter, translated and with a Preface by Paul Lehmann. Pp. 227. Chicago, University of Chicago Press, 1945.

*American Political Science Review,* XXXIX, 371, J. K. Pollack.
*Book Week,* (February 4, 1945), 2, E. Roettler.
*Booklist,* XLI, 192.
*Christian Century,* LXII, 682, G. Downum.
*Christian Science Monitor,* (February 2, 1945), 14, M. J. T.
*Current History,* VIII, 248, S. B. Fay.
*Ethics,* LV, 228, T. V. Smith.
*Foreign Affairs,* XXIII, 696.
*New Republic,* CXII, 565.
*New Statesman and Nation,* XXX, 28, H. Fraenkel.
*New York Times,* (April 22, 1945), 12, E. W. Fox.
*Saturday Review of Literature,* XXVIII, 7, R. Pick.
*School and Society,* LXI, 63.
*School and Society,* LXII, 111, H. S. Ficke.
*School Review,* LIII, 370, R. B. Browne.
*Survey Graphic,* XXXIV, 415, S. Neumann.
*Times* (of London) *Literary Supplement,* (April 21, 1945), 183.
*The Union Review,* VI, No. 2, 25, R. Niebuhr.
*Weekly Book Review,* (March 5, 1945), 5, W. A. Neilson.

*Ethics in a Christian Context.* Pp. 384. New York, Harper and Row, 1963.

*The Christian Century,* LXXXI, No. 1, 17-18, K. Cauthen.
*Dialog,* V, 147-50, G. H. Outka.
*Duke Divinity School Review,* XXIX, 141-43, H. L. Smith.
*Harvard Divinity Bulletin,* XXVIII, 97-99, G. D. Kaufmann.
*International Review of Missions,* 54, 110-12, M. M. Thomas.
*Nederlands Theologisch Tijdschrift,* XXII, 306-307, H. J. Heering.
*Princeton Seminary Bulletin,* LVIII, 44-49, C. C. West and M. R. Shaull.

*Reformed Theological Review,* XXIX, 23-24, A. W. Loy.
*Religion in Life,* XXXIII, 301-303, E. C. Gardner.
*Review and Expositor,* LXI, 356-57, H. H. Barnette.
*Scottish Journal of Theology,* XVIII, 92-94, W. Lillie.
*Southwestern Journal of Theology,* VI, 132-33, W. Pinson.
*The Student World,* LVII, 294-95, J. McCaughey.
*Studia Theologica,* XV, 490-93, G. C. Stead.
*Theologische Literaturzeitung,* XCIII, 700-703, H. van Oyen.
*Theology Today,* "Lehmann's Contextual Ethics and the Problem of Truth Telling," P. Ramsey, XXI, 466-75.
*Union Seminary Quarterly Review,* XIX, 261-65, J. Gustafson.
*Westminster Theological Journal,* XXXI, 110-13, P. G. Schrotenboer.

## 1936

DISSERTATION

*A Critical Comparison of the Doctrine of Justification in the Theologies of Albrecht Ritschl and Karl Barth,* Union Theological Seminary doctoral dissertation. [Positive microfilm of typewritten original, Rochester, N. Y.: Eastman Kodak Co., 1968.]

## 1937

ARTICLE

"Theocracy and Liberty," *Radical Religion* (became *Christianity and Society*), II, No. 3, 30-34.

## 1938

REVIEW

R. Niebuhr, *Beyond Tragedy,* "Preaching with Power," in *The Messenger,* January 13.

## 1940

ARTICLES

"The Authority of the Church and Freedom," *The Review of Religion,* IV, No. 2, 159-69.

"Barth and Brunner: The Dilemma of the Protestant Mind," *The Journal of Religion,* XX, No. 2, 124-40.

REVIEW

J. Haroutunian, *Wisdom and Folly in Religion,* in *Christianity and Society,* V, No. 5, 40-43.

## 1941

ARTICLE

"The Use of Christian Words," *The Journal of Religion*, XXI, No. 1, 46-48.

REVIEWS

R. B. Brandt, *The Philosophy of Schleiermacher*, in *Church History*, X, No. 4, 381-82.

J. Haroutunian, *Wisdom and Folly in Religion*, in *The Review of Religion*, V, No. 4, 472-78.

## 1942

ARTICLES

"The Promise of Theology in America," *The Student World*, XXXV, No. 1, 70-79.

"Obedience and Justice," *Christianity and Society*, VIII, No. 3, 35-39.

## 1943

ARTICLE

"Human Destiny—Reinhold Niebuhr: A Symposium," *The Union Review*, IV, No. 2, 18-20.

REVIEW

R. Niebuhr, *The Nature and Destiny of Man*, "Christianity and Contemporary Culture," in *The Student World*, XXXVI, No. 4, 317-32.

## 1944

ARTICLES

"Christian Foundations of the Peace," *Christianity and Society*, IX, No. 2, 36-41.

"Grace and Power" *Christianity and Society*, X, No. 1, 25-31.

"A Protestant Critique of Anglicanism," *Anglican Theological Review*, XXVI, No. 3, 151-59. [Reprinted 1948 in *The Churchman*, LXII, No. 4, 221-28.]

"Toward a Protestant Analysis of the Ethical Problem," *The Journal of Religion*, XXIV, No. 1, 1-16.

"The Christian Doctrine of Man," *The Journal of Religious Thought*, I. Man as Creature, I, No. 2, 140-56. II. Man as Sinner, II, No. 1, 60-77.

REVIEWS

E. Brunner, *The Divine Human Encounter,* in *The Journal of Religion,* XXIV, No. 3, 207.

R. L. Calhoun, *God and the Day's Work,* in *The Westminster Bookman,* III, No. 4, 12-13.

R. Niebuhr, *The Nature and Destiny of Man,* "A Watershed in American Theology," in *Theology Today,* I, No. 2, 234-54.

W. A. Visser t'Hooft, *The Wretchedness and Greatness of the Church,* in *The Student World,* XXXVII, No. 3, 266-69.

## 1945

ARTICLES

"The Rebirth of Theology," *Religion in Life,* XIV, No. 4, 575-85.

"The Christian Doctrine of Man," *The Journal of Religious Thought,* III. "Man as Believer," II, No. 2, 179-94.

REVIEWS

H. W. Clark, *The Cross and the Eternal Order,* in *The Journal of Religion,* XXV, No. 4, 290-91.

E. P. Dickie, *The Obedience of a Christian Man,* and L. Mumford, *The Condition of Man,* in *The Student World,* XXXVIII, No. 1, 70-77.

E. Frank, *Philosophical Understanding and Religious Truth,* in *The Westminster Bookman,* IV, No. 5, 10-11.

C. D. Kean, *Christianity and the Cultural Crisis,* in *The Westminster Bookman,* V, No. 1, 24-25.

L. Mumford, *The Condition of Man,* in *Theology Today,* II, No. 1, 125-27.

## 1946

ARTICLES

"Contemporary Reflections on the Epistle to the Romans," *The Journal of Bible and Religion,* XIV, No. 3, 158-63.

"The Reformer's Use of the Bible," *Theology Today,* III, No. 3, 328-44.

REVIEWS

E. Brunner, *Justice and the Social Order,* in *The Westminster Bookman,* VI, No. 1, 3-6.

V. Ferm, *Encyclopedia of Religion,* in *The Westminster Bookman,* V, No. 5, 16-18.

C. Van Til, *The New Modernism,* in *Christendom,* XI, No. 4, 528-30.

## 1947

ARTICLES

"The Direction of Theology Today," *The Duke Divinity School Bulletin*, XI, No. 4, 67-76. [Reprinted in *The Union Seminary Quarterly Review*, III, No. 1, 3-10.]

"Christianity and Community," Convocation Lecture published separately by the Committee on Convocations and Lectures of the University of North Carolina, Chapel Hill, N. C.

"Bible Studies," *The Westminster Fellowship Handbook*, September-December, 1947, for the Grinnel Assembly, June 30-July 5.

"Justification by Faith and the Disposition of Goods," *Christianity and Society*, XII, No. 4, 12-19.

"The Standpoint of the Reformation," *Christianity and Property*, Joseph Fletcher, ed., Philadelphia: The Westminster Press, Chapter 5, 100-123.

REVIEWS

C. Lowry, *The Holy Trinity and Christian Devotion*, in *The Journal of Religion*, XXVII, No. 2, 129.

N. Pittenger, *His Body the Church*, in *The Westminster Bookman*, VI, No. 4, 5-7.

H. N. Weiman, *The Source of Human Good*, in *Theology Today*, IV, No. 3, 429-33.

## 1948

ARTICLES

"Protestants, Liberals, and Liberty," *New Century*, (May), 8-10.

"The Bible and the Significance of Civilization," *Theology Today*, V, No. 3, 350-58.

"Where Liberalism Fails," *Theology Today*, IV, No. 4, 500-506.

"A Protestant Critique of Anglicanism," *The Churchman* (London), LXII, No. 4, 221-28. [Reprinted from *Anglican Theological Review*, XXVI, No. 3, 151-59.]

REVIEWS

J. Bennett, *Christian Ethics and Social Policy*, in *Theology Today*, V, No. 3, 447-49.

W. Cannon, *The Theology of John Wesley*, in *The Journal of Religion*, XXVIII, No. 2, 142-43.

F. Dostoevsky, *The Grand Inquisitor*, in *The Women's Press*, XLII, No. 10, 25.

E. Fromm, *Man For Himself* in *The Westminster Bookman*, VIII, No. 5, 7-9.

M. F. Thelan, *Man As Sinner*, in *Religion in Life*, XVII, No. 3, 453-54.

1949

ARTICLES

"On Being Fit For Freedom," *The Intercollegian,* LXVI, No. 5, 5-6.
"On the Meaning of Lent," *Discovery,* I, 16-17.
"The Mindzenty-Spellman Case," *New Century,* (Spring), 11-14, 29-30.
"The Meaning of the Resurrection," *Counsel,* I, No. 3.
"Truth Is in Order to Goodness," *Theology Today,* VI, No. 3, 348-60.

REVIEWS

J. Bennett, *Christianity and Communism,* and P. Scherer, *The Plight of Freedom,* in *Presbyterian Life,* II, No. 22, 26.
J. Haroutunian, *Lust for Power,* in *McCormick Speaking,* II, No. 3, 12-13.
J. L. Liebmann, ed., *Psychology and Religion,* in *Monday Morning,* XIV, No. 27, 21.
J. T. McNeill, *Books of Faith and Power,* in *The Journal of Religion,* XXIX, No. 1, 66.
W. Spurrier, *Power for Action,* in *Presbyterian Life,* II, No. 22, 23-24.
P. Tillich, *The Protestant Era,* in *Union Quarterly Review,* IV, No. 2, 35-39.
P. Tillich, *The Shaking of the Foundations,* and *The Protestant Era,* in *Interpretation,* III, No. 1, 112-16.
A. Toynbee, *Civilization on Trial,* in *The Westminster Bookman,* VIII, No. 3, 17-20.

1950

ARTICLES

"What Is Religious Liberty?" *Christianity and Society,* XV, No. 3, 10-13.
"Dynamics of Reformation Ethics," *Princeton Seminary Bulletin,* XLIII, No. 4, 17-22. [Inaugural address at Princeton, April 24, 1950.]

1951

ARTICLES

"Renewal in the Church," *Theology Today,* VII, No. 4, 472-85.
"Deliverance and Fulfillment: The Biblical View of Salvation," *Interpretation,* V, No. 4, 387-400.
"Christianity and Social Change," *The Intercollegian,* LXIX, No. 2, 7-8.

REVIEWS

P. Ramsey, *Basic Christian Ethics,* in *Princeton Seminary Bulletin,* XLV, No. 3, 35-47; and in *The Westminster Bookman,* X, No. 6, 12-14.

## 1952

ARTICLES

"The Presbyterian Churches," *The Quest for Christian Unity,* Robert S. Bilheimer, ed., New York: Association Press, 164-170.

"The Missionary Obligation of the Church," *Theology Today,* IX, No. 1, 20-38.

"Civil Liberties," *Christianity and Society,* XVII, No. 2, 5-6.

"The Christian Faith and Civil Liberties," *Social Progress,* XLIII, No. 4, 5-8.

REVIEWS

E. Carnell, *The Theology of Reinhold Niebuhr,* in *Crozer Quarterly,* XXIX, No. 1, 58-61.

D. Jenkins, *Europe and America,* in *Church History,* XXI, No. 2, 169-70.

A. Wilder, *Modern Poetry and the Christian Tradition,* in *The Westminster Bookman,* XI, No. 4, 11-12.

## 1953

ARTICLES

"The Foundation and Pattern of Christian Behavior," *Christian Faith and Social Action: Essays in Honor of Reinhold Niebuhr,* John Hutchison, ed., New York: Charles Scribner's Sons, 93-116.

"Willingen and Lund: The Church on the Way to Unity," *Theology Today,* IX, No. 4, 431-41.

"Biblical Faith and the Vocational Predicament of Our Time," *The Drew Gateway,* XXIII, Nos. 3 and 4, 101-08.

## 1954

ARTICLES

*Your Freedom Is in Trouble,* Study Booklet, National Student Council of the YMCA and YWCA, New York, N. Y.

"The Transforming Power of the Church," *The Intercollegian,* LXXI, No. 5, 5-7, 20.

"Light on Meetinghouse Hill," *Princeton Seminary Bulletin,* XLVII, No. 3, 17-26.

"Should the Church Speak Out on Social and Political Issues?" *This Generation,* VI, No. 3, 57-59.

"Academic Freedom in the United States," *The Student World*, XLVII, No. 2, 163-71.

"Evanston: Problems and Prospects," *Theology Today*, XI, No. 2, 143-53.

REVIEWS

R. Niebuhr, *Christian Realism and Political Problems*, in *The Westminster Bookman*, XIII, No. 2, 15-17.

R. L. Shinn, *Christianity and the Problem of History*, in *Monday Morning*, XIX, No. 8, 16.

### 1955

ARTICLES

"The Theology of Crisis," *The Twentieth Century Encyclopedia of Religious Knowledge*, Lefferts A. Loetscher, ed., Grand Rapids: Baker Book House, Vol. I, 309-12.

"Anti-Pelagian Writings," *A Companion to the Study of St. Augustine*, Roy Battenhouse, ed., New York: Oxford University Press, 203-34.

REVIEWS

J. Dillenberger and C. Welch, *Protestant Christianity Interpreted Through Its Development*, in *The Drew Gateway*, XXV, No. 4, 248-49.

W. Schweitzer, *Schrift und Dogma in der Oekumene*, in *The Ecumenical Review*, VIII, No. 1, 98-103.

### 1956

ARTICLES

"Betrayal of the Real Presence," *Princeton Seminary Bulletin*, XLIX, No. 3, 20-25.

"The Christology of Reinhold Niebuhr," *Reinhold Niebuhr: His Religious, Social, and Political Thought*, Charles W. Kegley and Robert W. Bretall, eds., New York: Macmillan, 252-80.

"The Changing Course of a Corrective Theology," *Theology Today*, XIII, No. 3, 332-57.

### 1957

ARTICLES

"The Context of Theological Inquiry," *Harvard Divinity School Bulletin*, XXII, 61-73.

"The Nature of the Unity We Seek" [Mimeographed Study Guide for the 4th Interseminary Movement; it does not indicate his contribution.]

REVIEWS

W. Elert, *The Christian Ethos,* in *The Westminster Bookman,* XVI, No. 4, 20-22.

J. T. Ellis, *American Catholicism,* in *Indiana Magazine of History,* LIII, No. 4, 454-57.

T. H. L. Parker, ed., *Essays in Christology,* in *The Christian Century,* LXXIV, No. 48, 1418.

G. F. Thomas, *Christian Ethics and Moral Philosophy,* in *Princeton Seminary Bulletin,* L, No. 4, 52-56.

## 1958

ARTICLES

"Law," and "Power," *A Handbook of Christian Theology,* Marvin Halverson and Arthur A. Cohen, eds., New York: Living Age Books, Meridian Books, Inc., 203-207 and 268-71.

"The Servant Image in Reformed Theology," *Theology Today,* XV, No. 3, 333-51.

REVIEW

H. Kraemer, *Religion and the Christian Faith,* in *The Ecumenical Review,* X, No. 2, 197-202.

## 1959

ARTICLES

"Religion, Power, and Christian Faith," *Religion and Culture: Essays in Honor of Paul Tillich,* Walter Leibrecht, ed., New York: Harper and Brothers, 243-58.

"Law as a Function of Forgiveness," *Oklahoma Law Review,* XII, No. 1, 102-12.

"The Environment of Authentic Selfhood," and "What Is a Christian Act?" *The Intercollegian,* LXXVI, No. 6, 8-9 and 11-13.

"Also Among the Prophets," *Theology Today,* XVI, No. 3, 345-55.

## 1961

ARTICLES

"Commentary: Dietrich Bonhoeffer in America," *Religion in Life,* XXX, No. 4, 616-18.

"Then What Did You Go Out to See," *Harvard Divinity School Bulletin,* XXV, No. 3, 4, 8-13.

## 1962

ARTICLES

*Ideology and Incarnation: A Contemporary Ecumenical Risk,* Geneva, Switzerland: The John Knox Association.

"Protestantism in a Post-Christian World," *Christianity and Crisis,* XXII, No. 1, 7-10, 12.

## 1963

ARTICLES

*Ideologie und Inkarnation: ein gegenwärtiges ökumenisches Risiko,*
Genf: John Knox Haus Gesellschaft.

*Idéologie et Incarnation: un risque actual de l'oecuménsime,* Genève,
Association du Foyer John Knox.

"An Ecumenical Venture in the Grand Manner," *Christianity and
Crisis,* XXIII, No. 9, 94-96.

"The Formative Power of Particularity," *Union Seminary Quarterly
Review,* XVIII, No. 3, pt. 2, 306-19.

REVIEWS

K. Barth, *Theology and the Church,* in *The Westminster Bookman,*
XXII, No. 2, 15-16.

J. A. T. Robinson, *Honest to God,* "A Call to Integrity," in *Christianity and Crisis,* XXIII, No. 19, 198-99.

## 1964

ARTICLES

"An Inadmissible Default," *The Christian Century,* LXXXI, 2, No.
29, 908-909.

"On Keeping Human Life Human," *The Christian Century,* LXXXI,
2, No. 43, 1297-99.

"The Logos in a World Come of Age," *Theology Today,* XXI, No.
3, 274-86.

"Integrity of Heart: A Comment Upon the Preceding Paper," *Ecumenical Dialogue at Harvard: The Roman Catholic-Protestant
Colloquium at Harvard,* Samuel H. Miller and G. Ernest Wright,
eds., Cambridge, Mass.: Harvard University Press, 274-79.

REVIEWS

E. Brunner, *The Christian Doctrine of the Church, Faith, and the
Consummation,* in *Union Seminary Quarterly Review,* XIX, No.
3, 256-58.

R. W. Jenson, *Alpha and Omega: A Study in the Theology of Karl
Barth,* in *Dialog,* III, No. 2, 148-51.

## 1965

ARTICLES

"Discussion: Christianity and Other Faiths," *Union Seminary Quarterly Review,* XX, No. 2, 184-87.

"The Shape of Theology for a World in Revolution," *Motive,* XXV,
No. 7, 9-13.

"Comments on a Critique," *Theology Today*, XXII, No. 1, 119-25.
"The Tri-Unity of God," *Union Seminary Quarterly Review*, XXI, No. 1, 35-49.

REVIEWS

H. Cox, *The Secular City*, "Chalcedon in Technopolis," in *Christianity and Crisis*, XXV, No. 12, 149-51.
F. Wendel, *Calvin: The Origins and Development of His Religious Thought*, in *Union Seminary Quarterly Review*, XX, No. 4, 393-96.

### 1966

ARTICLES

"The New Morality: A Sermon for Lent," *Dialog*, V, No. 1, 51-55.
"A Christian Alternative to Natural Law," *Die Moderne Demokratie und ihr Recht*. Festschrift für Gerhard Leibholz herausgegeben von Karl Dietrich Bracher, Christopher Dawson, Willi Geiger, Rudolf Smend, Tübingen: J. C. B. Mohr (Paul Siebeck) Erster Band, 519-42.
"Doing Theology: A Contextual Possibility," *Prospect for Theology: Essays in Honor of H. H. Farmer*, F. G. Healey, ed., London: James Nisbet and Co., Ltd., 117-36. A shortened version is reprinted in *Theology Today*, XXIX, 3-8.
"God in Three Persons," *The Covenant Companion*, March 21, 1966.
"The Function of Conscience in the Making of Decisions," *Conscience in Crisis*, Muskingum College, New Concord, Ohio, 1-36.
"Paradox of Discipleship," *I Knew Dietrich Bonhoeffer*, Wolf–Dieter Zimmermann and Ronald Gregor Smith, eds., London: Collins, 41-45.

REVIEWS

D. Bonhoeffer, *The Communion of Saints* and *No Rusty Swords*, *Union Seminary Quarterly Review*, XXI, No. 3, 364-69.
H. Cox, *The Secular City*, in *Religious Education*, LXI, No. 2, 140-42.
J. Fletcher, *Situation Ethics*, in *Bulletin of the Episcopal Theological School*, LIX, No. 1, 25-27.

### 1967

ARTICLES

"Contextual Ethics," and "Forgiveness," *Dictionary of Christian Ethics*, John Macquarrie, ed., Philadelphia: The Westminster Press, 71-73, and 130-31.

"Discussion: Communist-Christian    Dialogue," *Union Seminary Quarterly Review*, XXII, No. 3, 218-23.

"Jesus Christ and Theological Symbolization," and "Messiah and Metaphor," *Religious Studies in Higher Education*, Emerson I. Abendroth, ed., The Division of Higher Education, United Presbyterian Church, Witherspoon Building, Philadelphia, Pa., 12-24, and 25-33.

"Ecumenism and Church Union," *Realistic Reflections on Church Union*, John Macquarrie, ed., [Unpublished paper addressed primarily to American Episcopalians.], 57-63.

"Wilhelm Pauck," *Union Seminary Tower*, XIV, No. 11 (col. 1) and 33 (col. 1).

"Faith and Worldliness in Bonhoeffer's Thought," *Union Seminary Quarterly Review*, XXIII, No. 1, 31-44. Reprinted in *Bonhoeffer in a World Come of Age*, Peter Vorkink, comp., Philadelphia, Fortress Press, 1968, pp. 25-45.

REVIEW

E. Bethge, *Dietrich Bonhoeffer*, in *Union Seminary Quarterly Review*, XXIII, No. 1, 97-105.

## 1968

ARTICLES

"Dietrich Bonhoeffer," *Four Theological Giants Influence Our Faith*, [mimeographed] Union Theological Seminary, 1-12.

"A Theological Defense of Revolutions," *Africa Today*, XV, No. 3, 18-21.

"The Christian-Marxist Dialogue," *Social Action*, XXXV, No. 3, 17-22.

REVIEW

J. N. Hartt, *A Christian Critique of American Culture*, in *Religious Education*, LXIII, No. 6, 500-501.

## 1969

ARTICLE

"Christian Theology in a World in Revolution," *Openings for Marxist-Christian Dialogue*, Thomas W. Ogletree, ed., Nashville, New York: Abingdon Press, 98-139.

## 1970

ARTICLES

"Discussion: Theology and the Philosophy of Religion," *Union Seminary Quarterly Review*, XXV, No. 4, 494-99.

"A Christian Look at the Sexual Revolution," *Sexual Ethics and Christian Responsibility*, John C. Wynn, ed., New York: Association Press, 51-82.

Lecture at the National Campus Ministry Association Seminar on Problem Pregnancies. [United Ministry Board, 1514 East Third, Bloomington, Indiana 47401.]

"Karl Barth and the Future of Theology," *Religion Studies*, VI, No. 2, 105-20.

REVIEWS

R. W. Jensen, *The Knowledge of Things Hoped For*, in *Union Seminary Quarterly Review*, XXV, No. 4, 565-67.

G. D. Kaufmann, *Systematic Theology: A Historicist Perspective*, in *Religion in Life*, XXXIX, No. 2 294-96.

S. Keen, *Apology for Wonder*, in *Union Seminary Quarterly Review*, XXV, No. 3, 394-96.

1971

ARTICLE

"Foreword" to Milton Viorst, *Fall from Grace*, New York: Simon and Schuster.

REVIEWS

E. Bethge, *Dietrich Bonhoeffer*, and J. W. Woelfel, *Bonhoeffer's Theology: Classical and Revolutionary*, in *Union Seminary Quarterly Review*, XXVI, No. 4, 419-22; 446-48.

1972

ARTICLES

"Beyond Morality and Immorality in Foreign Affairs," *Theology Today*, XXVIII, No. 4, 489-94.

"Advent, Prisoners, and the Penal System," *Union Theological Seminary Journal*, January, pp. 2-3, 13.

"Contextual Theology," *Theology Today*, XXIX, No. 1, 3-8. A shortened and revised version of the essay "Doing Theology," 1966.

"Stranger Within The Gates," written with Ira Gollobin, *Christian Century*, LXXXIX, No. 15, 1149-52.

"Karl Barth, Theologian of Permanent Revolution," *Union Seminary Quarterly Review*, XXVIII, No. 1, 67-81.

1973

ARTICLE

"Theological Perspectives for the Practice of Collegiality in Union

Theological Seminary," *Union Seminary Quarterly Review,*
XXVII, No. 4, 287-89. A statement by Lehmann and other
Union faculty members.

## 1974

ARTICLE

"A Sermon: No Uncertain Sound!" *Union Seminary Quarterly Review,* **XXIX** (Spring and Summer, numbers 3 and 4), 273-77.

# Contributors

HORACE T. ALLEN is currently Director of the Office of Music and Worship for the Presbyterian Church (UPUSA and PCUS) and is the translator of *The Jewish Jesus.*

EBERHARD BETHGE is a lecturer in the theological faculty at the University of Bonn and Director of the Center for Continuing Education of Pastors, Rheinland-Westphalia. He is the author of *Dietrich Bonhoeffer: Man of Vision.*

HELMUT GOLLWITZER is Professor of Systematic Theology at the Free University of Berlin. His works include *The Existence of God as Confessed by Faith* and *The Demands of Freedom.*

CLIFFORD GREEN is an Assistant Professor of Religion at Goucher College and has taught at Wellesley. He is the co-author of *Critical Issues in Modern Religion.*

FREDERICK HERZOG is Professor of Systematic Theology at Duke University Divinity School. Among his writings are *Understanding God* and *Liberation Theology.*

JAN M. LOCHMAN is Professor of Systematic Theology at the University of Basel and Chairman of the Theological Department of the World Alliance of Reformed Churches. His works include *Church in a Marxist Society.*

JAMES LODER is Associate Professor of Christian Education at Princeton Theological Seminary. He is the author of *Religion and the Public Schools* and *Religious Pathology and the Christian Faith.*

ROBERT MATHEWSON is on the faculty of the Religion Department of Beaver College, Glenside, Pennsylvania, and was previously

Executive Secretary and Minister in Higher Education, Center City Christian Council, Philadelphia.

ALEXANDER J. McKELWAY is an Associate Professor of Religion at Davidson College and took his doctorate under the direction of Karl Barth at the University of Basel. He is the author of *The Systematic Theology of Paul Tillich*.

JÜRGEN MOLTMANN is Dean of the Faculty and Professor of Theology at the University of Tübingen. His works include *Gospel of Liberation* and *Theology of Hope*.

BRUCE MORGAN is presently Dean of the Faculty at Carleton College. He is the author of *Christians, the Church, and Property: Ethics and the Economy in a Supermarket World*.

BENJAMIN REIST is Professor of Systematic Theology at San Francisco Theological Seminary and the Graduate Theological Union at Berkeley. He is the author of *The Promise of Bonhoeffer*.

KRISTER STENDAHL is Frothingham Professor of Biblical Studies and Dean of Harvard Divinity School. Among his writings is *The School of St. Matthew, and its Use of the Old Testament*.

GEORGE WILLIAMS is Hollis Professor of Divinity at Harvard Divinity School. His books include *Anselm: Communion and Atonement* and *The Radical Reformation*.

E. DAVID WILLIS is Professor of Historical Theology at San Francisco Theological Seminary and has been an Assistant Professor of Systematic Theology at Princeton. He is the editor of *Baptism: Decision and Growth* and author of *Calvin's Catholic Christology*.

WIDENER UNIVERSITY
WOLFGRAM
LIBRARY
CHESTER, PA